Green Living

FOR

DUMMIES®

If

Green Living
FOR
DUMMIES®

by Liz Barclay and Michael Grosvenor

BICENTENNIAL
1807
WILEY
2007
BICENTENNIAL

John Wiley & Sons, Ltd

Green Living For Dummies®

Published by
John Wiley & Sons, Ltd
The Atrium
Southern Gate
Chichester
West Sussex
PO19 8SQ
England

E-mail (for orders and customer service enquires): cs-books@wiley.co.uk

Visit our Home Page on www.wiley.com

Copyright © 2007 John Wiley & Sons, Ltd, Chichester, West Sussex, England

Published by John Wiley & Sons, Ltd, Chichester, West Sussex

For general information on our other products and services, please contact our Customer Care Department within the U.S. at 800-762-2974, outside the U.S. at 317-572-3993, or fax 317-572-4002.

For technical support, please visit www.wiley.com/techsupport.

Wiley also publishes its books in a variety of electronic formats. Some content that appears in print may not be available in electronic books.

British Library Cataloguing in Publication Data: A catalogue record for this book is available from the British Library

ISBN: 978-0-470-06038-4

Printed and bound in Great Britain by TJ International, an ISO14001 Environment Management System accredited company; winner of the 2005 *Printing World* Best Environmental Printer award.

FSC
Mixed Sources
Product group from well-managed
forests and other controlled sources

Cert no. SGS-COC-2482
www.fsc.org
© 1996 Forest Stewardship Council

About the Authors

Liz Barclay has worked as an adviser, trainer, and manager with the Citizens Advice Bureau and still advises small businesses and sole traders on relationship management with staff and customers.

Liz is well connected within the media; she presents *You and Yours*, a factual radio programme on Radio 4, and has worked on a wide range of business and finance programmes for the BBC both on TV and radio. As a writer, Liz has written for the *News Of The World*, *The Express*, *Moneywise*, *Family Circle*, *Save Money*, and the *Mail On Sunday* personal finance magazine, and has also written *UK Law and Your Rights For Dummies* and *Small Business Employment Law For Dummies*.

Michael Grosvenor is a leading urban planning professional and freelance writer on sustainability. Through his work and writing, Michael promotes the benefits of making sustainable lifestyle choices. Michael has particular expertise in transport and advises the private sector and government on policies that promote increased public transport, walking and cycling facilities. Michael is a strong advocate for the important role that public transport plays in our cities and towns.

Michael is the director of his own consultancy and holds Masters degrees in Urban Affairs and Applied Social Research and a Degree in Town Planning. He is also a member of the Planning Institute of Australia and provides advice to the Institute on integrated land use and transport planning issues. Michael has also lived and studied in New York City, in the United States, but currently enjoys an inner-city lifestyle in Sydney, Australia.

Dedication

To my best friend and partner, Justine – thank you for your encouragement and support.

– Michael

Author's Acknowledgements

From Michael: My desire to talk to the general public about sustainable living motivated me to write this book. I'm often preaching to the converted in my consulting work. The environmentalists, planners, architects, social scientists, engineers and geographers I work with find ourselves saying the same things to each other, and we're often scribbling messages and ideas on whiteboards that no-one else gets to see.

Writing a book for an audience interested in living sustainably has been very rewarding. Hence, I am extremely grateful to Lesley Beaumont at Wiley Publishing Australia for supporting my idea for this book in the first instance and then giving the go-ahead for its publication.

This book covers a lot of ground – way too much ground for one person to have the required expertise on every topic. I have been able to carry out the necessary research for this book thanks to the thousands of committed professionals out there who have tested, researched, and published their findings about the problems facing the planet. This book could not be written without their passion.

I thoroughly enjoyed working with editor extraordinaire Maryanne Phillips and thank her for her brilliant guidance and direction. I'd also like to thank Giovanni Ebono for his excellent editorial contributions and ideas.

Publisher's Acknowledgements

We're proud of this book; please send us your comments through our Dummies online registration form located at www.dummies.com/register/.

Some of the people who helped bring this book to market include the following:

Acquisitions, Editorial, and Media Development

Project Editor: Rachael Chilvers

Special Projects Co-ordinator: Daniel Mersey

Content Editor: Steve Edwards

Commissioning Editor: Alison Yates

Copy Editor: Charlie Wilson

Proofreader: David Price

Technical Editor: Daniel James

Executive Editor: Jason Dunne

Executive Project Editor: Martin Tribe

Cover Photos: © GettyImages/Yoshio Sawaragi

Cartoons: Ed McLachlan

Composition Services

Project Coordinator: Jennifer Theriot

Layout and Graphics: Carl Byers, Denny Hager, Joyce Haughey, Heather Ryan

Proofreader: Jessica Kramer

Indexer: Aptara

Special Help

Brand Reviewer: Jan Simms

Manufacturing: Symmie Tyson

Publishing and Editorial for Consumer Dummies

> **Diane Graves Steele,** Vice President and Publisher, Consumer Dummies

> **Joyce Pepple,** Acquisitions Director, Consumer Dummies

> **Kristin A. Cocks,** Product Development Director, Consumer Dummies

> **Michael Spring,** Vice President and Publisher, Travel

> **Kelly Regan,** Editorial Director, Travel

Publishing for Technology Dummies

> **Andy Cummings,** Vice President and Publisher, Dummies Technology/General User

Composition Services

> **Gerry Fahey,** Vice President of Production Services

> **Debbie Stailey,** Director of Composition Services

Contents at a Glance

Table of Contents

Introduction

· ·

*W*elcome to *Green Living For Dummies!* If you're interested in the environment, want to know a bit more about why many people are concerned about the future of the planet, and what you can do to help, this is the book for you. I don't pretend to know how to save the planet – most scientists can't agree on how to tackle every aspect of that. But most people are agreed that human beings are using up valuable resources too fast to support everyone's demands and are putting back very little apart from rubbish, and that those habits can't continue at their present rate without some nasty side effects. This book aims to suggest a few ways you can help to reduce the damage you and your family cause to the planet.

About This Book

This book is about practical suggestions you can adopt to make your lifestyle greener. The first two chapters give a bit of background on what many scientists think the problems are, how they're caused, what impacts they're having on the planet, and what's likely to happen in the long term if human beings don't change their behaviour. The rest of the book is about what you can do to change. This is a book to dip into for ideas when you have the time.

Green living is leading the kind of lifestyle that will do as little damage as possible to the planet and the living things in it. In this book, all sorts of practical suggestions are made as to how you could be a bit greener – from using your car less, taking fewer flights, eating locally produced food, to using vinegar as a cleaner instead of cleaning products that contain a whole cocktail of chemicals.

Green living also means doing as little harm as possible to other people, animals, plants, insects. It's a whole way of thinking – making choices about what to buy so that you're as sure as you can be that animals don't suffer in order for you to have food, clothes, cosmetics, and medical treatment, and that people in far-flung parts of the world are fairly paid for producing the goods you buy and have decent working conditions and standards of living. Usually this is called *ethical living* and *ethical shopping* but for the purposes of this book I've put it all under the heading of green living.

Thinking about the environment, and how to be greener, changes all the time. Every day there are articles in newspapers and magazines that contradict similar articles written the week before. Many people argue that scientists are being hysterical when they say that human beings and the way they live are damaging the environment. Some scientists say that too. The prime minister may think that science will save the planet and that there's no need to stop flying to faraway holiday destinations, and in the long run that may turn out to be the case. But when you stop to think about it, billions of people can't possibly go on using up the planet's resources and creating endless streams of waste without having a negative impact. Even if you don't believe the worst-case predictions, it's worth living a greener lifestyle just to make the world a nicer place.

It's impossible to give you definitive answers, so this book aims to make you think, spark your interest, and get you started on a greener lifestyle. The idea is to do something rather than nothing. But don't set yourself unrealistic goals. You can't change your entire way of life overnight. Make simple changes to start with and make bigger changes as and when you can afford and manage to. When you start being greener it will become second nature and you'll discover that much of it is really just common sense. Caring about the environment you live in eventually leads you to care more about the wider environment and the people in it.

Conventions Used in This Book

To help you navigate this book I set up a few conventions:

- *Italics* are used for emphasis and to highlight new words or terms when they're defined for the first time – such as green jargon like *carbon neutral.*

- Web site addresses appear in a different typeface called monofont, such as `www.wiley.co.uk`. Be aware that if a URL is so long it wraps to a second line, you type it in exactly as if there were no break – no hyphens are inserted.

- Sidebars (the shaded grey boxes) contain information that, although interesting, may not be of interest or helpful to every reader. But if they don't apply to you now you may find them relevant at some point in the future.

Foolish Assumptions

They say that you should never assume as it makes an ass out of 'u' and an ass out of 'me', but I've dared to make a few assumptions, such as:

- You've bought this book because you are interested in being a bit greener.

- You're not a scientist or well clued up on all the latest thinking about the environment and the impact human beings are having on it.

✔ You want a few practical suggestions on how you can make your own lifestyle a bit greener rather than wanting to change the world overnight.

✔ You don't mind having a book 'For Dummies' on your bookshelf or in the loo because everybody has to start somewhere.

✔ You'll use the book as a guide rather than a source of definitive answers.

✔ You'll use the contacts and organisations given in this book to find out more, to give you all the information that's not covered in the following chapters, and to keep you up to date with all the latest green thinking and initiatives in the future.

How This Book is Organised

Green Living For Dummies is organised into six parts. The chapters in each part cover different aspects of green living and I've tried not to get too technical but keep it very practical instead.

Part 1: Your Environment, Your Responsibility

The first two chapters cover the problems faced by inhabitants of the planet and why scientists think that human beings may be responsible for causing damage to the environment.

These chapters contain much discussion about climate change. Scientists agree that weather patterns are changing – storms are getting stormier, floods getting more frequent, summers getting hotter and drier, and ice at the poles is melting. Many of them argue that's because of the pressure put on the planet by the billions of people living on it, using up irreplaceable fossil fuels like oil and coal and pumping carbon gases into the atmosphere as a result. Other scientists say that the climate changes are nothing to do with human behaviour and it's just what happens over thousands of years. This part covers the arguments of the first group of scientists who believe that people have to change their lifestyles and maps out what they think will happen in the long term if human beings don't become greener.

Part II: Living a Green Lifestyle

Green living starts at home and Part II of this book is all about what you can do at home to be greener. Maybe you're not completely convinced that human behaviour has to change, but feel that you'd rather make changes than risk your grandchildren blaming you for not taking the warnings seriously. Either way, I offer lots of simple, inexpensive ways you can change your habits at home that not only help you play your part but save you money.

Being green is cheaper than not being green because it's mainly about using and buying less of most things, including electricity and water, and reusing, repairing, and recycling as much as possible – all of which has the pleasing side effect of saving you money on bills.

There are also lots of ways of being greener at home that do cost money but they are likely to pay for themselves in the long run and this part covers those too. For example, you can invest in solar panels to heat your water and your home. They're still quite expensive to buy and install but they're an investment that saves you money on heating bills.

Nowhere in this book do I suggest that you have to make these kinds of big, expensive changes. I argue that even the smallest of changes makes you greener. Don't feel pressurised into green living – do what you can when you can, and do what you can afford. This part of the book has plenty of suggestions to fit all circumstances.

Part III: Green Shopping

While green living is fundamentally about using and buying less of everything, this part of the book recognises that you can't stop shopping altogether. You still need essentials like food and clothes. The chapters in this part look at what makes some items greener than others. Sometimes it can be a toss up between several options that have green elements and you have to make a choice. The labels have all the information but it can take time to absorb all that information. Green shopping can be time-consuming until you get used to it, and products change frequently. To keep on being as green as possible you need to keep an eye open for newer, greener versions of things you usually buy.

This part also looks at green financial products. These are more usually described as ethical products because they are about investing your money in companies or organisations that behave ethically – they don't invest in companies that sell arms or tobacco, for example. Being ethical is part of being green.

Part IV: Thinking Green Outside the Home

While green living starts at home, it doesn't have to end there. You can be greener outside the home too – at work, at school, and in the wider community. This part looks at how to spread the word. Just by behaving in a greener way, your greenness may well rub off on other people, but you can also ask for changes to be made. Talk to your boss at work about ways to make the workplace greener. Suggest changes that save money too – always something to make a boss sit up and listen. As a parent, you can talk to teachers about being greener in your child's school and if you offer to help make those changes happen you're sure to be welcomed with open arms. This part has practical suggestions that you can to put into action yourself.

Part V: Travelling Without Doing Any More Damage to the Planet

This part looks at travelling greener and taking greener holidays. The greenest way to travel is to walk or cycle so that you're not using up any fuel. You may need to eat a bit more to get the energy but then again think how lean and fit you can become if you leave the car at home. If you're near enough to a bus or train service, you can walk to the station or bus stop and take public transport the rest of the way.

Of course, not everyone is able to take public transport or walk or cycle to work, school, the shops, or to see friends and family. For many people the car is the only real option because there simply isn't any accessible or convenient bus or train service. But you can still reduce the number of car journeys by car sharing, lift sharing, or changing habits so that you do more of the things that have to be done by car with fewer trips. And if you can't reduce your car use any more than you have already, make sure that you buy as green a car as possible when you next change. There are greener, more fuel-efficient models coming onto the market just about every week.

More people are flying these days and low-cost flights mean more people are flying more often too. Air travel pumps out vast amounts of carbon gases into the atmosphere. If you can go by train, boat, or bus instead you'll be a greener traveller. If you have to fly, the only options are to take fewer flights or to try to make up for the carbon emissions your flight causes by paying to have trees planted. Perhaps technology will come up with greener flights and we won't need to worry but that hasn't happened yet, so do what you can to be a greener traveller.

Part VI: The Part of Tens

This part has five chapters, and between them they give you sources of more information, Web sites where you can get more ideas and keep up to date, fun things you can join in with or start up in your own area, and ideas for bringing up greener offspring.

Icons Used in This Book

If you flick through the book you'll notice some little icons in the margins. These highlight suggestions and remind you of useful information for the new greener you.

This icon is a target to aim for – it will be to your benefit.

You may have read it already or heard it before but the piece of information highlighted by this icon is well worth storing away in your mind for future use.

I've tried to use this icon sparingly in this book, using it to spell out what could happen if the worst comes to the worst.

This information explains technical phrases or procedures in a more reader-friendly way than you might find in other books.

This icon highlights actions you can take now or plan to do in the future to make you a greener person.

Where to Go from Here

Enjoy the book. You don't need to read it from cover to cover. Keep it handy and dip in and out. Even if you just read the cheat sheets at the front to start with you can be a greener person in no time. If you're a keen gardener start with Chapter 5; if food is your passion go straight to Chapter 7; if your local authority is insisting on recycling, Chapter 6 will be helpful; if you're booking your summer holiday, Chapter 14 is a good place to start.

I tried to make this book as easy to read as possible and to give you lots of sources of more information and ideas. I hope you'll enjoy the book, get a bit greener, spread the word, and follow up the leads I give you. But don't forget that by the time this book is printed there will already be newer, greener products on the shelves, so you have to keep up to date.

Part I
Your Environment, Your Responsibility

'He ain't singin' the blues – he's singin' the greens!'

In this part . . .

*I*f you want to keep the planet in good condition so that your grandchildren can enjoy it, you have to take responsibility for your actions now.

In this part I explain why problems are mounting up and why many scientists now agree that the planet is facing changes because of the impact of human activity. Whether you're aware of it or not, you have an impact. When you read this part and understand how your everyday activities could be contributing to that damage, you can start thinking about what you can do to stop it and even how to repair it. It's not too late as long as everyone accepts they have a role to play.

Chapter 1

Being Greener for the Good of the Planet and Its People

*I*f the world's inhabitants could consume the planet's natural resources – wood, fossil fuels such as oil and coal, water, minerals, and metals – at a rate that allowed the earth to keep on replacing what human beings took out, they would be living sustainably. But human beings use up resources much more quickly than the earth can replace them. As the world's population grows it becomes more difficult for the planet to support all its inhabitants. Anything you can do to cut down your consumption of those resources helps the planet and helps you lead a more sustainable – or greener – lifestyle.

In some cases it's possible to switch to using *renewable resources* – resources the earth can replace as quickly as they're used up. You can buy electricity generated using power from the wind, for example. Wind doesn't run out, so the electricity generated from it is sustainable, green energy.

Green living isn't just about trying to consume fewer of the earth's precious resources and living sustainably. It's about considering the greenest option in everything you consume, whether you're buying food, clothes, cleaning materials, or cosmetics.

Green living also entails trying to repair the planet when you have no option but to act in a way that causes damage to it – for example, taking steps to take some of that carbon out of the atmosphere when you have to take a flight. Being green extends to the way you deal with animals and other people. Most people who think of themselves as green want to be sure that animals don't suffer in order to give them the kind of food, clothes, cosmetics, and medical treatment they need. They also research the goods they buy to make sure that the people producing them in other countries are fairly paid and have decent working conditions and standards of living.

Understanding the Impact of Your Choices

A lot of greener living harks back to the way your parents and grandparents behaved. They bought less because they had less disposable income and reused, repaired, and recycled things because they couldn't afford new ones. Nobody called it green living because it was just the way things had to be done.

As more and more consumer goods became available at affordable prices, and incomes rose to give people more to spend, it became important to have the latest of everything. Old models were thrown away even though they still worked because everyone wanted to keep up with everyone else and have the newest and most fashionable things. No one gave much thought to how much of the earth's resources had gone into making the items in the first place and whether those resources would eventually run out. What happened to stuff after it went into the household rubbish bin and was collected by the bin lorry was of no concern to consumers.

All that's changing as it becomes more obvious that that way of living is having many different impacts on the planet – most of them negative. Resources are running out or are too expensive to extract from the earth's crust. Manufacturing processes use up resources and energy. In turn, those processes give off emissions that carry damaging gases and particles into the atmosphere. The same happens when cars, planes, and other transport vehicles use petrol and diesel to drive them along giving off exhaust gases, particularly carbon gases and particles. (Chapter 2 explains how the earth is being damaged by these emissions.)

Human beings are the deciding factor. You make decisions every day that have an impact on the planet. Some are more damaging than others. If you decide to fly rather than taking the train to your destination, you're responsible for releasing a much greater quantity of damaging carbon gases into the atmosphere. If you drive to work you make a negative impact on the environment; if you cycle you make no impact.

You're responsible for the energy and resources used in the making of everything you buy. If you keep using an item you already have, you're not responsible for the damage caused by the manufacture of a new one. But if you throw your old one away, you fill up landfill sites and are responsible for any toxic chemicals in it leaking into and contaminating the land around the site as well as damaging gases given off during the time it takes for the item to rot away.

It's a big responsibility to bear and it isn't always possible to go without, to keep on using an old item, or to put off buying more, but it's worth thinking about the impact each individual decision makes and weighing up the pros and cons.

Sometimes you can't win! If you go on using your old dishwasher you'll be using more energy and water than if you buy a new, more energy- and water-efficient one. Get as much information as you can before making any decision so that you can make the greenest decision possible.

Changing What You Can as You Can

You can't change the world and save the planet single-handedly overnight. Most people can't afford to change their car to a greener, more fuel-efficient model immediately, switch to organic food, or replace all their cleaning materials and light bulbs with greener versions all at once, but you can do your bit. You can make plenty of changes immediately – by deciding today to buy less and reuse and recycle as much as possible, for example. The idea is to take it a step at a time and not beat yourself up because there's something you can't make greener straight away.

Some of the changes, tips, and suggestions in this book are easier to adopt than others. What you can do sometimes depends on where you live, the type of home you live in, your budget, and even your job. It also depends on your beliefs and principles.

If you don't already recycle, maybe this is the place to start. You can recycle most paper and cardboard, glass and plastic bottles, drink and food cans, and there may be facilities for recycling other plastics in your area. Recycling gets everyone in the household involved and thinking about the need to change.

Taking those first small steps

An old saying points out that the only way to eat an elephant is bite by bite. The same applies to changing to a greener way of living. Accept that you have to make small changes as and when you can afford and manage them. Thinking greener is the most significant step.

The first thing to do is to consider where your priorities lie. For example, not everyone accepts that organic food is better than non-organic food or that it's better for the planet. Someone who lives in an area unsuited to a small car probably doesn't think that they should replace their bigger car with a smaller, more fuel-efficient model. Not everyone can afford to replace their household appliances with newer, more efficient models and they know that disposing of old appliances contributes to the rubbish going to landfill sites.

You have your own set of priorities and yours are as right as anyone else's. As you read through the book, make a list of changes you intend to make over time as well as the ones you'd like to adopt in an ideal world. Just tick them off the list as and when you can.

The government sees waste reduction as a priority. It wants everyone to reduce waste by producing less in the first place – buying goods with less packaging; reusing plastic bags when you go back to the supermarkets; and recycling as much as possible.

Read as much information as you can get your hands on in hard copy and on the Internet. Throughout this book, I give you Web addresses that can give you more information and direct you to other useful Web sites. If you don't have a computer, use one in your public library. The more you read the more you discover that there are still lots of arguments about how best to reduce the impact human beings make on the planet.

It can be a problem knowing exactly what to believe and how to be as green as possible. Don't let that put you off. Keep an open mind and be prepared to rethink your priorities as new information becomes available. Research is being carried out into most areas of green living and arguments will change. In the meantime take one small step every time you feel you can afford to or are ready to and keep aspiring to be greener.

Making it a habit at home

Just as charity begins at home, so does green living. Chapters 3 and 4 look at the green issues to take into consideration when you're moving, looking for a home, deciding on how big it should be and where, and at the everyday green issues that arise in the kitchen, bathroom, doing the laundry and washing up, and even in the bedroom.

Change little things as and when you can. Replace light bulbs with energy-efficient ones as your ordinary bulbs blow; replace broken appliances with energy-efficient ones when they need replacing. Adopting some – or even just one – of the green-living suggestions in this book is a good start. The book focuses on practical tips and information that help you adopt a greener lifestyle over time. Do just one thing and you'll be greener!

Looking for ways to be greener becomes habit-forming. You take one small step and then you look for the next and before you know it green living is second nature and part of your everyday life:

- You get out of bed to have a shower instead of a bath so that you use less water and less energy heating the water. Next time you cut down your shower time to conserve water still further.

- You dress in organic cotton clothes, and have organic cereal for breakfast with free trade coffee.

- You walk to work or to the nearest train station and leave the car in the garage.

- At work you use recycled paper, print on both sides, then dispose of it in the recycling bin when you've finished. You switch off lights and computer equipment when you're out of the office and before you go home – making sure that your colleagues do the same.

- On your way home you buy organic food for dinner so you don't have to make an additional trip to the shops by car.

- You wash up the heavy pans and dishes in the sink with biodegradable detergent. The rest goes in the energy-efficient dishwasher and you switch it on when there's a full load.

- Before going to bed, you make sure that all the lights and electrical appliances are turned off at the wall and not left on standby.

Green living needn't be complicated and as you go through this book you'll find all these points and more, and the reasons why they are good green steps to follow. But there are many more positive steps you can take and if you're still not convinced that human beings can or need to make a difference, Chapter 2 explains how the planet is being damaged and what will happen if everyone doesn't do their bit.

When you introduce green living at home, everyone can be involved. Children learn from adults and pass the word on to their friends who pass it on to their parents. Give everyone a role to play by putting them in charge of some aspect of your greener household.

Measuring your environmental footprint

A useful way to understand the impact you have on the environment is to measure your *ecological footprint* (the amount of land needed to support your consumption of goods and resources). Think of it as a way of describing the amount of land required to farm your food, mine your energy sources, transport your goods and services, and hold your waste.

The Earth Day Network – a network of environmental organisations and projects – estimates that there are only 1.8 biologically productive global hectares per person left on the planet. The average ecological footprint in the UK is 7.6 global hectares per person, so the average Briton is consuming more than their fair share of what the earth has left to give.

You can measure your own ecological footprint by inputting some information at the Earth Day Network Web site at www.myfootprint.org.uk. Start by looking at how many hectares of earth you're using to satisfy your lifestyle and thinking about how to cut down your personal impact on the planet.

Becoming carbon neutral

When you fly or drive, carbon is released into the atmosphere. When you heat your home or turn on the lights or buy new goods carbon is released into the atmosphere at some point in the process of producing the electricity or during the manufacturing process. As the end user, that carbon is your responsibility.

Being *carbon neutral* means reducing your carbon footprint (see the previous section) as much as possible and then offsetting unavoidable carbon emission. The Carbon Neutral Company at www.carbonneutral.com helps organisations to reduce their carbon footprint. *Offsetting* means paying to help develop schemes and technologies to reduce carbon produced or paying for or planting enough trees to absorb the carbon you're responsible for releasing into the atmosphere. Take a look at the Future Forests Web site at www.futureforests.com for more information on how to go about having trees planted.

The problem with offsetting carbon emission by planting trees is that the whole of the earth's surface would eventually have to be covered in trees. The only real way to stop so much carbon being pumped into the atmosphere is to use less fuel and energy, take fewer flights, leave the car at home more often, and buy less. Paying for trees doesn't let you off the hook.

Conserving is the Key

Using is old hat – *conserving* is the new watchword. If you conserve electricity, water, fuel, and resources, fewer of them need to be extracted from the earth and processed into usable forms. Not only are the original natural materials like coal and oil extracted at slower rates but less energy is needed to process them and fewer damaging gases released in the process. The only way to conserve what the planet has to offer is to consume less.

Water and energy are the two resources that you can effectively conserve in significant quantities. Very few people in the UK had to think about conserving water until the dry winters in the early 2000s led to hosepipe bans in the south-east of England. The average person wastes 15 litres of water each time they brush their teeth by letting the tap run. Just turning the tap off while brushing your teeth, having showers instead of baths, and flushing the toilet only when there's brown matter there saves gallons of water a day. You can conserve even more water if you collect rainwater for washing the car and watering the garden and reuse dish and bath water for flushing and car washing.

Having a water meter installed, and devices that can show you how much energy particular appliances use, concentrates the mind. You can see the bills ticking up and can make decisions about where to make savings. By saving yourself money you're also conserving precious natural resources and vice versa. There's more on energy and water conservation in Chapters 4 and 5.

Energy use, along with recycling, is where you can make most difference, both for the environment and your bank account. Replacing all your ordinary light bulbs with energy-efficient ones can cut your energy use and your bill – you can save up to £9 a year on your electricity bill for every energy-efficient light bulb you use; turning the heating down by just one degree at the thermostat can save you a tenth of your electricity bill; switching TV, computers, and mobile phone chargers off at the wall when not in use instead of leaving them on standby or still plugged in and switched on without an appliance on the end can save you a lot of money. Many appliances use on standby as much as 85 per cent of the energy that they use when switched on fully. If you save energy you are helping reduce demand overall but you're also saving on your bills. You can find more information about energy efficiency at home from the Energy Saving Trust at www.est.org.uk/myhome.

Reducing, reusing, repairing, and recycling are the four most important words when it comes to adopting a greener lifestyle. Much of what you throw in the rubbish bin can be reused:

- **Plastic bags** are easy to reuse over and over again for your supermarket shopping rather than chucking them out and asking for new ones. When they're no longer safe enough to carry shopping home in, use them as rubbish bags, for dirty cat litter, or cleaning out the budgie's cage.

- **Plastic cartons** from the Chinese takeaway can be washed and used as storage boxes for the freezer or lunch boxes.

- **Sandwich bags** can be washed and used again.

- **Plastic bottles** can be filled with water and kept cool in the fridge.

- **Computer paper** has two sides, remember, so use both to print on. Use shredded paper for bedding for the hamster or rabbit.

✔ **Old towels and tea towels** are ideal for washing the car, windows, and floors.

✔ **Coffee grinds** and other organic material can be reused by making them into compost which you can use in the garden (more on this in Chapter 5).

You can repair and reuse clothes and electrical appliances as well. If there are things you can't reuse, remember that there may be someone else who can. Giving things to the charity shop or to friends is another way of reusing and recycling them.

When all other avenues have been exhausted, sort your waste into stuff that can be recycled and the stuff that has to go into household rubbish. Reduce the waste element as far as possible.

When you've worked out what goes into your rubbish you can work out ways of reducing the amount of that material you bring home with you. If a lot of it is packaging that can't be recycled or reused, look for equivalent items in the shops that come with less packaging. Chapter 6 has much more information about reducing, reusing, repairing, and recycling.

Shopping Greenly and Ethically

Strictly speaking shopping isn't just about buying green products. Ethical issues play a big part for most consumers who want to be green. Green shopping is about buying the greenest possible options – food produced using as few chemicals as possible, grown locally in season, and transported over as short distances as possible to reduce the amount of transport fuel used, for example. Clothes made from organically produced materials, goods made from recycled materials rather that resources that have to be mined from the earth, second-hand or vintage goods, and those made from biodegradable materials are all green options.

But the other important aspect of green shopping is the ethical one; looking at how the people and animals involved in the production were treated. Shoppers are keen to know that the workers, producers, suppliers, and farmers involved in the production chain are paid fairly, have good working conditions, and can sustain production because they had enough left after feeding themselves and their families to maintain their premises, or buy new equipment and seeds. People are concerned about child labour and sweatshop working conditions and want to make sure that they aren't buying goods produced in that way.

There are also concerns about animal welfare. Meat eaters, as well as people who don't eat meat, are increasingly concerned that the meat comes from animals raised in humane conditions rather than intensively farmed in dirty overcrowded pens and cages. For that reason sales of organic and free range food products are growing. Chapters 7 and 8 have more on green and ethical shopping in food and non-food sectors and they explain how the Fairtrade scheme works – set up to ensure that producers keep a fair slice of the price the customer pays so that they can live a better lifestyle and stay in production.

Being Environmentally Sound at Work

Sometimes people leave all their principles behind went they go to work. It's easy to be green at home and forget that you can be just as green in the office. You can influence even more people in the workplace than at home – persuading your bosses and colleagues to be green too and take the green-living message out to their own families and friends.

All the measures you put in place at home – energy-efficient appliances and equipment, water saving and energy conservation devices and strategies, recycling and reusing schemes – can translate to the workplace.

Your boss won't thank you if you ask for a meeting and simply complain that the working environment isn't green enough for your liking, but if you ask for a meeting and have a host of changes that can be made, you have thought through how they can be made, and justified the need and the money-saving potential of them, your boss will be hooked. Just printing on both sides of the printing paper cuts the paper bills in half! You may not get all you want but you can make a start. Even if your employer can't afford to buy new energy-efficient equipment he or she will usually welcome a visit from an energy-saving expert who can identify savings that will cut the bills.

Even if your boss won't consider green practices, you may be able to persuade colleagues to start up a car-sharing scheme, use both sides of computer paper, and make sure that lights and equipment are turned off when not in use. Think through how your workplace can be greener with the help of Chapter 10 and give it a try.

Travelling Smart

The biggest problem for the environment is the carbon emissions given off during travel. Cars and other vehicles using internal combustion engines burn fuel to propel the vehicle and emit damaging greenhouse gases into the atmosphere in the process. The fuels used come mainly from coal and oil, which are becoming scarcer and more expensive. There are alternatives being worked on, such as biofuels and hydrogen as explained in Chapters 12 and 13, but at the moment few vehicles use them.

Cars and planes are the biggest culprits. More and more cars are taking to the roads as developing economies grow rapidly and more people can afford to desert public transport. Flights are affordable as the no-frills airlines offer more routes and cheaper seats and so more people can choose to travel by air and to fly more often. Chapter 12 looks at the future on the roads and in the air. Some scientists believe that new technologies will provide more efficient engines that will cause less damage to the planet. Others think that the increase in demand for car and air travel will outstrip those technological advances and congestion on the ground and pollution in the air will bring the planet to a standstill.

In the meantime, the greener traveller cycles or walks instead of taking the car and if that's not possible uses public transport. Flying is out if the train can take the strain because the train is the greener option. The section 'Becoming carbon neutral', earlier in this chapter, explains how to offset your travel emissions.

Banking Better

You can change your life for the greener even when it comes to money. Whether you're spending it or saving and investing it, you can affect the planet and some of its people. You can help harm them if you buy or invest in the wrong things. You can avoid causing harm and may even do some good by making ethical investment decisions.

If you choose to buy only green and ethical products, demand for them goes up and more producers get the message. Consumers with money have power. If producers are persuaded to switch to greener production methods and there are more green options on the market, prices come down so more people can buy greener products.

Just as customers can drive change by spending money, they can drive change by refusing to buy certain goods. If you refuse to buy goods and services you believe are damaging the planet or harming people or animals, the firm selling them may get the message and be forced to change for the better.

If you prefer to save your money on the grounds that being truly green means buying less, you can save in green accounts or investment products. Think carefully about what you do and do not want your money to be used for and take ethical financial advice from an independent financial adviser. You can get a list from the Association of Independent Financial Advisers on 0207 628 1287 or www.unbiased.co.uk. Chapter 9 has more information on the kinds of investments that count as ethical or green investments and the different green accounts on offer from the banks and other financial institutions.

Creating a Green Society

You can't save the planet by yourself but by making small changes to your own behaviour you influence family and friends, who each influence their network of family and friends, and the word spreads.

Society changes because the people in it change and lead by example. If more people want locally produced or organically grown food in the supermarket, the big chains will buy more from their suppliers who will in turn adapt their farming methods to meet the demand. Shoppers are making greener choices and the supermarkets are gradually changing.

You can do the same by talking to your children's teachers and other parents about adopting greener methods in schools – buying and using recycled paper, printing on both sides to cut down wastage, recycling more of the school's rubbish, and growing vegetables for school lunches on that unused piece of land by the football pitch. There's more on helping to make your children's schools greener in Chapter 11.

Anywhere people gather and form a community – at work, church groups, organisations like the Women's Institute, or the golf club – you can help to make things greener. As separate organisations become greener in their thinking, running, and planning, you're helping to create a greener society.

You can't do it all yourself but you can encourage and motivate other people to join with you to live greener lifestyles and do their bit for the planet. Your children will thank you for helping to create a greener society that they can bring their own children up in.

Setting up community projects that work

If no community projects in your area are addressing local environmental problems, set one up. It's highly unlikely that the environment you live in is perfect. There will be stretches of rivers or canals that need cleaning up, neglected pieces of land that can – with the owner's permission – be turned into a wildflower meadow to attract birds and insects, or an old building that should be restored. Community projects that get people from all age groups and sections of society involved work best as people learn from each other and there's always someone to raise flagging spirits when the going gets tough. Chapter 19 has ten types of environmental projects to get the community pulling together, from setting up a local trading system or a recycling project to virtual volunteering and car-sharing schemes.

Take stock of the environmental problems in your area and check relevant national organisations and their Web sites for information. There are dozens of them mentioned throughout this book and in Chapter 19. Contact existing organisations you think may be interested in becoming involved, such as schools and community groups. You need just a few willing volunteers to get things started.

Make sure that you take good legal advice about how best to set up your organisation, as you're likely to need insurance to protect workers on some projects and there may be other checks required if buildings or children are involved.

Supporting the local agenda

In 1992 the United Nations released a ground-breaking action plan for sustainable development called *Agenda 21* (The United Nations action plan is called Agenda 21; local schemes and projects come under the title of Local Agenda 21), a blueprint that sets out what can be done to contribute to global sustainability in the 21st century – hence the name. The idea was to encourage people to act in a sustainable or green way at their local level, involving local government, business, and the community.

Two results that an Agenda 21 programme should deliver at a local level are:

✔ Community involvement in the development and implementation of a sustainable programme

✔ Support for local people and businesses and equal access to the opportunities generated by the programme

Basically, a Local Agenda 21 project should involve the local community in deciding what needs to be done, what changes to make, and help the local community make them.

It's usually up to local councils to develop and put these programmes into action. The kinds of programmes your local authority may come up with include:

✔ Energy and water efficiency projects

✔ Recycling and waste reduction schemes

✔ Worm farms, composting, and green gardening systems

✔ Alternative energy projects, such as solar lighting in local parks

✔ The promotion of public transport, walking, and cycling schemes

✔ Public information on unique flora and fauna and local ecosystems, which may include giveaways such as plant seeds

✔ Exhibitions on low-energy design for homes

✔ Educational programmes for people in different local communities

✔ Raising awareness of opportunities in green jobs, such as in council nurseries, parks, and gardens.

If you type 'Local Agenda 21' into a search engine you will find a whole list of local authority Web sites outlining their individual projects – including what's going on in your area.

Supporting local traders

You can support your local community socially and economically by buying your food, gifts, crafts, items for your home, and clothes from local producers and local traders. You can even think about investing some of your spare cash in local companies involved in green industries.

Reaping the Rewards of a Sustainable Lifestyle

As with most things that are done with the best possible motives – you reap what you sow! There are plenty of benefits of living a green lifestyle. Being green can improve your life on all sorts of levels.

Saving the environment can save you money too

You can save money by going green. Here are some examples:

✔ You start consuming less. For example, turning off lights reduces your electricity bill and taking showers instead of baths and recycling your grey water reduces your water bill.

✔ Growing your own fruit and vegetables in your greener garden is much cheaper than buying them from a shop.

✔ Walking, cycling, and using public transport is much cheaper than running a car.

✔ Recycling and reusing your home appliances and clothes saves a packet.

Being green means being profitable

It's becoming increasingly clear to many businesses that the more positive the contribution they make to the environment and to the community, the more likely they are to find loyal customers and make money. Customers no longer tolerate firms that damage the environment by pumping toxic chemicals into nearby rivers, killing fish. Increasingly, they want to know that they're buying goods from producers who don't waste the earth's natural resources and who pay their workers fair wages and give them decent working conditions. It can take a while for companies to realise what their customers want and become greener and more ethical traders – but some short-term financial pain will ultimately bring long-term gain. Regulations are also getting stricter when it comes to businesses and the environmental impact they have, so firms would do well to follow the best practice in their industry and stay ahead of the game.

This economic realisation grows as more people support those businesses that are ethical and responsible. Ways in which you can encourage businesses to be greener include:

✔ Buying products from green and ethical firms.

✔ Investing your money in ethical firms.

✔ Boycotting those companies that continue to compromise the planet's long-term future, especially those companies that spend money on some environmental and social initiatives while continuing to be involved in unsustainable industries.

Living a green lifestyle keeps the doctor away

Many of the green tips in this book can make you healthier if you follow them! Here are some examples:

✔ Walking or cycling instead of using the car is a great way of getting essential exercise when you're working long hours and are too busy to go to the gym. The more people stop using their cars, the less smog and pollution there is – which can help people with conditions like asthma.

✔ There's no scientific proof that organic food is better for you but if you buy organic fresh food it is produced using fewer chemicals.

✔ Outfitting and decorating your home with natural products reduces the amount of toxic chemicals that you breathe in.

Leaving a legacy for future generations

If all human beings consumed the planet's resources at the same rate as the Americans, it would take six planets to support everyone. As the economies of developing countries grow, their populations get richer and want what people in the West have – cars, air travel, electronic gadgets, and plentiful good food – and who can blame them? But one planet simply can't cope in the long term. If you want to have anything left on this planet for your grandchildren to look forward to you have to act now.

If you go on being greedy and ignoring the plight of the planet, some examples of what may happen are

✔ Rising sea levels resulting from warmer seas melting the polar icecaps will result in the loss of land, with smaller islands disappearing first and then possibly whole coastal regions.

✔ Stronger storms and floods may wipe out large communities in their path.

✔ Increased flooding due to rising sea levels will wipe out prime low-lying agricultural land, which places greater pressure on existing areas to mass-produce food.

✔ Increased mass production of food could lead to lower-quality foods and have major health implications on the population.

✔ Changing ecosystems may result in new viruses continuing to be introduced into largely populated areas.

✔ Existing dry areas will become drier, reducing water supply to urban areas and limiting agricultural production in rural areas. In developing nations, this would result in increasing levels of poverty.

If you start to consume only what you need, stop wasting, do things more naturally, and invest locally, you have gone a long way to leaving future generations a planet that they can benefit from.

Chapter 2

Understanding the Environment and Its Problems

*T*he headlines over the past few years speak for themselves: *Arctic meltdown just decades away; Global warming fuelled 2005 hurricanes; Natural disasters becoming more common; Earth hottest it's been in 2,000 years; Global warming may take economic toll.* Most scientists believe that climate change is caused by human beings and their behaviour. But there are still some scientists who disagree about the extent of the problem, and if scientists can't agree how are you supposed to know what's going on?

Public opinion seems to be shifting towards the idea that human beings and their lifestyles are having a negative impact on the planet. More and more people are feeling that it's important to make some changes – however small – to do their bit in the hope of saving the planet, as it is, for future generations. You have probably reached that opinion or you wouldn't have bought this book.

This chapter explains the damage being done to the planet and what can be done to reverse it.

Considering Consumption

When you don't take care of something, it often becomes unreliable and if you don't service or repair it, it's likely to break down. Human beings haven't been taking care of the planet very well and it's time to stop causing damage and start repairing it.

The basic problem is that human beings aspire to what they see as better lifestyles, owning more and more goods like cars, TVs, computers, dishwashers, toasters, and so on. As demand increases it takes more of the earth's resources to provide raw materials to make those goods and more energy to put them through the manufacturing process.

The more people there are making more demands, the worse the situation gets. More people want more goods, cars, and airline flights. Not only are precious resources being used up, but damaging gases are being pumped out into the atmosphere through the burning of fossil fuels like oil and coal to create energy. And once all those goods are finished with, the waste generated has to be disposed of.

The warning signs suggest that the planet is being damaged as a result of all this consumption, and the damage is showing up in the form of changing weather patterns – the kind of weather that results in floods, hurricanes, the melting of Arctic ice caps, drought and famine, and other natural disasters widely reported around the globe.

Changing Climate

How often have you thought that every summer seems to be hotter than the last one; or what a mild winter you seem to be having? Maybe you're getting older and your mind is starting to play tricks or maybe it is getting warmer.

The issue of climate change has been a hot topic of debate scientifically and politically for some time now. The debate is not so much centred on whether climate is changing – science shows that it is – but on the extent to which this will cause problems in future and what if anything can be done to stop and reverse those changes.

Statistics from the United Nations' Intergovernmental Panel on Climate Change show the extent of the problem:

- Average global surface temperature has increased by approximately 0.6 degrees centigrade since the late 19th century.
- The warming rate since 1976 has been 0.17 degrees a decade.
- Alpine and continental glaciers have reduced in size as a result of 20th-century warming.
- Northern hemisphere lakes and rivers are covered in ice for two weeks less than they were in the 1970s.

The reason the planet has a climate change problem is because humans add too much carbon dioxide and nitrous oxide to the atmosphere. These form *greenhouse gases* – a layer of gases that hold heat between themselves and the surface of the earth – that heat the earth up.

Burning fossil fuels is the main culprit in creating greenhouse gases (see the sidebar 'The damaging impact of using fossil fuels', later in this chapter). Fossil fuels are burned to refine and manufacture products in factories, produce electricity, and to drive cars or fly planes.

Cutting down trees makes the situation worse. Trees help to take carbon dioxide out of the atmosphere as part of the photosynthesis process. They hold that carbon dioxide until they are cut down. If and when those trees are then burned the carbon dioxide they were holding is released into the atmosphere. Planting more trees helps to reduce the amount of carbon dioxide in the earth's atmosphere – but if trees aren't planted and don't grow as quickly as others are being chopped down that makes the situation worse.

Warming up the globe

Climate change is probably the most serious of current environmental problems. The earth has been warming faster than at any stage in history. Many scientists blame this warming for rising sea levels, unnatural weather patterns, and changing ecosystems. The polar ice caps have started melting and sea levels are rising. If the ice caps continue to melt at current rates, some countries will see their coastal towns and villages vanish and some smaller island countries may cease to exist. Not everywhere gets warmer as a result of this rise in the earth's temperature: some areas get colder because of water from the melting ice caps mixing with the sea water.

Burning and refining fossil fuels like oil, coal, and gas for electrical energy, and for use in transport (especially cars and aeroplanes), is the main culprit because, when processed, fossil fuels give off or emit greenhouse gases like carbon dioxide. They're called greenhouse gases because they act like a greenhouse around the earth – creating a blanket that traps heat between it and the earth.

Ignoring the weather – at your peril

The UN's Intergovernmental Panel on Climate Change says that the impact of climate change is increased exposure to variations in temperature, rainfall, and frequency and severity of weather-related events like storms and floods. Other effects will be rising sea levels, and more danger of big bush fires, pest infestations, and infectious diseases – all a result of a 0.6-degree average increase in global temperatures.

This would all be okay if human beings had the capacity to adapt to the changing conditions. Although improved technology makes it possible to predict storms and floods more accurately, in many cases there's very little people can do to stop them or get out of the way of them, and they can only wait for the disaster to strike and then react to the result.

If the earth continues to get warmer you may see more:

- Big forest fires close to urban areas because of extreme heat
- Infectious disease epidemics created in tropical areas
- Years of drought in dry regions
- Coastal erosion and building collapses due to increased and more intense rainfall
- Flash floods due to monsoons and freak storms

Bringing more natural catastrophes

The incidence and power of weather-related catastrophes is increasing, with scientists agreeing that the increase is directly related to rising ocean temperatures. Recent hurricanes in the USA such as the one that hit New Orleans in 2005 and the floods in South-East Asia and Europe are the kinds of natural catastrophes many scientists predict will be a lot more common in future.

Drying up the earth

One of the effects of increased global temperatures is to make arid areas even drier and droughts last much longer. This increases pressure on urban and rural water supplies. This pressure is made worse by the huge amounts of water wasted in homes, at work, in the factory, on the farm, and in leisure facilities like golf courses.

The traditional method of damming natural waterways, creating new reservoirs, and concreting streams and rivers is just not effective any more in the driest parts of the earth. Water sources are drying up so there is a need to think of other ways to supply people with the water they need.

Seeing the climate change warning signs

You probably know from watching the news that the following areas of the world have serious problems because of climate change:

- **Africa:** Africa is well known as having low *food security* – another way of saying that starvation is a part of everyday life in many countries across the continent. Obviously increased drought conditions do nothing to improve the situation. Many inland lakes and rivers that provide much of the fish are almost dried up.

- **Asia:** Large proportions of low-lying land in Bangladesh and India are becoming more susceptible to flooding due to sea levels rising, the increasing intensity of rainfall, and the lowering of the water table due to over-irrigation. It is now commonplace for Bangladesh, in particular, to have major floods every year that force millions of people out of their homes.

- **Australia and the Pacific:** Nearly every year there are serious bushfire threats around several of the major cities and towns due to a drop in rainfall. Rising sea levels are jeopardising the future of many Pacific islands, with fears that several more islands will join the queue of those that have already drowned, such as Tebua Tarawa and Abanuea. Islands identified as being in danger include Kiribati, Tuvalu, and the atolls that form the Marshall Islands.

- **Europe:** Annual floods are now the norm in many parts of Europe due to the rapid melting of snow in alpine regions when the warmer temperatures arrive. Some floods have also been caused by freak rainfall – such as the one that rampaged through Prague in 2002.

> ✔ **Latin America:** The Amazon rainforest, which is home to diverse species of frogs and mammals, and an enormous range of plant life, is in trouble because of urban and agricultural encroachment and dry weather caused by global warming.

> ✔ **North America:** Many in the United States are now starting to take notice of the whole climate change issue as a result of the increasing number of severe weather-related events in recent years. Hurricane Katrina, which devastated the low-lying city of New Orleans, was a result of the combined impact of increasing sea levels and a massive storm surge. Other regions of the North America have completely different issues, such as bushfires in California and Oregon, shortages of water in Arizona and California, and the ever thinning ice cover in the sub-arctic and the arctic regions of northern Canada.

Investigating Human Impact

Ecosystems change not only as a result of global warming but from direct human impact from production methods, urban sprawl, land clearing, and tourism.

Irreversible changes are taking place in some of the planet's oldest and most valuable ecosystems, such as the Amazon rainforest in South America, the Everglades in the USA, and the Great Barrier Reef off the Australian coastline. Animals, plants, birds, and insects are affected by such changes, with many species becoming extinct as a result.

Emitting toxic waste

Exhaust pipes and factory chimneys emit more than greenhouse gases. The other dangerous gases and particles they put out can bring on respiratory infections and illnesses.

Then there are the nasty by-products resulting from increasing chemical production. Industries that manufacture medicines, plastics, textiles, detergents, paints, and pesticides have to be much more careful today how they dispose of these by-products but, not long ago, they were released uncontrolled into the air, rivers, streams, and wherever companies could hide them. Modern production methods can reduce the amount of waste produced as a result of manufacturing processes but these still have to be disposed of.

Many waste materials, and much of the packaging and most of the products when they've outlived their useful life, end up in landfill sites or are burned in incinerators. In either case they eventually end up emitting the toxic chemicals they contain back into the land or the air.

Using up energy

Electrical energy is the most popular form of energy supplied around the world. The cheapest and most reliable way of providing electricity to cities and towns has been from power plants that burn fossil fuels such as coal. The energy required for transport comes from refining oil – also a fossil fuel. Burning fossil fuels causes much of the greenhouse gas problem that many scientists think is responsible for climate change. See the sidebar 'The damaging impact of using fossil fuels', later in this chapter.

There are now *alternative energy sources* (such as wind, hydro and solar power) that produce little to no greenhouse gas emissions and if the market for them increased, they would also become more affordable. But even if you stick with electricity and petrol, there are some simple lifestyle changes you can make to greatly reduce your reliance on them. There are practical tips on how to do that throughout this book.

Wasting away

One of the great examples of how humans take the planet for granted is waste disposal. Historically, waste is incinerated or sent to landfill sites hidden away on the edges of cities and towns.

Burning waste in big incinerators has been stopped in many countries, as it's a major source of air pollution and greenhouse gases. The alternative, however, is to send more waste to landfill sites. But now many large urban areas are running out of suitable landfill sites as the amount of waste produced continues to rise. Land in the areas around landfill sites becomes contaminated from the toxic chemicals leaking from the waste in the site.

Most countries are now focusing on reducing the amount of waste that goes into landfill sites by using the carrot-and-stick approach to get people to reduce the amount of waste they're responsible for, to reuse as much as possible, to recycle what can't be reused, to turn household and garden waste into compost, and to throw away only what's left. Chapter 6 deals with waste reduction and disposal.

Growing urban populations

One of the big consequences of economic growth in developing countries is movement of poor people from rural areas into the urban areas in search of work. That causes a whole raft of ethical as well as environmental problems.

Moving into the cities

It's estimated that in the not-too-distant future there will be more than ten world cities with populations over 20 million people. Currently there are only four – New York (USA), Tokyo (Japan), Seoul (South Korea), and Mexico City (you guessed it – in Mexico). The new megacities will include Beijing in China; Cairo in Egypt; Jakarta in Indonesia; Mumbai and Delhi in India; Lagos in Nigeria; and São Paulo in Brazil.

As poor rural populations flock to the big cities where global investment is taking place, the result is that vast conurbations of poor people looking for jobs live with their families in confined spaces. The resulting social, health, and environmental issues can be impossible to control. Many of these *mega-cities* become perfect incubators for many modern-day viruses that kill large numbers of people, including AIDS and flu.

Large populations put pressure on water and energy supplies. Food and other essential products have to be transported into towns and cities to support people who no longer produce their own food and clothing. Mass production farming methods are required to produce the food needed. The amount of waste that has to be disposed of grows, and as wealth grows so does demand for products and the energy required to make and power them . . . leading to further carbon emissions and pollution. On the other side of the coin rural areas become depopulated and less productive.

Increasing the number of cars

More people moving to urban areas causes those areas to sprawl. Having a car allows you to live on the outskirts of an urban area and drive everywhere you need to go – which means cities can sprawl even farther. And the farther out you live the more you feel you need to have a car! It's a catch-22 of modern life.

If more people decided to live in areas close to public transport and within walking distance of community services and facilities, there would be less demand for cars. Chapter 3 looks at some of the factors to consider when deciding where to live and the type of home that is the greenest choice.

The damaging impact of using fossil fuels

Fossil fuels are energy-rich substances formed from long-buried plants and micro-organisms. Often found under the sea bed, they include oil, coal, and natural gas. Fossil fuels have been influential in powering the growth of modern society, especially giving the ability to industrialise and transport people and materials from one place to another. In 2002 it was calculated that the world used 29 billion barrels of oil, 5 billion metric tons of coal, and 2.6 trillion cubic metres (92 trillion cubic feet) of natural gas. Around 84 million barrels of oil were used every day in 2005.

These substances are extracted from the earth's crust and are mostly refined into suitable fuel products, such as petrol, heating oil, and kerosene. One of the biggest environmental impacts is the burning of these fossil fuels. When fossil fuels are burned, sulphur, nitrogen, and carbon combine with oxygen to form compounds known as oxides. These form gases that cause numerous environmental problems, including climate change, particle pollution, and acid rain.

Fossil fuels are being consumed at much faster rates than they are produced in the earth's crust and, as such, will eventually run out. Alternative energy sources that have minimal impact on the environment include solar and wind power.

Taxing energy supplies

If you look around your home town at night think about the number of office blocks fully lit even though everyone's gone home. Empty shops, streets, and car parks stay lit all night while all the people who used them in the daytime are at home with the lights burning in their homes.

The more people move into towns and the more the urban areas sprawl, the more demand there is for electricity to light areas that almost no one uses at night. The more people move into urban areas to work in factories and offices the more demand there is for heating, air conditioning, and office equipment, all of which runs on electricity. Big sprawling cities put pressure on energy supplies.

Counting the cost of global trading

One of the big impacts of economic growth is western companies relocating their manufacturing plants to developing countries to take advantage of cheaper resources and labour and so increase their profits. Companies that have made that move produce many of your household appliances, clothes, and kitchen goods.

People in developing countries work for these firms for little money because they have no real alternatives. But local economies in western cities and towns lose industries that once specialised in manufacturing these goods – leaving people unemployed. The cost of welfare benefits for increasing numbers of unemployed people is a problem for western governments, but the social problems that result from high levels of unemployment such as drug use and antisocial behaviour are very significant and difficult to deal with in growing urban areas.

These are all ethical issues that you may want to consider when you're making decisions about how to be greener. Buying goods produced abroad by workers on very low wages may seem like exploitation but if those people don't get those wages they may not be able to feed their families. The cheaper products are, the more likely people are to be able afford to buy them, and as demand increases so does the amount of energy used in total production. That in turn pushes up carbon emissions. Being green is about deciding what's most important for you and it brings with it many of these kinds of dilemmas.

Facing Health Problems

Part of green living is about bringing benefits to other people in other parts of the world rather than damaging them and their local environments, so reducing the spread of disease is an important green issue.

Growing world populations increasingly grouped together in large urban areas means more and more people living close to sources of pollution and sources of infection. More and more world travel means more opportunities for diseases to spread over greater distances. Medical advances have saved millions of lives and given people in many parts of the world greater life expectancies and better standards of healthcare but new health problems keep arising.

Spreading virulent viruses

For several years, world health experts have worried about the possibility of a flu pandemic – an outbreak that they predict could kill hundreds of millions of people around the world. In the past viruses spread more slowly because people travelled very little outside their own communities and so outbreaks were isolated. Today, viruses spread at the speed of air travel. One unsuspecting disease carrier flying from Thailand to the UK can spread a virus freely among a huge urban population and the millions of commuters and visitors who can spread it around the UK and the rest of the world within hours.

When viruses spread in this way they can cause devastation to animals, birds, insects, and other wildlife, causing damage to natural ecosystems and environments.

Gasping for air

Countries that don't control the amount of exhaust and factory emissions face huge health bills. People living close to industrial sites in countries with little or no environmental regulation on emissions and pollution of air, land, and water are at risk of all sorts of health problems including asthma and other respiratory diseases.

Even in countries like the UK, where environmental regulation is taken very seriously, sheer volume of traffic in urban areas can leave people at risk from diseases caused or made worse by air pollution. There's more information in the section 'What You Can't See Can Harm You' about the types of particles that can make their way into the air around you and causes illnesses.

Turning the water bad

Toxic chemical leaks from industrial sites into nearby water ways still happen in the UK occasionally despite rigorous enforcement of environmental regulations. These leaks leave people at risk of toxic poisoning.

In parts of the world where factories routinely get rid of their waste into the nearest stretch of water and where local people are dependent on that water for everyday use, the dangers are huge. In many parts of the world, human effluent also finds it way into the nearest stretch of water.

More and more people are at risk from contaminated water in areas where environmental regulations haven't caught up. There's more information in the section later in this chapter on 'The seeping giant – toxic waste your water'.

Poisoning food

The need to feed the world's growing population and the demand for cheap food has led to mass food production. Intensive farming methods have developed to meet demand and to get food onto plates quickly. Chemical additives, antibiotics, and artificial hormones are used to make animals and birds grow more quickly and prevent disease in herds and flocks. Pesticides and artificial fertilisers raise the quantities of crops that can be produced per acre of land.

The long-term health effects of these methods aren't always clear immediately, but they are cause for concern. For example, antibiotics in the food chain cause people to become resistant to them, which causes problems when they're essential to the treatment of a medical condition. The BSE (Bovine Spongiform Encephalopathy) outbreak, which led to the death and illness of several people in the UK, was as a direct result of the use of particular bone meal products in the food given to beef cattle to keep the costs of beef production down. Chapter 7 looks at the food you eat and how to buy the greenest food available.

Running Out of Resources

The equation is simple: The planet is struggling to support its population because people are consuming resources faster than the earth can provide them, and damaging the earth more quickly than it can regenerate itself. Those two factors added together give a negative result. Many scientists believe that the earth will run out of resources some time this century if the current rate of consumption continues.

The western world is largely to blame. The following figures from the anti-consumerism campaign group Enough (www.enough.org.uk) speak volumes:

✔ The USA, with just 6 per cent of the world's population, uses 30 per cent of its resources.

✔ One-fifth of the world's population consumes over 70 per cent of the earth's natural resources, and owns over 80 per cent of its wealth – they are mainly concentrated in the USA, Canada, Western Europe, Saudi Arabia, Australia, and Japan.

✔ The world produces enough grain to supply every person on the planet with over 2,500 calories per day and yet starvation is still rife in many developing nations.

✔ One-fifth of the world's population, (again its wealthy consumer class), is responsible for over half of the greenhouse pollutants and 90 per cent of the ozone-depleting gases pumped out into the earth's atmosphere.

These statistics show the western world, including the UK, is using more than its fair share of the world's resources.

It doesn't take a rocket scientist to see that there is only so much the earth can take. It can't replenish and grow at the same rate that human beings consume. Some resources are in danger of running out:

- **Land:** The amount of land available in the world for growing crops is less than half the amount needed to match average western demands. This is largely a result of urbanisation, land clearing, and the large amount of infertile land (deserts, forests, and unsuitable climates).

- **Water:** Water supplies are dwindling because of rapid population growth in the developing world and because of the way people waste water in the western world. The total amount of water that falls as rain is enough to provide the world's current population with fresh water, but much of the total rainfall is concentrated in specific regions, leaving other areas without enough.

- **Energy:** Energy use has been growing faster than the world's population. There has been an overreliance on fossil fuels such as coal and oil to supply the world's energy and many scientists agree that there may be only 50 years' worth of oil left if it continues to be used at current rates.

- **Biological resources:** Studies show that people depend on approximately 10 million other species on earth to support the food production process. Many of those species, which exist within the food chain to produce, protect, or enhance food production, are in danger of disappearing because of the impact human behaviour has on the ecosystems they live in.

Two hundred years of increasing prosperity and pollution

The timeline here shows the progress of pollution:

1800-1860 – Manufacture by Machine: New engineering techniques lead to the advent of more modern machinery and factories. Steam power and railways increase the size of urban areas.

1830-1900 – Growth of the Industrial Town: Cities grow remarkably due to increases in manufacturing and related employment opportunities. Housing and social problems evolve, as do the first serious environmental problems.

1870-1914 – Second Industrial Revolution: The advent of electricity and medicine creates a new wave of industry.

1914-1930 – World War I: The war drains global resources but the era of mass production helps the world recuperate.

1930-1968 – Modernism: World War II and its advancement in weaponry is soon followed by nuclear power, space exploration, and a better understanding of DNA and the structure of life. The post-war period is characterised by rapid urban expansion. Consumption rises.

1960-2000 – The Age of Ambivalence: The impact of unchecked consumption leads to the birth of the environmental movement. The advent of computers enhances the amount and distribution of information.

What You Can't See Can Harm You

Global warming is just one of the effects of uncontrollably burning fossil fuels for a variety of energy, transport, and industrial needs. The gases produced can also pose serious health risks. Then there are the many hidden toxic chemicals emitted into the environment, whether into the air, the ground, waterways, and even through the food you eat.

All you need is the air that you breathe

You may not see it, but some of the pollution floating around in the air is a major health hazard. Carbon dioxide and nitrous oxides are a major contributor to the greenhouse gases that cause global warming. Some of the dangers in the air include:

- **Ozone:** Good ozone is the layer that exists between 10 and 50 kilometres above the earth's surface and protects you against the sun's ultra-violet rays. Bad ozone is formed when pollutants emitted by cars, factories, and refineries react chemically in the presence of sunlight. Ozone can bring on respiratory infections and increase the incidence of asthma.

- **Particle pollution:** Most fine particle pollutants are visible only through a microscope but together they form the smog you see on windless days. They are emitted directly (from car exhausts and manufacturing plants, for example) or formed in the atmosphere when other pollutants react and can also cause major respiratory difficulties and have even been linked to lung and heart illnesses.

- **Carbon monoxide:** Carbon monoxide (CO) is an odourless, colourless gas that's hard to detect. It forms when the carbon in fuels doesn't completely burn. Cars contribute a high proportion of CO, especially in winter when you start your engine and the combustion process doesn't work quite as well as it should. Industry and bushfires also contribute to CO emissions. CO in the body restricts blood flow and affects those with cardiovascular problems.

- **Sulphur dioxide:** Sulphur dioxide is also colourless but is the gas that smells like rotten eggs so you know when you're near it. It's a reactive gas that's produced when coal and oil are burned in places like power plants and industrial boilers. The smell is the main reason that people stay away from industrial areas using these fuels but besides being offensive to the nose, it's offensive to the lungs and heart.

When you next watch your local news service on TV, pay attention to the weather report and a thing called the air-quality index. This index measures the extent of major gases and particles delivered into the air on a given day.

The seeping giant – toxic waste in your water

Another nasty that is quite visible but usually out of sight until it's too late is toxic chemical pollution. The biggest users of toxic chemicals are industries that manufacture medicines, plastics, textiles, detergents, paints, and pesticides. When the manufacture of these chemicals began decades ago, the toxic mess produced was invariably released into nearby waterways, emitted into the air, or simply just dumped on the ground.

Some of the major toxic problems include:

- **Brominated flame retardants:** These are used in plastics for computer casings, white goods, car interiors, carpets, and polyurethane foams in furniture and bedding. They can end up in the dust of homes and offices and are linked with cancer and reproductive problems.

- **Dioxins:** A by-product of PVC (Polyvinyl Chloride, made into anything from window frames and plastic), industrial bleaching, and incineration, dioxins can create diseases of the immune system, reproductive and developmental disorders, as well as cancers.

- **Metals:** Toxic heavy metals that don't break down in the environment and aren't destroyed at any temperature include lead and mercury. Lead is the most prevalent industrial toxin released into the environment and therefore causes the most environmental related health problems. It is released into the atmosphere through petrol and paint. Low levels of lead and mercury can cause mental illness, learning disabilities, and stunted growth in children.

- **Organochlorine pesticides:** This type of pesticide includes DDT, dieldrin, heptachlor, chlordane, and mirex, which are used in farming and gardening and can end up in soils, the water table, and rivers and streams. Most have been banned in many countries including the UK as they can cause cancer and are toxic to the immune system.

- **Perfluorochemicals:** These are acids used in the manufacture of everyday items such as clothing, stain resistants, and cosmetics. They're linked to cancer and liver damage.

Government regulations dictate that industries are a lot more careful how they get rid of their toxic waste, with guidelines now in place to minimise the impact on people and the environment.

Thinking Globally, Acting Locally

Is it possible to stop and then reverse the destruction of the planet? The answer is yes, but it will take a combined effort from individuals, businesses, and governments.

This book includes all sorts of tips on how you can make a difference in your own home and community and thereby contribute to making a difference globally.

Taking the global view from Kyoto

The Kyoto Protocol explained:

In 1990 The Intergovernmental Panel on Climate Change reported that a 60 per cent reduction in harmful emissions into the earth's atmosphere was needed to redress serious damage that had been done to the planet.

In 1998 in Kyoto, Japan, 141 world leaders agreed that industrialised countries would work to reduce their own greenhouse gas emissions to 5.2 per cent below 1990 levels, for the period 2008 to 2012. The United States of America pulled out of the agreement in 2001. One of the reasons President George Bush gave for doing so was that India and China, considered developing nations, were not participants in the agreement. Through sheer population size, these nations will obviously have an impact on increasing greenhouse emissions but realistically they still have extremely low per capita emissions. The USA, on the other hand, contributes a quarter of the world's total greenhouse gas emissions and the total carbon dioxide emissions from one US citizen in 1996 were 19 times the emissions of one Indian citizen. USA emissions in total are still more than double those from China.

The statistics suggest that not having the USA on board reduces the global effectiveness of the Protocol but it may only be the start of a very long-term process of making a global difference. Politicians and politics change rapidly and as climate change becomes too big an issue to ignore the Kyoto Protocol may be seen as the agreement that started the ball rolling.

Some changes you can make to you own lifestyle without asking anyone for permission. As well as that, you can play your part in helping other people around you to adopt a similar green approach, such as:

- ✔ Volunteering for a community action group that has similar interests to you, such as a cyclists' user group or a group representing local conservation

- ✔ Writing letters to the editors of newspapers, magazines, Internet Web sites, your council, and your local member of parliament

- ✔ Joining a political party that represents your views and in which you think you may be able to have an influence.

Getting involved in actively promoting greener living makes it more likely that the politicians responsible for policy-making will take environmental issues more seriously.

People who don't budget wisely tend to spend for the short term and ignore the longer-term implications. The same goes for the environment. Many people use what they need for the short term and have little concern for future consequences.

Many of the tips in this book are simple and can be started immediately without making huge differences to your lifestyle. If you take action you'll be helping to turn the tide and provide hope that the planet can sustain its future generations – your grandchildren and great-grandchildren.

Part II
Living a Green Lifestyle

'I just hope our eco-friendly, environmentally green cottage we built meets the approval of our neighbours.'

In this part . . .

1 look at what it takes to live a greener lifestyle. Some of the steps you can take are very quick and simple and won't cost you a penny. Many of them can save you money. Bigger changes can cost money – such as changing all your light bulbs to energy-efficient ones and having insulation put in, or even a wind turbine installed on your roof – but even these can save you money in the long run.

However, some of the most effective steps to green living are common sense and only need a change in habits and thinking. All the family can play their part, whether in the kitchen, living room, or garden. The key to being greener is to reduce the number of goods you buy, reuse things or give them to someone who can make use of them, repair instead of buying new, and reduce the amount of waste you produce to a minimum with recycling and composting.

Chapter 3

Living in a Green Home

. . . .

In This Chapter

▶ Picturing perfect green living

▶ Examining alternative energy solutions

▶ Looking at location

▶ Changing behaviour to make your home greener

▶ Constructing a green home

. . . .

*N*o matter what kind of a home you're looking for, you have to make decisions about renting or buying, living in a house or a flat, how much to spend, and where to live. Whatever you end up deciding, the choice of where you live and what you live in is a major influence on the impact you have on the planet.

This chapter explores why your home is so important environmentally, and what makes a home planet-friendly. It also looks at how to make your existing home greener by conserving precious resources like water and energy; switching to more efficient devices and appliances; and even moving towards generating some energy of your own.

You don't need to spend thousands of pounds to go greener at home. The simplest and most efficient ways to get greener are to become more *energy efficient* – cutting down on the electricity and gas you use (saving money on bills into the bargain!) and changing to a green energy supplier.

Imagining the Ideal Sustainable Home

Whether you're moving home, trying to adapt your existing home to a greener lifestyle, or building a new one, size and location are two major things to think about:

- The size of the house dictates the energy that's needed to heat and light it, the number of appliances that are used, and to some extent the amount of water that's used.

- The location dictates to a great extent other resources that are used – petrol for driving if you're not close to public transport, local infrastructure like roads and shops. Location also has a bearing on the kind of power supplies you have access to, and the infrastructure needed to get those supplies such as gas and electricity, along with water and telecommunications systems installed in your home.

Both of these points are worth considering if you want to keep your impact on the environment to a minimum.

Sizing up size issues – bigger isn't always better

Housing that uses less space – high-density housing such as flats and townhouses – encourages a lifestyle that is less demanding on the environment. Such buildings require less land and less space and are generally in the most accessible locations and so encourage less car use.

Housing that takes up a lot of space, such as big suburban semi-detached houses or detached properties with big gardens in quiet residential streets – so-called *low-density housing* – uses up a lot of urban space and has become increasingly difficult to reach with good public transport and community services. In big cities like London, Birmingham, and Manchester roads leading into the centre from these areas are congested with commuters driving to work.

Then there are the modern-day big houses on blocks of land hidden away amongst rows and rows of other large houses. They give you more living space but demand more appliances, more roads, more cars, and more of just about everything. These huge houses use every bit of land they sit on, with grand entries and multiple bedrooms, reception rooms, bathrooms, and garages – 'McMansions' as they're called in America because they all look like someone ordered them from a generic mansion menu ('I'll take three baths, a great room, workout room, five bedrooms, and a Jacuzzi – super size that, please'). When you drive through these neighbourhoods, you wonder where the local shops and the nearest train and bus services are.

Unfortunately, many of these new suburbs have been built without a lot of thought for infrastructure and services, so you end up with plain-looking areas with not much greenery, very little community open space, and the need for Mum and Dad to drive family members to wherever they want to go because there is no other transport choice.

Just how much space do you need? It's not an easy question to answer and many people go for bigger each time they move just for the joy of having extra space. Think carefully about the needs of each member of your family. Look around the home you're living in be quite realistic about whether or not it meets those needs. Often the real reason a home seems too small is because there's too much in it and a lot of it is surplus to requirements. Instead of spending a fortune moving to a bigger house, declutter your living quarters. Give away or recycle things you really don't need including clothing, furniture, books, electrical appliances, and when you can see the floors again your rooms will seem much bigger. Think about whether you really need a spare bedroom; if you don't have guests staying over very often why not have a sofabed in the living room?

Home Information Packs

When you're buying a home you may find it difficult to get information about how energy-efficient it is and most sellers haven't given the green issues much thought. That's about to change though. The government and a European Union directive are forcing home owners to think about increasing energy efficiency. Home Information Packs will be introduced in England and Wales in June 2007. These packs will be prepared by the seller of a property to give prospective buyers information about the home they are considering buying. The aim is to speed up the selling/buying process. However, the original proposals have been watered down and it won't, as originally intended, be compulsory to include a Home Condition Report on the state of the property. It will, though, be compulsory to include an Energy Performance Certificate.

Energy Performance Certificates will give each home on the market a grading according to how energy-efficient they are. The grades will run from A to G – very much the same as energy efficiency ratings on fridges and washing machines – with A the most efficient and G the least energy-efficient. Home Inspectors are being trained to carry out inspections on homes to grade them for energy efficiency. These will also become a legal requirement for rented properties from the beginning of 2009.

Inspectors for Energy Performance Certificates will be able to give a list of practical things you can do to cut your fuel bills and carbon emissions, and the Energy Savings Trust estimates that by following those tips the average householder should be able to save £300 a year on fuel bills. The government also hopes the information will be used to support applications for green mortgages (see Chapter 10 for more information on green mortgages).

Designing a home for energy efficiency

Homes use about 15 per cent of the energy consumed within cities. You can live comfortably while working together with your community to reduce this percentage.

Home may be where the heart is but it can also be the place where most of your CO_2 emissions are generated. The car usually gets the blame for being the biggest generator of harmful emissions but many homes are responsible for emitting more carbon dioxide in a year than the cars parked outside. Buildings use around 40 per cent of the earth's energy and 16 per cent of the water consumed, so by becoming greener you'll be doing your bit to reduce those figures.

An *energy-efficient* home is one where everything possible has been done to use energy as efficiently as possible and reduce energy use (for example, ordinary light bulbs have been replaced by low-energy ones and appliances are all the highest efficiency rating available). Another way of being greener is to use green energy, produced from *renewable sources* (those that aren't used up by the process of generating power like electricity and gas – such as the sun or wind farms) for hot water and heating or – increasingly important as summers appear to be getting hotter – cool the home. You can buy green energy from your power supply company or even – if you have the money – install equipment to generate your own. A green home is one that

- ✔ **Captures the power of the sun:** Solar panels on the roof can heat water and produce electricity for other uses. The design of the building can help as well. Placing living areas on the south side of the home, with as many windows as possible, naturally captures the sun's rays to help heat the house.

- ✔ **Is well insulated:** Depending on whether you want to trap the warmth or be cool, the internal building structure, the type of windows used, the way the rooms are decorated, and how well the place is insulated will all reflect on how green the house is.

- ✔ **Lets light through the windows:** Although thick glass is very efficient at keeping out the heat, glass is probably the biggest generator of heat in your home. Covering your windows or keeping your curtains closed to protect your rooms from the summer sun is the most effective way of keeping the heat out. Installing awnings and screens, and even planting vegetation in the line between the sun and the window, works wonders.

✓ **Makes use of shade-makers:** Outdoor trees, hedges, and bushes can shade the house in summer and act as a wind-break in winter. Place them between windows and the direction of the sun. Awnings and screens on south-facing windows keep the temperature down when it's hot.

✓ **Goes with the airflow:** New buildings can be designed so that there's an energy-efficient airflow through them. If you're renovating your home you can create that airflow by placing your rooms, walls, doors, and windows to take advantage of any breezes that come in, and by making your rooms connect in such a way that air flows from one end of the building to the other.

The sidebars 'Home Information Packs' and 'Assessing new home energy efficiency' give advice if you're looking to move into a greener home.

Assessing new home energy efficiency

The main indicator used to show home buyers the energy efficiency of a property for sale is the SAP (Standard Assessment Procedure) calculation. The SAP rating scale is from 1 to 100, the higher the score the more efficient the property. It's an important tool for new home buyers to use when assessing and comparing new properties. The more energy-efficient the building, the higher the SAP rating, therefore ensuring lower fuel bills and lower CO_2 emissions. The SAP ratings take into account:

✓ Levels of thermal insulation

✓ Types and efficiency of the heating system

✓ Ventilation of the property.

Current legislation requires all house builders to display the SAP rating of all new homes.

An alternative exists in The Building Research Establishment's EcoHomes voluntary code. This has greener credentials than the SAP calculation, and independently evaluates new or re-developed houses over a wide range of environmental issues and presents the results in one straightforward rating – pass, good, very good, or excellent. This includes everything from how close a home is to public transport, how thermally efficient it is, how well it tackles recycling to whether it's built with sustainable materials. It covers new, converted, or renovated houses and apartments. The minimum EcoHome rating is higher than that required by building regulations. Some developers now design their homes to meet EcoHomes standards. The government intends to use the code to form the basis of further revisions to building regulations in 2010 and 2015, so buying an EcoHome certified home will put you ahead of the game.

Exploring Renewable Energy

You can be so much more energy-efficient by reducing your reliance on electricity from the mains and converting to sustainable and renewable alternative energy sources. (Chapters 1 and 2 explain why these are so important for the future of the planet.)

The majority of the electricity you get in your home at the flick of a switch is produced at power plants that burn fossil fuels such as coal. Some electricity is also produced at hydroelectric plants, using water, but this forms only a small percentage of the overall electrical energy delivered to your home. The main point to remember about the sustainability of electricity is that a lot of coal and oil is mined and drilled to meet your electrical energy demands.

Generating your own green power

The green alternatives to powering your home with electricity from the national grid are

- **Solar power:** Energy from the sun is converted by solar panels (technically called photovoltaic panels) into electrical energy.

- **Wind power:** Energy from the wind propels the blades on a wind turbine to create energy within a generator that in turn creates electrical energy.

- **Hydro power:** Water flow creates enough force within a generator to create electrical output.

- **Biomass:** Waste material, such as waste, straw, and other organic material, can be burned to create energy.

- **Ground heat:** Heat trapped in the ground from the sun, pumped out of the ground to use for heating and hot water.

You can install the equipment needed to generate your own green power and use that to reduce the amount of conventional electricity you buy from your electricity supplier. The most easily adapted alternative energy source in urban areas is solar power, especially for your water heating needs. In rural areas, especially on farms, many people are creating their own cheaper electrical power source by connecting to small domestic wind and hydro power generators.

Tapping into the sun's rays

Solar energy is just one of the alternatives to traditional electrical power. You may not be able to generate all the power your household needs using solar energy but the more solar power you do use, the less electricity you need, and so the less fossil fuel you're using. That means you'll be responsible for fewer greenhouse gas emissions.

There are three ways to generate power from the sun:

- ✔ **Passive solar energy** is most effective in new homes because it relies on installing glass doors and windows to make the most of the passing sun. Glass doors and windows on south facing walls can significantly increase the temperature of the whole house. Adding a glass conservatory has a similar effect. It's not so much about generating power as trapping the power of the sun allowing you to rely less on other energy supplies.

   As summers get hotter, you may need to add shades to windows and doors to keep the indoor temperatures down. And in winter, you may need heavy curtains to stop heat escaping and making your home too cold.

- ✔ **Active solar panels** installed in the south-facing roof of your home allow the sun's rays to heat water in the small pipes in the panels, which is then pumped into the water tank.

   It can be fairly expensive to install solar panels – anything from £2,000 upwards. Your installation will pay for itself eventually but it can take 15 to 20 years.

   How much hot water you get depends on the size of the panels and how much sun is around. It also depends on the climate, the model of heater, how much hot water you need, and the size of your hot water tank. The more panels you install, the more water you can heat in this way.

   The bonus is that your electricity bills come down accordingly.

   One big high-street electrical chain launched solar panels in the summer of 2006 and estimates that the average household would need to install nine panels at a cost of £9,000 in order to cut its fuel bills in half. Other retailers are likely to follow suit and so prices may well come down.

   You can find a lot more information at www.greenenergy.org.uk, the Web site for the Solar Trade Association which represents the solar panel industry, and also on the Green Energy Web site of the National Energy Foundation at www.nef.org.uk. You may be able to get a grant for buying and installing solar panels. See the sidebar 'Getting the money for energy-producing products', elsewhere in this chapter.

✓ **Photovoltaic Panels** convert the sun's rays into general purpose electrical energy. These panels, which are like large sheets of glass, are placed on a frame outside the house or within the roof.

You can generate up to half of your energy needs with one of these panels but they're still expensive and take a long time to pay for themselves. But the good news is, if you install enough panels to generate more electricity than you needs you can sell it back to the national electricity grid.

Small versions of these types of panels are increasingly being using in things like burglar alarms to recharge the batteries and you can buy solar mobile phone chargers which use similar technology.

Blowing up energy from wind

The UK can, in theory, generate all the energy it needs using the power of the wind.

The debate rages on about the size and location of wind farms both on- and offshore. Some people argue that they're noisy and a blot on the landscape. Others want to see more of them built as quickly as possible to reduce our dependence on fossil fuels and imported gas.

While that debate goes on you can install your own wind turbine if you have enough space for one in your garden. You can also get small ones that attach to the roof of your house. You can forestall neighbours' complaints by choosing one of the very small and quiet models coming onto the market.

It takes a turbine with a blade span of about five metres to generate enough power for an average household, so unless you're in the countryside with lots of space around you, you'd probably have to install a smaller one that would generate just a portion of your energy needs.

You need planning permission from your local authority before you can get your turbine up and running but the planning regulations are geared to support small-scale energy generation and the government has promised to remove planning barriers. Talk to your local authority planning department for more information.

The cost of the turbine and installation may take several years to pay for itself in terms of the amount it saves you on your electricity bills, but think of it as a long-term investment. It will cost you between £2,500 and £5,000 for every kilowatt of energy your turbine produces, but as demand increases and the systems become mass produced, the costs are likely to come down. That's enough energy to power your dishwasher and TV at the same time.

Look for answers to all your questions on wind turbines on the British Wind Energy Association's Web site at www.bwea.com. The site has information on firms that build and install small wind power generators, and also on costs, planning permission, and grants. (For more details on grants, see the sidebar 'Getting the money for energy-producing products', elsewhere in this chapter.)

Heating from the ground up

Even in the UK heat from the ground can be used to heat buildings and water. An electrical ground source heat pump installed in a borehole or a trench on your property pumps out heat from the ground (created by the sun's warming) that you can use to heat water or generate electricity.

A typical system will generate up to four times as much energy as it uses in electricity to drive the pump. There are grants available and you can get more information from the Ground Source Heat Pump Association through the National Energy Foundation Web site, www.nef.org.uk/gshp, or by calling 01908 665555. A typical 8kW system costs £6,400–£9,600 plus the price of connection to the distribution system.

Burning biomass

Biomass, renewable organic material burned to produce energy, is all around you in fast-growing trees like the willow and poplar, wood chips, the straw left after crops have been harvested, manure, and litter from poultry farms. If you think about it, your ancestors burned biomass to heat water and do their cooking – and many people in the developing world still do this.

You can buy biomass for use at home in the form of logs or wood chips, or pellets you then use to fuel a wood-burning or biomass-burning stove. And not only can you use it at home, but it can also fuel power stations.

Biomass meets the renewable standard because as you burn one lot, another lot is being grown. The beauty of biomass is that when you burn it, the carbon dioxide released is equal to the amount of carbon dioxide the plants took out of the atmosphere while they were growing. Then the new plants growing absorb the carbon dioxide the burning process releases, so biomass is the ultimate in renewable power sources if the source of the fuel is managed sustainably.

Peat is organic material that can be burned but it takes millions of years to form. Like coal, peat is a fossil fuel and not renewable or sustainable.

Getting the money for energy-producing products

You may be able to apply for a grant to help with the costs of solar panels and domestic wind turbines. The maximum grant an individual can get for a wind turbine is £5,000 but the amount depends on the size of the turbine you install and how much power it generates.

The places to contact are

✔ The Low Carbon Buildings Programme, funded by the Department of Trade and Industry, at www.lowcarbon buildings.org.uk or by calling 0800 915 7722.

✔ The Energy Saving Trust, which runs the programme, at www.est.org.uk or on 08457 277200.

✔ The Scottish Community and Householder Renewables Initiative at www.est.co.uk/schri in Scotland.

Contact British Biogen at www.r-p-a.org.uk or on 020 7235 8474 for more information on biomass systems that can be installed at home, or go to the Green Energy Web site of the National Energy Foundation, www.nef.org.uk/greenenergy/biomass.htm.

Buying and selling green electricity

If you can't produce your own energy from wind or solar power, it's still possible to be a green energy consumer. You can choose to buy electricity produced from renewable wind, solar, and hydro power sources. Most of the big supply companies now have green energy schemes.

Talk to your present supplier, and if you're not happy with what it has to offer, switch to another supplier. You can buy your energy from any supply company now and it's easy to switch. You can get more information from the National Energy Foundation's Web site www.nef.org.uk/gshp or by calling 01908 665555.

If you install your own green power electricity generator and produce more power than you can use or store, you can connect into the national electricity grid and sell your surplus electricity to the grid. Most domestic green power generators at the moment don't generate electricity on that scale and are just big enough to supply a portion of the electricity a household uses, but in a few years, who knows?

Surveying Green Places

It's not just the kind of home you live in that affects the impact you have on the environment, but also where that home is located. If you want to live a green lifestyle you need to consider the location of your home.

Closing in on being close

Where you live has a big influence on how green you are likely to be in the years to come. You're more likely to lead a green lifestyle if you live near facilities and services such as shops, schools, doctors' surgeries, public transport, and leisure clubs.

Keep in mind that the closer you are to these amenities, the smaller the homes available. Homes are smaller to allow as many people as possible access to the public transport network or to walk or cycle to nearby shops and services. It takes a lot of people living in a relatively small geographic area to justify the cost of providing expensive public transport such as a rail network.

Planning agencies have recognised the importance of providing as many people as possible with accessible yet affordable housing choices across the urban area. Many councils now encourage developers to provide housing around established centres with railway stations in preference to developing further out on the edge of the urban area. There has been a huge increase in apartments in most of our big cities, which is a direct result of an increasing number of people willing to trade space for a location near good public transport links or within walking or cycling distance of work.

The most sustainable housing locations are those close to – preferably within walking distance of – the following characteristics:

✔ **Transport:** Proximity to good transport networks, such as bus stops and railway stations, reduces your need to travel by car. A sustainable area has safe, well-lit, and good-quality walking and cycling paths, and low levels of vehicular traffic.

New development located close to public transport is called *transit-oriented development*. The inner-city areas of big cities and regional towns, where there is a concentration of shops and jobs, are most accessible for public transport systems and are beginning to actively promote walking and cycling. Even country towns, where most of the residents live within walking distance of the main street and its shops and services, provide much greater accessibility than most cities with large spread-out and sprawling suburban areas.

✔ **Essential services:** The ability to walk or cycle to services such as schools, churches, public open spaces, community services, care facilities, libraries, and shops makes life easier and greener for everyone, especially children who don't have to rely on you driving them to get everywhere.

✔ **Cultural and recreational facilities:** Access to open space, parks, sports facilities, and recreation areas keeps you in tune with Mother Nature's greenery, and nearby concert halls and theatres feed your artistic soul.

✔ **The centre of the local community:** You can tell you're in a vibrant sustainable community when many people of all ages and cultures walk the streets; all the shops and services are open; the streets and paths are clean; and there is a good mix of housing styles and types, which implies there may be a good socio-economic mix as well.

Comparing country versus city life

It's estimated that at some point in 2007, the tipping point will be reached where for the first time more than half of the world's population live in urban rather than rural areas. That means that many highly accessible urban locations have become quite expensive to live in, and buy or rent homes in.

Not everyone can afford to, or wants to, live in highly accessible inner-city areas. The question then, if you are looking for a greener lifestyle, is whether the suburbs or the countryside is the better location in terms of sustainability.

Hopping aboard transport issues

One of the key characteristics of increasingly sprawling urban areas is the distance from your home to just about anywhere. If there are no footpaths on your street and it's too far to walk to a local shop or school, travelling the distance in between becomes the biggest challenge.

One of the major issues with sprawling outer urban areas is the bias that exists against those who don't have access to a car. It's a big problem when one family member takes the car to work for the day and there are no other realistic options to get anywhere.

Catering for the kids

When children are young, their ideal location is wherever you are, but growing children need to be ferried to and from nurseries, playgroups, schools, or their baby-sitters or childminders may have to come to you. As their social life becomes more important to them you may have to make endless journeys to and from parties, out-of-school activities, sports events, youth clubs, friends' homes, and the nearest bus or train stations.

The farther you are from all these the more you will have to use public transport or, if that isn't accessible and convenient, your car. So it's not just your needs that have to be considered when choosing the greenest possible location for your home.

Choosing the other option – living in the countryside – makes distance issues loom even larger. In the country, you can make your home green and grow your own vegetables if you have a big enough garden, but public transport is likely to be scarce and you may spend a lot of time in the car.

Buying the groceries and having things delivered add to the impact you make on the environment. You have to factor in having water, electricity, gas, telephone, and postal services laid on, the wear and tear your activities cause to roads, and the cost to the environment of keeping all that infrastructure in good repair. Many people dream of living in the middle of nowhere away from the rat race but if you want to be green, you have to add all this into the equation. However, deliveries are often better in terms of carbon emissions – one van can deliver to 30 houses rather than 30 cars driving to a shop.

Consuming suburban life

Living in the suburbs leads to high levels of *consumption* – using up resources like energy and petrol – that put much greater pressure on the environment than other types of housing. For example:

- ✔ Living on the outskirts of cities means there's less vegetation and agricultural land. Urban areas have expanded out and green land has been concreted and tarmacked. When it rains heavily or there's a storm the water can't seep away into the earth as it once did, and this causes erosion and flooding.

- ✔ The need to drive everywhere increases the demand for petrol and oil.

- ✔ The desire to have large houses with all the mod-cons such as large entertainment systems, air conditioning, swimming pools, and lots of fully furnished rooms puts increased demand on energy supplies.

Greening urban enclaves

At the same time as demand has grown for big homes in the suburbs there has also been growth in apartment living and a regeneration of inner urban areas. Measures are now being put in place to reverse the unsustainable sprawl of outer urban areas and towns. These include:

- ✔ Developing new areas in a more integrated way, around village centres, shops, services, and transport systems, with such facilities and services being provided at the same time that the housing is provided.

- ✔ Increasing the mix of homes available, with apartments and town-houses being built within more traditionally developed residential areas.

- ✔ Developing networks of roads that allow bus and train services to get to the majority of the population, and footpaths so children can be less reliant on their mum and dad's car.

Checking out your council

Getting the location right is all well and good but if your local council doesn't offer recycling, or doesn't encourage sustainable development, then that can outweigh many of the advantages your chosen location offers in terms of a greener lifestyle.

Once you think you have found a sustainable housing location check the policies of your local authority. Have a look at its Web site and check what it says about the following:

- ✔ **The State of the Environment:** Most councils now produce a yearly State of the Environment Report that shows how the local area is performing on environmental issues such as water efficiency, pollution, energy efficiency, transport, air quality, greenhouse gas emissions, waste management, recycling, and noise.

- ✔ **Community Services:** The majority of councils list the range of community facilities available in their area. You can find the location and number of childcare centres, community activity venues, and services for elderly and disabled residents, and young people. Most sustainable residential areas will have a lot of these services located near your house.

✔ **Development:** One of the key functions of all councils is to work on strategies and plans that will guide future development. Have a look at the council's future plans. If there is an emphasis on economic growth and more development with little reference to environmental protection this may not be as green a place as you thought. Councils supporting sustainable principles are more likely to talk about promoting the environment, accessibility, vitality, and social fabric with any growth and development promoted within that context.

Adapting Your Existing Home to Be Greener

If your relatives and friends are already in the same area; your children are firmly ensconced in local schools; shops, places of worship, and entertainment venues are nearby; and public transport gets you to work quickly and easily, staying put may be your best option. Adopting a greener lifestyle may mean adapting your present home and your habits to do your bit for the environment.

The most limiting factor when it comes to making changes around the house is cost. Prices for green household equipment and appliances are coming down as demand is going up, and you may be able to get some help in the form of grants (see the sidebar 'Getting the money for energy-producing products', elsewhere in this chapter).

You can spend a lot of money making your home greener but you can help the environment without spending a penny. Changing the behaviour of everyone in your home – including you – will make the biggest impact, even if you live in the most unsustainably designed home in your area. Just because you've replaced all your appliances with the most energy-efficient models available isn't an excuse for using them round the clock. If you do that you negate the reason for having them in the first place.

Not only is changing your behaviour kinder on the environment, it saves you money on energy bills. With electricity and gas prices rising steadily that's got to be welcome.

This book is full of information on conservation; the following sections cover just the basics.

Reducing fuel use

If every person in the UK cut their electricity use by half, there'd be a noticeable reduction in greenhouse gas emissions. Although you're just one person, following these suggestions can pay dividends, even if you don't try any of the energy-efficient alternatives suggested elsewhere in this chapter.

- ✔ Put a jumper or jacket on in the winter and turn the thermostat down. Spend more time in your cooler rooms in the summer and leave the air conditioner or electric fans off.

- ✔ Use your appliances only when you need to, which may not be every day of the week. If your dishwasher isn't one of the latest models that uses less water than hand-washing, try doing at least one manual wash and dry a week.

- ✔ Think seriously about turning the light on. It may be a matter of just opening the curtains and letting the natural light come in so saving energy. When you need to replace light bulbs, replace them with energy-saving ones.

- ✔ Look into washing and drying your clothes more naturally. It only takes about five minutes to place clothes on a drying rack or clothes-line and even if space is a problem, just hang some of the smaller clothes on a rack and put a few clothes in the dryer. They'll dry quicker because there are fewer items to dry, so you save energy.

Turning it off after you turn it on

People tend to leave things on regardless of whether they're using them or not. Here are some general tips for using electrical power only when you need it:

- ✔ Turn electrical appliances off at the power point. Many electrical appliances, in particular entertainment systems, still draw power when they're on standby.

- ✔ Turn off all the lights in rooms you're not using – even the Queen does that! Use timers to make sure you don't use your lights unnecessarily.

Fluorescent lights use less energy then normal light bulbs. When you have to use light bulbs, use the lowest wattage you can and replace worn-out normal light bulbs with low energy ones – they may be more expensive initially, but they use up to two-thirds less energy and last eight to ten times longer than non-green light bulbs and so save money in the long run. It's a simple measure that has real impact.

- ✔ Use timers around the house for things that you find impossible to check all the time, like hot water heaters and televisions you regularly fall asleep in front of.

Turning it down!

Turn your heating down a notch or two at the thermostat. Turning it down by just one degree centigrade can save up to a tenth of your heating bills. Turn down your hot water so that it's at the right temperature for showers rather than having to cool it down with cold water. Dimmer switches, lower wattage light bulbs, or better still old-fashioned beeswax candles enable you to turn the lights down and create a romantic atmosphere!

Cutting down on water consumption

In some areas in the south of the UK water supplies can get very low following dry winters and hot summers. Aquifers, reservoirs, and rivers can all become seriously depleted. The hot summer of 2006 proved that if our climate does get hotter, water will be a very important issue. Even without water shortages it's worth cutting down on water use because every time you turn the tap on energy is used to get the water out of it. It all contributes to the impact you have on the environment.

You can do your bit by turning off the tap while brushing your teeth and having showers instead of baths, but there are many more small things you can do to conserve supplies. Here are just a few (there are more in Chapters 4 and 5):

- ✔ Stop the dripping tap – it can waste as much as 90 litres a week.

- ✔ Rinse your mouth and teeth using a tumbler and save 9 litres of water a minute from the running tap.

- ✔ Keep drinking water in a container so you don't have to run the tap every time you fancy a drink. However remember that every time you open the fridge door you're using energy unnecessarily – get used to drinking water at room temperature!

- ✔ Use your washing machine only when you have a full load. A full load uses less water than two half loads.

- ✔ Water your houseplants with the cooled water after boiling an egg – or veg. (Plants like cold tea too apparently, and you can use the dirty water from cleaning out your fish tank as well. It's rich in nitrogen and phosphorus, and is an excellent fertiliser.)

- ✔ Fit a water-saving device in your cistern and save up to three litres a flush. If your cistern is old think about replacing it with a more modern water-efficient version.

- ✔ Have a water meter installed by your water company. You'll be charged for every drip you use but you can keep an eye on how much you're using – you'll soon be looking for savings!

✔ Shower for five minutes instead of taking a bath. That uses about a third of the water and saves up to 400 litres a week.

✔ Lag your pipes to avoid bursts and leave your heating on a low setting while you are out in cold weather to prevent pipes freezing.

Insulating for savings

Putting in good insulation is one of the best ways of making your home – new or old – more energy-efficient. If you can afford to do only one thing, and installing an alternative energy generator is beyond your reach (see the section 'Generating your own green power', earlier in the chapter), think insulation. Around half of the heat lost in a typical home is lost through the walls and loft.

Insulating your roof, ceilings, and walls is one of the most effective ways of keeping the heat in and the cold out, and vice versa. Get more information from the Energy Saving Trust at www.est.org.uk or on 08457 277200.

Many builders and architects suggest lining walls and ceilings with reflective foil before laying the insulation as an additional measure to keep humidity out in the summertime.

Insulating your boiler keeps your water hot for longer, and don't forget that double glazing your windows is insulating too.

Draught-proofing is another way of stopping heat escaping during the cold months. Make sure that your doors and windows are well sealed so that cold air doesn't get in and the warm air inside doesn't get out. Rugs, carpets, and curtains are very good at keeping the heat in your rooms for longer into the night, instead of it seeping away through the floors, ceilings, and windows.

You can get more information about all types of insulation from the National Energy Foundation at www.nef.org.uk/gshp or by calling 01908 665555, or from the Energy Saving Trust at www.est.org.uk or on 08457 277200.

You can be even greener by using *green insulation*:

✔ **Cellulose fibre loft insulation.** Manufactured from fire-retarded recycled newspaper, this is designed for loose filling lofts (where it offers a real cost-effective alternative to mineral fibre insulation).

✔ **Sheep's wool thermal insulation.** This is suitable for sloping ceilings and roof slope insulation, as well as stud walls and dry lining.

You may be entitled to a grant to help with the cost of some of your insulation, particularly if you are elderly or have a disability. Talk to your local authority and power company.

Using appliances efficiently

Your electrical appliances can be replaced with newer, more energy-efficient models. But you also need to think about the energy that goes into building new appliances and balance the two. A well-functioning second-hand appliance is the greenest choice; if you are buying new make sure your old appliance is reused or recycled. Whatever the efficiency of the appliance you're using think about how you use it. There's no point in having the most efficient washing machine in the world and using it more frequently than you need to with only a few items tumbling around inside.

Checking the ratings

The appliances you buy – such as the boiler, washing machine, fridge freezer, tumble dryer, electric oven, and dishwasher – come with an energy efficiency rating (the EU Energy Label). Appliances are rated with a letter from A to G, with A being the most efficient. The majority of modern appliances are A so you shouldn't settle for anything less. When you go shopping for new appliances ask for information about the various products on offer and check the appliance itself for its rating letter.

There is an Energy Efficiency Recommended Database, set up by Defra (the Department for the Environment, Food, and Rural Affairs). You can access the database through Defra's Web site at www.defra.gov.uk, or go to the government's information service at www.direct.gov.uk/HomeAndCommunity/ InYourHome/SavingEnergy/SavingEnergyArticles. In late 2006, the government also launched a new environment information line for consumers called Environment Direct. You can find more information about this on the Defra Web site.

In England and Wales you can get information on energy-efficient appliances at Energy Efficiency Advice Centres. You will get put through to your nearest one if you call 0800 512012 or take a look at the Web site at www.saveenergy. co.uk.

 There is also a voluntary *energy star* scheme for other products such as televisions, computers, and office equipment to promote their energy efficiency. For people who just leave things on, *energy star* products do save energy. They also have a *sleep* mode which uses 75 per cent less energy than standby mode. Find out more from www.eu-energystar.org.

 Appliances in standby still use a large proportion of the electricity they use while fully functioning. Only by turning them completely off at the wall do they stop using any electricity. And don't believe people who tell you that turning an appliance off uses more energy than leaving it on standby. Off is *the* most energy-efficient mode for an electrical appliance.

Calculating your energy efficiency

Many of the energy supply companies help you to calculate your energy efficiency using online calculators. The Energy Savings Trust has a simple one that takes you on a tour of a virtual house and shows where you can take steps to become more energy-efficient – such as insulation, installing the most energy-efficient appliances, and replacing existing bulbs with low-energy ones. It shows you how much you can save in a year for each of those efficiency suggestions you implement. It also have an online home energy check. You put in some information and you get an analysis back online – or you can call for a paper version.

My calculation shows that I can save half my bills by having very energy-efficient electrical appliances, replacing the boiler with a new condensing boiler, and using energy-efficient light bulbs. If you'd like to know more go to the website at www.est.org.uk/myhome/whatcan and click on 'Online home energy check'.

Ditching the energy guzzling boiler

If your boiler is more than 15 years old, it's using more energy than you want it to. The newer boilers are much more energy-efficient and not only will you do the environment a power of good by replacing it, you'll cut your electricity bills by as much as a quarter and save money in the long run. If you go for a new condensing boiler you can save even more. The Energy Saving Trust can give you more information on the types of boilers available and their efficiency. You can contact the trust at www.est.org.uk or on 08457 277200.

Doing without air conditioning units

If summers are set to get warmer, as predicted, the use of air conditioning will rise. Energy suppliers used to assume that demand for electricity would be at its peak in the winter months, but as the summer of 2006 showed, the demand for electricity can be just as high in the hottest weeks of the summer because more offices and homes are installing air conditioning. But there are lots of other steps you can take to keep cool instead of investing in air conditioning, which uses valuable energy and results in more carbon emissions.

Keep curtains and blinds closed during the day to keep rooms from warming up too much. If you have a garden, plant hedges and bushes to protect windows from the sun and keep them in the shade. Open windows and doors, so that air can circulate and any breeze creates a through draught. Fit exterior shutters or canopies to keep the sun from south facing doors and windows, and keep windows open at night (but make sure they are secured to stop intruders).

You can buy yourself a solar powered fan – great because it works using the power of the sun, which is exactly when you need a fan.

Building Your Green Dream Home

It's certainly not for everybody, but one way of getting the green home of your dreams is to build it from scratch – either doing it yourself or buying from a developer's plans. You can be as green as your pocket will allow.

The first thing to think about is the materials. Wood is a renewable resource but it's one of the natural resources used at a much faster rate than it grows. Reducing the number of trees on the earth affects air quality and has an influence on global warming. Use as little wood as possible; use recycled timber or make sure that the timber you do use comes from a managed plantation which only releases timber at the same rate that it's being produced. Wood should be sourced from suppliers accredited by the Forest Stewardship Council (FSC); there's more information on the FSC's Web site at www.fsc-uk.org. Greenpeace has a 'Good Wood' guide which is worth looking at or printing off from its Web site at www.greenpeace.org.uk.

Other building materials should be from sustainable sources too:

- **House supports (beams, decking, and so on):** Very innovative timber alternatives are being developed today, such as composite wood made from reclaimed hardwood sawdust, and plastic formed from reclaimed/recycled plastic.

- **Insulation:** Many insulation products such as roofing batts, wall and floor linings, and cellulose are made from recycled materials such as glass and fibreglass.

- **Paints:** Most eco-sensitive paints are water based (acrylic) paints with fewer chemical additives and toxic materials, no animal testing, and recycled packaging. Some paints are even developed using recycled materials, but there are no regulatory standards for eco-friendly paints so be careful of over-exaggerated claims on the tins.

- **Tiles:** Tiles can now be made of recycled glass and porcelain.

- **Walls:** It is possible to buy gypsum and fibreboard planks for walls made of recycled material such as recycled gypsum and waste paper.

There are green homes being built in the UK from various materials such as recycled tyres, straw, and bricks made from recycled ash. There's a whole wealth of information on the latest green building technologies on the Internet. Type 'building a green home' into a search engine and you'll find more information than you can imagine. Try www.sustlife.com, which is a not-for-profit Web site promoting sustainable living.

Chapter 4

Acting Green at Home

Creating a green home with good insulation, energy-efficient appliances, and solar panels as explained in Chapter 3 is part of leading a green lifestyle. The other part is thinking and acting green around that home. Even if installing a new greener fridge and an energy-producing domestic wind turbine are beyond your budget, you can help protect the planet by behaving in an environmentally friendly way throughout your home. This chapter gives tips and tricks for ecofriendly living in every room of your home.

Working in a Green Kitchen

The kitchen is the heart of any home and probably the place where you can do the most energy saving. The food you buy, how you store it, the way you cook it, and how you clean up afterwards all make a difference to the amount of energy you use, how many greenhouse gases you produce, how many chemicals you release down the drain, and how much water you use.

Reducing your reliance on appliances

It's hard to live without some kitchen appliances but by reducing the number of electrical appliances you use and changing the way you use them, you become greener – and save money on your bills.

In the back of your cupboards there's sure to be at least one appliance that you just had to have at one point but soon realised wasn't as essential as you thought. If you decide to get rid of such an appliance, try to pass it on to someone else who wants it rather than throwing it out to end up in a landfill site. Ask your local council what recycling facilities they have as your appliance could perhaps be recycled; if not they will tell you how to dispose of it.

Try selling appliances you don't want at a car boot sale, on an Internet auction site, or by Freecycling them (there's more information on freecycling in Chapter 17).

The fridge is fairly essential. You must keep a lot of the food you buy in it – especially after it's opened. But a few small changes to the way you use your fridge make it less of an environmental hazard:

- Take frozen food out of the freezer the night before and defrost it in the fridge instead of using the microwave or oven to thaw it out.

- Buy fresh food that doesn't have to be kept in the freezer. If you're within easy reach of the shops you may find you don't need a freezer at all. But if you have to drive to the shops a freezer may be greener than using your car to shop more frequently.

- Buy food that keeps in cupboards and get a smaller, more energy-efficient fridge. There's more information on these in Chapter 3. Things like bread, peanut butter, condiments, cordial, some fruit and vegetables, and water can be stored at room temperature.

- Set the thermostats in both the fridge and freezer to the optimum energy-efficient temperatures (3 to 5 degrees for the fridge and -15 to -18 degrees for the freezer). If the temperatures are set any higher or lower the appliances use more energy – unnecessarily.

Other appliances such as electric ovens and kettles also use up a lot of energy but using them differently means greater energy efficiency too:

- Cook on your gas hob rather than the electric oven. Even a microwave oven is a more energy efficient than an electric oven.

- Boil only as much water as you need in the kettle rather than filling it up each time.

There's often an alternative way of doing things that doesn't require electricity. Use the dust pan and brush for small clean up jobs instead of the vacuum cleaner, and create a romantic atmosphere with candles instead of electric lights. Think before you flick the switch!

Using water well

Most tap water is used for flushing, washing, and cleaning even though it's all high-quality drinking water. Don't waste good-quality water by letting it run down the drain into the sewers from where it has to be reprocessed back into drinking-quality water.

In some southern parts of the UK, people have been banned from using hosepipes to water their gardens and wash their cars since 2005 due to water shortages. The Government and the water companies are debating whether to build more reservoirs, transport water from the wetter north of the UK to the drier south, or to build desalination plants to process salty sea water into water for domestic use. Some scientists argue that this is just a sign of things to come and that water must be used more carefully.

Another reason to be careful with water use is the energy involved in getting it from reservoir to your tap. Water has to be pumped at various stages along the way and that takes energy. It has to be treated and that process uses energy. If you conserve water you also conserve energy, and that helps keep down the number of carbon emissions pumped into the atmosphere (which, as you can read in Chapters 1 and 2, are credited with causing climate changes and all the problems associated with those changes).

Conserving every day

In the meantime you can conserve water by cutting down the amount you use every day:

- Fix leaking taps straight away. While you're waiting for the plumber to come, collect the water in a bowl or bucket to use for something else. You'll be surprised by how much collects. Don't waste it – use it for washing the windows or car, or watering your garden.

- Check the lagging around water pipes to be sure that they won't burst in cold weather. Bursts waste a lot of water and can cause a lot of damage inside and outside your home.

- Ask your water supply company to fit a meter. You pay for the water you use and that gives you the incentive to cut down.

- Keep a bottle of water in the fridge, if you prefer your drinking water cold, rather than wasting water by running the tap until the water is really cold.

Washing-up – choosing the basin or the dishwasher

Washing up by hand or using the dishwasher isn't an easy decision. Use the following points to help make it:

✔ The newest dishwashers use as little as 9 litres of water per load; older machines use around 20 litres. The average human washer-upper in the UK uses 63 litres of water for every set of dishes and that can run to as much at 150 litres if you wash up under running water.

✔ As well as water consumption you have to add in the electricity used to operate the dishwasher when deciding which is the greener way to wash up. The newest dishwashers use less energy to heat the water than the average gas boiler.

✔ The third factor to add into the calculation is that it takes a lot of energy to make a dishwasher. (And someday you may have to dispose of it.)

These tips help you be as green as you can while washing up:

✔ Fill a plastic basin or bottles with the cold tap water that would normally go down the drain while you're waiting for the hot water to come through. Use this cold water for drinking water, cooking, or to rinse off the dirtiest dishes.

✔ Use a washing up bowl rather than the kitchen sink to do the washing as you'll use less water.

Fill the washing up bowl with warm water. The washing up water doesn't need to be very hot if you've already rinsed off the dirtiest dishes.

✔ Use a natural detergent so the water can be used to water the garden. You can also recycle water used for rinsing onto the garden.

✔ Wash the cleanest dishes first, working your way up to the dirtiest so that you don't have to change the water so often.

✔ Fill a second basin with tepid water for rinsing the dishes rather than rinsing under the running tap. Use this water to wash windows, floors, or the car, to flush the loo or water the garden.

If you go with the dishwasher, follow these tips to reduce your environmental impact:

✔ Load the dishwasher carefully and make sure that it's full before you press Start.

✔ Turn the dishwasher off as soon as it has finished washing, before it starts the drying cycle, so that the dishes dry naturally rather than using the dishwasher's heater, which comprises a large portion of the dishwasher's energy drain.

✔ Buy a dishwasher that's as energy efficient as possible for your needs – one with an economy cycle and which uses cold and hot water. That way you can set loads that just need a light wash at a lower temperature and save on energy.

Sorting kitchen waste

Disposing of waste is one of the most important green issues because governments are running out of space for landfill sites (waste is discussed in detail in Chapter 6). Kitchen waste – mainly food scraps and packaging – makes up a large part of the total household waste generated. Getting to grips with what you put in the kitchen bin can help reduce the need for landfill sites and large incinerators.

Chapter 6 covers more about reusing and recycling, but here are some things you can do in the kitchen to help out:

✔ **Pay attention to packaging.** Fresh food straight from the counter in a butchers or deli can be wrapped in paper and biodegradable bags rather than in pre-packed plastic containers. If you are buying pre-packed foods look for recyclable packaging. Put fruit and vegetables straight into your trolley or basket without putting them into a plastic bag first.

✔ **Carry out compost.** Reuse your food scraps and peelings for composting in the garden (Chapter 5 tells you all about how to compost) and use leftovers for tomorrow's lunch instead of throwing them in the bin.

✔ **Recycle the rigid materials.** You can recycle much of your kitchen waste including paper, cardboard, plastics, food and drink cans, and glass jars and bottles.

✔ **Bring your own bags.** Take canvas bags or baskets to the shops rather than accepting the plastic carrier bags offered; ask for a cardboard box to take stuff home in, or reuse carrier bags.

When it comes to waste, reduce it as much as possible and when you've done that, reuse or recycle what's left. What's waste to you may be useful to your friends and neighbours or to a charity shop (see Chapter 6).

Bottling out – the damage done by bottled water

Nearly half of the bottled water sold is just processed tap water. Yet on average each person in the UK drinks about 15 litres a year. The tap water in the UK is at least as good as bottled water according to water inspectors.

The biggest problem with bottled water is that it is transported around the world – often in heavy glass bottles – so a lot of energy is used up getting it into the shops. That energy use results in greenhouse gas emissions, which in turn are blamed for leading to climate change, which in turn threatens water supplies. On top of that the glass and plastic bottles the water comes in end up in landfill sites unless they're recycled. So, keep in mind that you're not conserving water by drinking the bottled versions.

If you use bottled water on long walks or while out running, keep a bottle handy and refill it from the tap each time rather than buying a new bottle.

Splashing About in Your Green Bathroom

The bathroom is probably the room you spend the least time in, but by nature of what you do in there, it can also be the least environmentally friendly part of your home. The most obvious way to make your bathroom greener is to cut down on the amount of water you use. But you can also make a big difference by changing your cosmetics and toiletries for green versions. You can also use greener cleaning materials, which are addressed later in this chapter in the section 'Cleaning the Green Way'.

Keeping water usage to a minimum

One of the most effective ways to save water is to turn the tap off while you're brushing your teeth. Letting the tap run constantly for the three minutes you're advised to clean your teeth for uses approximately 15 litres of water. That's almost as much as the average dishwasher uses. If four people clean their teeth for three minutes twice a day and leave the tap running, that wastes enough drinking water to fill the bath.

Showering versus bathing

A shower uses about a third of the water it takes to fill your bath. However, how much water you use depends on the depth of the water in the bath, whether or not you use a power shower, and how long you stand under the running water. Cut down the time you spend in the shower to about five minutes at the most.

Other tips to conserve water while you bathe are:

- Bathe with your partner or use the bath after each other.
- Take a shower instead of a bath but be aware of how long you let the water run. A ten-minute shower under a power shower uses even more water than taking a bath.
- Shave in the basin instead of in the shower.
- Fit special shower heads that restrict the water flow or aerate the water, to reduce the volume you use.
- Make sure that there are no dripping taps or shower heads, leaks, or overflows from the bathroom.

If you use less water you use less energy to heat it up. And setting the shower to a slightly lower temperature also cuts your fuel bills.

Reducing the flush factor

Toilet flushing accounts for about a third of all the household water you use. Most toilets have a half-flush and full-flush option – or a dual-flush. Use the half-flush when you can.

Think before you press the button or handle whether you need to flush. If you're at home all day by yourself, and there's no one outside the family to use the toilet, save it up and flush at one go. Or adopt the policy of flushing when there's brown material in the toilet bowl and not if there isn't. If it's yellow, let it mellow; if it's brown, flush it down! Each time you don't flush you save water.

Use recycled water to flush the toilet – such as rainwater collected in the garden. Using drinking-quality tap water to flush the toilet makes no sense environmentally. There are water-saving devices you can install to recycle used water from the shower, bath, or wash hand basin into the cistern so that it's reused to flush the toilet.

Waterless toilets are another option, although they're expensive to fit into existing homes. Modern waterless composting toilets collect waste in a container below the house and treat it to make compost for fertilising your garden. There's more information on water saving on the Environment Agency's Web site at www.environment-agency.gov.uk.

Going green with your toiletries and cosmetics

The green cosmetics and toiletries industries are flourishing. There are greener versions of everything, from perfume and lipstick to cotton buds and hair dye, soap, shaving cream, and deodorant. The choice is huge and can be quite confusing.

To be as green as possible, you can pursue several paths:

✔ Stop using anything that isn't essential. It is possible to stop using shampoo and conditioners for your hair, for example, without ill effects (see Chapter 17).

✔ Reduce the amount of cosmetics and toiletries you use. Most people use far more toothpaste than necessary – a blob the size of a small pea is enough.

✔ Consider the container. Choose items that are have little or no packaging, come in recyclable or refillable containers, and contain as few chemicals as you can find. Shop around for the ones that suit you best.

✔ Make sure as far as you can that ingredients are all natural products – plant or vegetable extracts for example.

Also make sure that the ingredients

• Haven't been tested on animals. Animal testing for cosmetics and their ingredients hasn't been allowed by the UK government since 1988 but both ingredients and complete products that have been tested on animals in other countries can be sold here and UK firms can get their new products animal tested abroad.

• Don't contain chemicals. This isn't easy as there are nearly 900 chemicals used in cosmetics and toiletries, many of which are toxic according to the National Institute of Occupational Safety and Health. These include sodium laurel sulphate, used in shower gel and shampoos (also used to degrease engines!), and propylene glycol, which is used in skin cream (and as anti-freeze!).

There are plenty of natural products you can use instead of potions made with lots of chemicals. Tea tree oil is a natural antiseptic and disinfectant, for example. There are ranges of plant and herb extracts such as lavender and coconut that can be used to replace products such as shampoos and oils that have chemicals in them. Ask at your local health food shop for natural products and they can tell you what to use in what circumstances. You'll find shops in most towns that specialise in natural cosmetic and beauty care products and if you type 'chemical-free cosmetics' into an Internet search engine you'll find a whole array of different companies selling 100% chemical-free products.

A couple other tips to keep in mind:

- ✔ The cotton industry is one of the biggest consumers of agrochemicals in the world and the cotton is usually treated with chlorine. Buy organic cotton wool if you can.

- ✔ Use electric razors or razor blades so that you're not throwing out disposable ones with plastic handles which aren't recyclable.

The places where you can get these products are expanding almost daily. The high street has health food shops that carry ranges of green toiletries and cosmetics as well as their food ranges, and supermarkets are getting in on the act. You'll find green ranges in the big chains of chemists shops, and even specialist chains dedicated to natural ranges. If you can't find a greener version of something in the shops try the Internet. Get more information on green cosmetics at www.wen.org.uk, the Web site of the Women's Environmental Network.

Some green items may be more expensive than their less environmentally friendly equivalents, but the more demand there is for them the quicker prices come down. In addition, you can save some money by choosing greener products to replace your usual ones as they run out rather than replacing them all at once. That way the shock to your wallet isn't so great and you're not disposing of half-used products that end up in landfill sites.

You can't replace everything with alternatives that are completely free of chemicals. For example, hair dyes are a problem because they use a lot of potentially toxic chemicals, but there are herbal versions with fewer chemicals coming onto the market.

Don't worry if you still use some items that you are aware could be greener. If you can't do without them and can't finder greener ones, at least you've still made a lot of changes and are greener than you were.

Entertaining Green Ideals in the Living Room

The living room – if you use it for living in rather than spending most of your time in the kitchen – is a large consumer of energy. Entertainment systems such as music and DVD players and television sets use a lot of electricity. If you're reading, the lights are usually on. If you're sitting relaxing the heating may be on. And if you want a pleasant environment to live in you probably spend quite a bit of effort keeping it clean.

Chapter 3 shows that insulating your home reduces the heat that escapes as well as keeping unwanted heat or cold out. That means your rooms need less energy to keep them warm or cool. But that's not the only way to reduce energy consumption in the living room.

Finding entertainment system solutions

Big and loud isn't always beautiful when it comes to the amount of energy used. Modern LCD (Liquid Crystal Display) and high-definition television sets, digital radios, and digital televisions use more energy than smaller, older models with fewer functions. If you're replacing an older model ask the retailer for details of energy consumption.

Don't turn televisions, radios, and music players on unless you're listening to or watching them, to prevent using energy unnecessarily.

Switching to the television of the future

The government is going to phase out current broadcast television transmitters. Sometime between 2008 and 2012, depending on which part of the UK you live in, you will need to have a digital television or set top box in order to watch the telly.

These set top boxes can't be unplugged and switched off but designers are working on reducing the power they use. Hang on to your old-fashioned small-screen TV until you have no choice but to buy a new one to keep your energy consumption down.

The fewer new items you buy the more you reduce the total numbers that will be manufactured and the damage the production process causes.

Every time you buy a new piece of equipment, think about the amount of energy it took to make the new item and how many potentially damaging gases such as carbon dioxide were generated by the manufacturing process. There's more on carbon emissions in Chapters 1 and 2.

When you buy new equipment, give away older models to people who will use them – to friends, members of the freecycling system (talked about in Chapter 17), or to charity shops. That way they're reused and recycled rather than ending up on landfill.

Getting out of the standby habit

Make sure you turn everything off at the wall rather than leaving it on standby if you leave the room and before you go to bed. Electronics go on using a high proportion of electricity while on standby, in fact, some appliances – especially older ones – can use up to 85 per cent of the power on standby that they do while in use.

It's not just in the living room that you must get out of the habit of leaving everything on standby when you're not using it. Check around the kitchen, study, utility room, and bedrooms, too, for appliances plugged in and switched on but not being used. They may have been that way for days. Make it someone's job to check, every night before bed, and turn off every switch that doesn't have to be on. Don't forget to switch off all those mobile phone chargers. Just about the only items you can justify leaving on overnight are fridge and freezer, the heating and hot water heating timing controls, and the alarm.

Turning down the thermostat – woolly jumpers rule!

Most living areas in homes are hotter than they need to be in winter. You get used to having central heating and use it as an excuse to shed layers of clothes. The Energy Saving Trust says the living room will be comfortable for most fit and healthy people at around 21 degrees but that most will be happy in a range of temperature of around 5 degrees (so 19–23 degrees). By turning the thermostat down by just one degree you save anything up to a tenth of your heating bills, not to mention adding your might towards saving the ozone layer. Turn it down by another degree and add a jumper to save even more energy and money. You can get more information from the Energy Saving Trust website at www.est.org.uk.

More tips that can keep you greener and a bit warmer are:

✔ Put shiny foil behind your radiators to reflect the heat out into the room rather than have it heating the walls.

✔ Block up any open fireplaces and chimneys you don't use to prevent heated air escaping up them and draughts of cold air blowing down – or buy a chimney balloon to attach to the top of the chimney. They stop draughts, reduce heat loss, and save you money.

✔ Make sure that your home is well insulated as explained in Chapter 3.

✔ Turn off the heating and water heating if you're going away, although in cold weather you may want to set them to come on for a few hours every day to stop the pipes freezing up.

Check with the Energy Saving Trust for more tips on using less energy and keeping the bills down at www.est.org.uk.

Sleeping Soundly in Your Green Bedroom

The bedroom is often overlooked when it comes to going green. After all, the thing you spend most time doing in there is sleeping and you're not using up much energy while you're asleep. But there's still room for improvement.

If you leave the heating, electric blanket, air conditioning, or electric fan on all night, you have scope for cutting down your energy consumption. In winter turn the heating thermostat down and put an extra blanket on the bed. Take a hot water bottle to bed rather than leaving the electric blanket on all night.

In summer, if you feel safe with the windows open, open them at strategic points around the house to allow a flow of air. Opening just your own bedroom window may not be as effective.

In warm weather keep your curtains closed during the day to keep the sun out and the room cool, and in winter keep them closed to keep the heat in.

Turn off the television and any other electrical appliances in your bedroom at the wall before you fall asleep.

Laundering Your Green Credentials

The washing machine and tumble dryer are two power hungry appliances that most people find they can't live without. Reduce the amount you use them – especially the tumble dryer – and change the way you use them, and your laundry can be greener.

Using ecofriendly products

Some washing powders on the market are less harsh on the environment than others when they enter the water system after the wash. Most supermarkets have ranges of ecofriendly products. Go for as green a powder as possible and use about half the recommended amount. Try not to use heavy-duty powders that promise to obliterate every stain under the sun because they're likely to have more potentially damaging chemicals in them.

Deciding between terries or disposables

The debate goes on over whether disposable nappies or washable ones are best for the environment. The Women's Environment Network (WEN) says that disposable nappies have twice the impact on the environment as washable ones. (You can get more information from WEN at www.wen.org.uk or 020 7481 9004.)

If you use disposables buy brands that have as much recycled and biodegradable material, and as few chemicals, as possible. About 8 million disposable nappies are thrown out every day in the UK, and the majority of them end up in landfill sites where even biodegradable ones take hundreds of years to break down.

How green washable nappies are depends on what they're made from, how you wash and dry them, which products you use in the washing machine, and how energy-efficient you are when you do your washing. If you use washable nappies your greenest option is those made from organic cotton.

If you can afford to have your nappies washed by a nappy-laundering service you are being very green. Because they're washing nappies on a big scale these services are most efficient in terms of energy and water used. For more information on using washable nappies take a look at the Web site of the Women's Environmental Network at www.wen.org.uk/nappies.

Even if you stick to your normal powder, and reduce the amount you use, then you're greener than you were last time you did a wash.

Do the washing only when you can do a full load. But don't overload the machine or the clothes won't move around freely enough to get clean.

Keeping the temperature down

Front-loader washing machines generally use less water and detergent than top-loading ones, and allow cold-water washes, which use less energy than hot-water washes. You can do most of your washing at 30 degrees – especially if it's clothes that have been worn to work once and then tossed into the laundry basket. Washing at lower temperatures means you can put colours together without the dangers of them running – so you're more likely to wash more clothes at once. Sixty-degree washes use almost a third more energy than 40-degree washes and the colours fade faster.

Not all clothes need to be washed every time they're worn. If something's a bit smelly rather than dirty, put it on a coat hanger and hang it on the clothes line or by an open window to freshen up.

Drying naturally

Hanging your clothes on a clothes line or drying rack enables you to cut down on the use of your dryer. Line drying isn't always possible, particularly if you live in a small flat where space is at a premium, or where there are restrictions on what you can hang outside or on balconies.

Clothes dried on the line, on coat hangers, or folded and dried in a warm cupboard by the hot water tank are less likely to need ironing.

When you do have to iron, do it when clothes are still slightly damp or use a hand spray to dampen them rather than a steam iron. A steam iron wastes energy heating up the water in its tank.

If you need a dryer go for the most energy-efficient one you can find. Stop the dryer just before the clothes are completely dry. They can finish drying while they're hanging up or as you iron them. About a third of all the energy used in tumble dryers is used when the drying programme carries on after the clothes are dry.

Dry off slightly damp clothes by putting them into the cupboard (if you have one) by your hot water tank, if you have one and there's room.

Cleaning the Green Way

When it comes to cleaning you can find a greener way to clean just about everything in the home. If you're lucky enough to have a cleaner who comes in for a few hours a week you may not even know what cleaning materials lurk in your home. Do a stock take and resolve to replace each cleaning item with a greener one the next time it needs replacing. If you do have a cleaner get him or her involved, too, or you may have a rebellion on your hands. The basic rules of green cleaning are:

- Use as little detergent as possible and use those with the fewest additives you can find.
- Use natural cleaning agents such as vinegar, lemon juice, borax, and bicarbonate of soda.
- Save old toothbrushes for scrubbing dirt and stains out of small, difficult-to-reach areas.
- Clean up as you go along so that dirt and grime doesn't get too dried out and encrusted to be removed by natural cleaners.
- Use a carpet sweeper or dustpan and brush instead of your vacuum cleaner for small cleaning operations.

Arguing the case against air fresheners

Air fresheners contain chemicals and cover up smells rather than removing them. Plug-in air fresheners use energy while they're pumping their chemicals into the air. Some people find air fresheners make them short of breath and give them headaches.

Fortunately, you can still enjoy a nice-smelling home because natural alternatives abound. Both vinegar and bicarbonate of soda dissolved in water absorb bad smells. Lemon slices in a pan of boiling water make another good air freshener. If you have smokers in your house leave a small bowl of vinegar hidden under a piece of furniture and it will deodorise the room. Burning candles takes the cigarette smoke out of the air and stops fabrics getting smelly.

Use essential oils to make rooms smell nice. Get an oil burner, some small candles, and your favourite naturally scented oils to get a more natural smell or fill up a bowl with petals from flowers and herbs from your garden.

Cleaning without chemicals

You can use everyday items you probably already have in your cupboard to clean almost everything in your home – from the cooker to the floors, wooden furniture to glass windows, and more. The following list offers just a few examples of some natural cleaners and how to use them.

- **Borax** is a natural mineral which is a disinfectant and great in the laundry and as a kitchen cleaner. Add it to your washing powder drawer to whiten and soften discoloured towels and other whites. You can buy it in leading high street chemists and online.

- **Baking soda** is a mild abrasive. Use it as you would an abrasive cleaning powder. Some suggestions are:

  - Brighten up taps and other chrome fittings with water mixed with a little baking soda.

  - Clean worktops, appliances, and other surfaces with a small amount on a damp cloth.

  - Clean your fridge inside and out with a solution of three tablespoons of baking soda dissolved in half a cup of warm water and wipe over with a damp cloth.

  - Moisten the inside walls of your oven with a damp cloth, then sprinkling baking soda over the oven and leave for an hour, before wiping off with a cloth. If the stains are too stubborn try an oven cleaner that contains as few chemicals as possible.

  - Soak dirty pots and pans in a basin of hot water with two or three tablespoons of baking soda for about an hour, and then scrub off with an abrasive scrubber.

  - Use it on mildew in the shower and on shower curtains – use an old toothbrush for cleaning the grouting between tiles.

  - Pour half a cup of baking soda down your kitchen or bathroom drain followed by half a cup of vinegar and then some boiling water. This breaks down fatty acids that block up drains.

You can get larger quantities of bicarbonate of soda and borax from hardware stores than in the supermarket. If you have difficulty finding either ask your chemist or hardware store to order them for you.

- **Vinegar** takes away grease and deodorises. Use normal white vinegar (not your expensive balsamic) to

- Clean limescale marks off the bath, wash hand basin, and kitchen sink. Soak the shower head in vinegar and then brush the built-up limescale off with an old toothbrush.

  Lemon juice also works on limescale. If the stains are stubborn leave some lemon juice on the mark for a few minutes – or soak a tissue in lemon juice and set it on the problem area. Bottled lemon juice is less trouble than squeezing fresh lemons.

- Wash your windows. Use a mixture of vinegar and water and wipe them with old crumpled-up newspaper to shine them up (if the print comes off the newspaper onto your hands, it's not yet old enough, so don't use it for cleaning with). Use the same on your car windows. Vinegar cuts through the accumulated grease. The more greasy the glass the more vinegar you'll need – try half and half to start with.

- Brush around the toilet bowl. For more stubborn marks sprinkle the toilet bowl with baking soda and follow by pouring some vinegar on top of it. Be prepared for the bubbling froth that results. Use a toilet brush to scour the bowl clean.

✔ **Olive oil** takes finger marks off stainless steel and mixed with a little vinegar – about one part vinegar to three parts oil – makes a good floor polish (or salad dressing!).

Use a mixture of lemon, water, and olive oil instead of furniture polish. Use it like you would any other polish and smooth off with a dry cloth. The proportions you use will depend on the wood and how dirty it is – try a spoonful of each to start with.

You can also try natural wax polishes, great for wooden surfaces. You can buy *beeswax* polishes from antique furniture shops.

✔ **Castor oil** is good for conditioning leather. As a massage makes tired muscles feel better, so a bit of elbow grease applied with this natural cleaner brings tired leather to life again.

✔ **Soda water** helps remove carpet stains; blot some on and dab the stains away.

For wet red wine or coffee stains, pour baking soda on the stain, rub it in and then brush it off. Try cornflour on more stubborn stains. Rub it into the wet stain and brush off.

Experiment with the mixtures and ingredients until you find the ideal mix for cleaning every item in your house. When you find a mixture that works for you, make up a batch, put it into an empty jar or bottle, label it, and keep for future use.

Using natural products may call for a bit more effort on your part because they're less abrasive and may be slower acting than the chemical-laden alternatives. On the plus side, the exercise is as good as going to the gym.

Replacing aerosols with green versions

The objections to aerosols are that the spray cans are filled under pressure and when the button is pressed the products are carried farther – carrying the chemicals into the air. This can trigger allergic reactions in some people and bring on asthmatic attacks as well as making a contribution to polluting the atmosphere. The cans are also dangerous if they're exposed to heat. Even an empty one can explode if it gets too hot.

If you want to spray your natural polish or cleaning solutions onto surfaces, buy from the garden centre a plastic spray-pump container meant to spray water onto plants.

Getting greener cleaning products on sale

Although you may try many natural recipes for creating your own cleaning products, you may still want to purchase some greener cleaning and washing products. Some of the top sellers are washing powders, toilet cleaners, recycled toilet paper and rubbish sacks, washing up liquid, fabric softener, and recycled aluminium foil.

If life is too short to make up your own versions, or you can't make a natural version of the product you need, buy these instead. If you have difficulty finding them in supermarkets or hardware shops try the Internet. Just two of the sites you can try are www.ecotopia.co.uk and www.greenshop.co.uk.

Bringing up Environmentally Friendly Children

Being green works best when the whole family is involved, understands, and is signed up to the idea. There's little point in your using less water and energy, leaving the car at home, and trying to keep the household waste down to a minimum if everyone else is undoing all your good work. As with most principles you apply around the house, being green works better if everyone, even children as far as they can for their age, understands why it's necessary.

Younger children learn from your example, so bring them up to be as green as you are and answer any of their questions as you go along. They grow up accepting that recycling and composting are a part of everyday life and that you walk or cycle if at all possible.

As children get older they become more aware of the ranges of toys and gadgets available. They see what their friends get for presents. Advertisements on television, in magazines and on the Internet make an impact on them too. You can't blame them for wanting new things. Sometimes it's easier to give in to your pestering child than to explain yet again that buying all those new things is bad for the planet. Don't beat yourself up about giving in to a treat every now and again. The problems arise as they get older if their friends go everywhere by car and eat convenience food in lots of packaging, while they don't. Don't be too strict – some junk food once in a while won't do any harm – but explain why that kind of food isn't the best to eat and also that producing it causes problems for the planet, the animals, and other people.

Remembering that pets can be green too

If you own one of the UK's 30 million pets – goldfish and hamsters through to pot-bellied pigs and Shetland ponies, not to mention UK favourites dogs and cats – make them greener too.

If you decide to buy a puppy or a kitten make sure that the breeder has a good reputation and that the animal won't suffer painful health conditions as it gets older because it has been highly bred. There are hundreds of puppy farms where the animals are kept in very poor conditions and are just a money-making exercise. Ask friends and local vets for recommendations and visit the breeders to check them out. Not all pet shops look after animals well either. Check that any pet shop you buy from is a member of the Pet Care Trust. Look on the Trust's Web site for more information at www.petcare.org.uk or call on 0870 062 4400. The Web site also has information on taking care of pets. Another source of information is the RSPCA (the Royal Society for the Prevention of Cruelty to Animals) at www.rspca.org.uk.

Be sure that you have the time and patience to give an animal the love, care, and training it needs and that your home has the space and facilities necessary. It's cruel to keep a big dog in a small flat all day by itself while you're at work. Cats love to be outdoors, but you can't let them out if they'll be in danger from traffic. And, fit them with a collar with a bell so the birds are warned off instead of stalked and killed.

Animals are getting fatter. Many owners don't know how to feed them and give them too many treats. They often don't get enough exercise. It's cruel to allow animals to become overweight. Take advice from your vet about how best to feed and exercise your animal – which is, after all, your best friend.

When it comes to feeding and grooming apply the same green principles you apply to the rest of the family. If your children aren't allowed food with additives and artificial colouring and preservatives, or use natural shampoos without chemicals, why should your dog be treated any differently?

Older children understand if you explain why it's important to look after the welfare of the planet. They understand even better if they can see how the way they live can make a difference to a child their own age in another part of the world. If there are floods in a part of Africa that scientists are attributing to climate change as a result of carbon emission in rich countries, explain the connection between your capacity to buy goods and the rain that falls to cause the floods.

Children love animals. Give them information about the work of the various charities and other organisations to make the environment a safe place for animals and to protect endangered species. You can find more ideas in Chapter 18 and some useful Web sites to visit in Chapter 16.

If your children are old enough, allow them to share in decisions about how the family can be more green. Give them responsibility for some aspect of the green operation of the household.

Furnish you children's rooms with furniture made from renewable and sustainable materials such as wood from recycled timber and sustainable plantations (see Chapter 1). Explain why some wood is greener than others.

Make children feel that their contribution is as important as anyone else's. But if there's the odd slip when someone forgets to turn the TV off at the wall or runs the tap when still half asleep in the morning, give them a break. It's about being greener not being perfect.

Planning Your Green Funeral

Green funerals are among the fastest-growing green businesses in the UK. For just about every aspect of a traditional funeral there's an environmentally friendly alternative way that's kinder to the planet.

Most people don't want to talk about death but if you want a green funeral, you must do your research, make your plans, draw up a list of do's and don'ts and talk to your nearest and dearest about your wishes. Write all the details down and keep them with your will.

The average funeral costs in the region of £800. You can have a green funeral much more cheaply, and keep the bills down for your family, as well as protect the planet.

If you want a wooden coffin choose one that's made from wood certified to come from a sustainable forest – one where trees are being replaced as they are cut down. You can get more information from the Forest Stewardship Council at www.fscus.org. Alternatives are wicker or cardboard coffins, which are biodegradable. You can have a cardboard coffin inside a wooden shell that goes back to the undertaker when the funeral is over. Visit www.eco-funerals.com or www.memorialcentre.co.uk for more information. In some cases you can be buried or cremated without a coffin at all.

Your relatives will want to know whether you want to be buried or cremated. They are green arguments for and against either decision. There's a problem of space for conventional burials in cemeteries and the problem of damaging gases released into the atmosphere by cremation. Conventional burials use embalming fluids which can pollute the ground and any water nearby.

A third option is to be buried in a green or natural burial site. These sites don't usually allow the use of embalming fluids and you must use biodegradable coffins. Because bodies are not encased in lead-lined coffins they degrade quickly. There are no headstones – most graves have trees planted on them – so you have a doubly green send-off. There are about 200 of these woodland or meadow sites around the UK. The Natural Death Centre has all the information about environmentally friendly funerals. Call the centre on 0871 2882098 or visit the Web site at www.naturaldeath.org.uk.

Chapter 5

Getting Green in the Garden

In This Chapter

▶ Looking at your whole garden

▶ Turning off the taps

▶ Using your garden to grow food

▶ Saying goodbye to chemicals and hello to muscle power

▶ Turning your waste into compost

▶ Caring for your lawn and your surroundings

▶ Designing a sustainable garden

*H*ow green does your garden grow? The UK is often hailed as a nation of gardeners, and the vast majority of the UK population has access to a garden or patch of green of some sort. For many people, the garden is an extra room – a beautifully manicured place they can relax and enjoy in warm weather. For others a garden is functional – somewhere they can grow food and create a haven for wildlife.

However you see your own little bit of outside space there are lots of ways you can make it greener, and this chapter tells you about some of them.

Sue Fisher, Michael MacCaskey, and Bill Marken's *Gardening For Dummies* (Wiley) gives plenty of additional gardening advice.

Balancing the Garden Ecosystem

Left to its own devices, any area becomes a complex ecosystem. Plants attract insects, which in turn attract birds and animals. Everything lives off something else in the ecosystem. Everything you do in your garden has a bearing on how that ecosystem evolves. The less negative impact you have, the greener your garden.

The basic principles of being green in your garden are:

- Keeping the amount of water you use to a minimum and relying on sources other than the tap.
- Growing plants and vegetables to benefit the whole ecosystem.
- Reducing the garden's consumption of energy and chemicals. Cut the use of chemicals right out and use natural materials such as home-made compost, bone meal, and some types of animal manure as fertiliser.
- Feeding your plants with your own compost.

Each species in your garden will eventually establish a natural balance. Snails will keep down algae in the pond; the birds will keep down the insect population; some good insects like ladybirds devour bad insects like greenfly. To attract certain good insects into your garden to help you keep the bad ones at bay, grow the plants that will attract them.

The Royal Entomology Society has masses of information about insects and how to create suitable environments for them in your garden, including a useful booklet you can download called *Garden Entomology*. Take a look at www.royalensoc.co.uk.

Green gardening requires a bit of research, planning, and experimentation to get it right. The idea is to get to the point where you have the garden you want without having to take drastic action with chemicals.

Getting the whole family involved

Gardens are places where the whole family can practise being green. Put each person in charge of some green aspect of your outside space. The children will probably love the compost and the worm farm. Give each an area to grow their own vegetables or wild flowers. People get very competitive with each other as to who can grow plants most successfully. Give someone the job of counting all the different species that come into your garden and of spotting each new arrival. Someone else in the family may be happy to do research into alternative green materials and native plants that can be used – even if they can't or won't do any of the hard work outdoors.

Even if you don't have a garden there are jobs to be done – planting window boxes and pots with herbs and salad leaves, or sorting out kitchen waste for composting in a compost bin or worm farm. There's something that everyone can contribute and the more involved they are the more green the whole family becomes.

Watching Your Watering

Water is a big issue for most gardeners and depending on where you live in the UK you're likely to complain of having too much of it or too little of it at certain times of the year. If you're in the latter category, you can safeguard your garden from drying out by setting up water collection systems in preparation for any hosepipe bans. Look at ways of using *grey water* (water used already in your home for something else like washing up, bathing, or showering) in the garden, and you can design the sort of garden that can stay green without a lot of water in the first place.

Reflecting on water sources and methods

Your aim should be to water your garden as infrequently as possible and to use water you've collected rather than putting treated drinking water on your plants. Several tips can help you water more greenly and efficiently:

✔ Collect rainwater in a water butt. You can get all sorts of water butts made to look like garden features such as rocks.

You can collect water that runs off your roof and down a drainpipe. You may be able to divert your bath or shower water into water butts rather than letting it run down the drain into the sewage system.

Even if you don't have a water butt you can use basins or buckets to carry water from your washing up or bath to water your plants.

✔ Water your garden at the coolest part of the day to reduce evaporation. If you have to water, do it in the early morning or late evening and water only the areas and plants that need it.

✔ Use a trigger nozzle instead of a sprinkler. Sprinklers can be wasteful. A sprinkler can use as much water in an hour as a family of four uses in a day! It doesn't take long for a sprinkler to soak your lawn thoroughly. Using a trigger nozzle only when needed can save up to 225 litres a week.

Mulch to keep moisture in the garden. Adding a layer of tree bark, compost, coconut husks, or even newspaper keeps the sun off the soil and holds in moisture.

Taking plants' water needs into account

Xeriscape means to landscape for water conservation. The idea is to use plants that require less water. Ask your local garden centre about how much water different plants need. Some thrive in drier conditions.

Lawns can take a lot of water to keep them green and lush. To reduce the amount of water you use in the garden cut down on the area of lawn and grow plants that need less water. Established trees and shrubs don't usually need to be watered.

Instead of water-hungry plants, utilise objects such as rocks, bricks, benches, and gravel for decorative effect.

Growing Your Own Food

You can grow your own food just about anywhere as long as you have a bit of sun and a water supply. Even if you live in a tiny flat with only a windowsill you can still grow some of your own.

Growing organic

As I explain in Chapter 7, eating locally grown food in season is the greenest way to eat, and if that food is organically produced, even better. Growing food in your own garden using organic methods ticks all the green boxes, and you have the satisfaction of having done it all yourself.

Some of the principles of organic gardening include:

- ✔ **Rotating:** Traditional methods of rotating crops – growing different vegetables in different parts of the garden each year – enrich the soil. Different nutrients are taken from the soil by different crops and rotating crops each year, and leaving part of the land unplanted each year, gives the soil time to recover and replenish depleted nutrients.

- ✔ **Fertilising:** Plants need nitrogen, potassium, and phosphorus. If your soil is a bit low on these nutrients, you can add them using blood and bone meal – crushed or ground blood and bone; rock potash or liquid fertiliser from nature; or a wormery (see the section below 'Setting up a worm farm'). The next point and the 'Giving Your Waste a New Lease of Life' section, later in this chapter, talk about compost as a nutrient source as well. Your local garden centre or nursery can advise you about your soil type and how to enrich it.

Rely on natural fertilisers rather than artificial chemicals that can get into your food and into nearby streams.

✔ **Composting:** Use you own home-made compost to energise and fertilise your soil. If you don't have enough of your own compost to start, you can buy compost, preferably organic compost if you're growing organic fruit and veg. The upcoming 'Giving Your Waste a New Lease of Life' section digs into all the composting dirt.

Resist the temptation to use any materials based on peat. Gardeners use nearly 3 million cubic metres of peat-based planting and growing compost each year, and, as a result, very little of the original UK peat bogs now remain. Peat can't be replanted and regrown – it's not sustainable. Ask your garden centre for green alternatives or make your own compost.

✔ **Mulching:** Mulching keeps down the weeds and helps keep the moisture in the soil. The most basic mulch is a plastic sheet, but its organic equivalent is a layer of natural material such as compost, wood chips, grass cuttings, straw, or rotted manure. These organic mulches add organic content and nutrients to the soil as well as keeping the weeds in check so that you don't have to use chemical weedkillers.

Hoeing stimulates the growth of plants, reduces water loss from the soil surface, and removes weeds that take up valuable water and nutrients.

Looking at organic standards

Organic products have to comply with standards set out by the European Union on the use of pesticides and other chemicals. Organic food produced in the UK doesn't have to be completely chemical-free but instead of the 450 pesticides that can be used in conventional farming only seven can be used in organic production.

For more information, take a look at the Department for Environment, Food, and Rural Affairs (Defra) Web site at `www.defra.gov.uk/farm/organic` or at the Soil Association Web site at `www.soilassociation.org`.

The Soil Association is one of the organisations in the UK that can certify that a food is organic and you will find its logo on many UK-produced organic products in the shops. Producers who are certified as organic by the Soil Association are only allowed to use four pesticides on their produce and there are plans to restrict that to two in the future.

As long as you aren't selling your produce as organic you don't have to comply with the standards but the closer you can get to them the more organic your home-produced food will be.

If your garden was used by previous occupants to grow fruit and vegetables, it may contain a whole range of chemicals. It takes time to get those chemicals out of the soil so that your produce is organic. You can get more information on making your garden organic from Garden Advice at www.gardenadvice. co.uk. Talk to your local nursery or garden centre staff about the types of plants and seeds you need for organic production or try The Organic Gardening Catalogue at www.organiccatalogue.com.

Growing small

Even if you don't have what could be called a garden, you can grow a surprising amount in pots, window boxes, on your balcony, or on windowsills. Even if there's only enough space for a few herbs or salad leaves that's a start, and it takes surprisingly little space to grow a few tomatoes.

Talk to your local garden centre or nursery about the best kinds of plants to grow in the conditions you have.

Keep growing in a confined space simple by following these steps:

1. **Buy clay or terracotta pots, which are the most naturally made of the pots on the market.**

    If they're locally made, even better. Make sure that the pots are deep enough to allow adequate root growth (about 20 to 25 cm) and that there are some holes in the bottom so water drains right through the soil.

2. **Buy organically grown seeds, available from most hardware stores and nurseries.**

3. **Plant the seeds in pre-packaged or home-made organic potting mix, which contains natural ingredients such as soil, plant mulch, compost, manure, and sand, until your own compost is ready to use.**

4. **Place the pots in the best position to make the most of sun and rain.**

As your tiny garden grows, use the following tips to keep it growing greenly:

✔ Feed your plants organic fertiliser that contains rock minerals and animal manure produced from sustainable farming methods. You can also use the liquid from the bottom of a worm farm.

✔ Use organically made insecticides such as those made from a mix of garlic, chillies, and dried *pyrethrum* (a plant of the daisy family).

Find out more about gardening in pots at www.container-gardens.com.

Growing under cover

If you have space for a greenhouse – or glasshouse as it should more accurately be called – you can produce a whole different range of plants to those you can grow outside:

- ✔ In summer, the glass makes the interior temperature warmer so that plants that would die in the outside temperatures can flourish. You can take advantage of the heat to grow more exotic plants, fruit, and vegetables than you can grow in the garden. If you live too far north to successfully grow strawberries outside you could grow them under glass. Many people use their greenhouses to grow tomatoes because they live in areas where even in summer it's too cold for them outside or because they can grow different varieties.

- ✔ In winter, the greenhouse can be the place to keep fragile plants alive that would otherwise die in the garden. You can heat the greenhouse and grow a whole range of plants, but that's not very green as you're using energy and causing carbon emissions. Depending on where you live you may be able to grow new young plants from seeds, seedlings, or bulbs and then plant them out in the garden in the spring.

Use the same principles – seeds and plants grown using organic methods with natural fertilisers and insecticides and home-produced compost – in your greenhouse. You can find more useful information from Garden Advice at www.gardenadvice.co.uk.

Growing community

If you really don't have access to any space of your own but like the idea of gardening and growing some of your own food, consider joining a community gardening project – or even setting up one in your area. *Community gardens* are gardens on land donated to the local community usually by the local council, a church, a school, or healthcare facility. After you've got the land you can set up a team to manage the project. Volunteers who want to take part agree to contribute their time and energy to running the garden as well as growing their own and communal plants.

If you type 'community garden projects' into a search engine, dozens of local schemes in all parts of the UK pop up. Go to www.gardensforpeople.com for more information and help on planning your garden and getting it up and growing. The joy of community gardening is that you don't have to do all the work yourself.

Growing an allotment

An option for would-be gardeners without space of their own is to rent an allotment. When you travel around the UK – particularly by train – you see areas dedicated to allotments on the outskirts of most towns and cities. They are very popular. You may be able to rent half an allotment or share one with some friends.

Many allotments are abandoned because they are hard work. Don't get carried away. Ease yourself into allotment life. Do a bit of work on your allotment regularly rather than spending a whole day digging and ending up exhausted with a sore back. Nothing's guaranteed to put you off more than backache.

Grow the things you know your family like best but try to grow as wide a variety as possible or everyone will get sick of carrots or courgettes and go back to buying different vegetables from the supermarket.

Set aside an area for a compost heap and use organic production methods to keep your allotment super green.

Other allotment holders on your site are wonderful sources of information on what will grow and what won't. Most people don't mind being asked for their opinions! Another good place to find information on allotment sites around the UK and for help with your allotment in general is www.allotments-uk.com.

Shedding the Chemicals and Energy-Guzzling Tools

The shed at the bottom of the garden has become the butt of many jokes, but when you look at how toxic the contents of the average shed are it's no laughing matter. Most tool sheds or garages harbour some of the least green garden products on the market – chemicals for keeping down weeds and pests, petrol powered lawnmowers, electric tools, and old tins of paint and wood preservative.

As you establish your green garden, you can cut down the ungreen materials you use. Downsizing your lawn and developing your own sustainable garden ecosystem allows you to rid yourself of toxic chemicals and you can replace your engine mower and other petrol-powered landscaping machines with hand-held, human-powered versions.

Cut down the energy you use in the garden by replacing your power tools with manual alternatives. Table 5-1 offers suggestions.

Table 5-1	Green and Non-Green Garden Tools
Replace This . . .	*With This . . .*
Electric or petrol lawnmower	Push reel mower
Electric lawn edger	Foot-powered lawn edger
Electric strimmer	Long-necked grass shears
Electric or petrol chainsaw	Manual pocket chainsaw
Electric or petrol leaf blower	Garden rake
Electric drill	Rechargeable battery drill

Dispose of any chemicals safely – call your local authority waste management department to find out where you can take them to get rid of them safely. Sell or give away the electrical and petrol-powered tools – so that they are being reused and recycled.

Giving Your Waste a New Lease of Life

Organic gardeners regard compost as the key to a green sustainable garden. Composting is the link between the inside world and the outside world – by composting your own household waste and using it to nourish your garden, you create your own mini-ecosystem. It doesn't get much greener than that!

Compost is decayed organic material which is used as a fertiliser for your garden soil and growing plants. It's made from anything that can rot naturally and break down with the help of the tiny organisms that live in it, materials like leaves, grass cuttings, wood chips, and manure. If you pile your organic material for composting into a heap or a pile in the garden or put it into a composting bin (which you can get from a garden centre) it eventually decays and becomes brown and crumbly. When you dig it into your garden soil it adds nutrients and makes the soil richer and easier to work with. You can buy compost from garden centres ready to use if there's no space to create your own.

Compost puts back into the soil nutrients that plants take out. It helps your soil do a better job for the growing plants by:

✔ Allowing the soil to hold moisture so you can do less watering

✔ Stopping nutrients leaching out of the soil, which means plants get more of the nutrients they need

✔ Keeping the soil healthy and reducing the likelihood of soil-borne disease

The added attraction of composting is that you get rid of your kitchen waste in the greenest possible way. It doesn't travel miles and fill up landfill space unnecessarily.

Composting your waste away

Between a third and a half of all household waste can be turned into compost for use in the garden rather than put in the rubbish bin to end up in landfill. Anything in your home that eventually decomposes can go into your compost bin or heap. Banana skins and egg shells, paper and cardboard, vegetable peelings and tea bags – much of the stuff you throw in the bin to be collected by the bin lorry can be composted instead. Avoid meat, fish, newspapers, and cooked food, and make sure no cat and dog dirt, glossy magazines, or disposable nappies get into the mix.

The two key ingredients of compost are carbon and nitrogen. You can find the carbon in your household recycling bin – paper and cardboard for example – and find the nitrogen in your kitchen bin in the form of fruit and vegetable peelings. Add some grass cuttings, manure (farmyard animal or chicken manure with straw in it is best), and weeds (nitrogen-producing materials) to the mix and you'll eventually have some great compost. Equal proportions of carbon and nitrogen materials give you the best mix. Try www.gardenorganic. org.uk for help with your compost.

Chop everything into small pieces so that the composting process can work more quickly and effectively. It takes longer for the material to break down into compost the bigger the pieces are.

Put the whole lot into a composting bin which you can get from your local garden centre, hardware store, or from your local authority – some provide them for free. Otherwise, leave an area of your garden for a composting heap that you can keep adding material to. The BBC has a guide to building your own compost heap at www.bbc.co.uk/gardening.

The key to a good compost is balance – don't overdo it with any one ingredient as it will oversupply some of the nutrients, which can sometimes do as much harm as good.

In order for the waste material to turn into compost, it needs air and water:

✔ Keep the festering compost moist to allow the thousands of bacteria and fungi to do their work. If there's too much moisture the heap will be fairly smelly but if it's too dry nothing will happen.

✔ Turn the compost over regularly with a garden fork and allow as much oxygen to enter the process as you can. The more often you turn it, the quicker the compost will be ready.

As composting materials rot, they produce heat and micro-organisms that speed up the rotting process. Larger organisms, such as flies, worms, and other insects live in your compost and contribute to the rotting process as well.

Eventually you get broken-down material that looks like dark earth. It can take up to a year for small-scale composting of household material to produce compost you can use in the garden but covering the compost heap with old carpet keeps the heat in and speeds up the composting process.

If you live in a flat and don't have anywhere to keep a compost bin, think about joining or forming a community composting project. Get the neighbours together to collect and compost household waste. Ask your local authority if there is a scheme in your area. There's more information at www.communitycompost.org.

You'll find more information on composting at www.wasteonline.org.uk or from the Composting Association at www.compost.org.uk.

Setting up a worm farm

Worm farms are an ideal way to deal with small amounts of household waste and are perfect if you don't have much outside space. A *worm farm* is basically a series of small bins or crates stacked on top of each other with holes in the floor of each for the worms to crawl up through. The worms munch the vegetable and fruit peelings, paper, and cardboard you put in the top of the worm farm and process it through their digestive systems to come out the other end as worm castings – creating very effective compost. You can set up your own worm farm:

1. **Construct a worm farm.**

   Buy a worm farm or box from your local council or garden centre, or make your own from scratch using storage boxes or crates that aren't being used for anything else. You need four for maximum effect.

   Make plenty of holes or perforations at the bottom of three of the boxes for the worms to move up through – leaving the box that will be at the bottom without holes so the worms don't wriggle away.

2. **Supply your worm farm with all the necessary start-up material.**

   You need the right types of worms – most experts recommend either red worms or tiger worms. The average garden worm isn't right for the job.

   You also need ordinary garden soil, and fruit and vegetable scraps.

3. **Lay the materials and introduce the worms.**

   Line the bottom of the first (bottom) box with soil and newspaper, add fruit and veggie scraps, then the worms.

   Block as much light to the box as you can by placing a hessian cloth or some more newspaper over the top.

4. **Add additional boxes on top of the first one.**

   Monitor your farm for a couple of weeks to make sure that the worms are growing larger and multiplying. If they aren't you've probably not given them enough material to work with, so add some more to the mix.

   Add the same mix as in Step 3 to a second box and put that box on top of the first one. As the worms leave the bottom box and move to the new scraps in the second box, they leave behind an accumulation of compost material that you can spread over your garden or through your pot plants.

   As the original scraps and soil mix begins to look like compost add your next box. You can also use the liquid that accumulates in the bottom box as a liquid fertiliser.

For more information about how to set up your own worm farm have a look at your local council Web site or buy a worm farm from www.greener gardening.co.uk or www.originalorganics.co.uk.

Maintaining Lawn, Trees, and Wildlife

After you've designed and planted your garden, you've got the job of caring for it. A neat lawn with healthy plants, shrubs, trees, and an abundance of wildlife is a joy to behold but the aim is to be as green as possible in an environmental sense as well as having green and pleasant land.

Keeping the grass in shape

Grass is much better for wildlife than concrete but your grass doesn't have to be all manicured lawn. If you decide that some lawn is essential, and that turning your whole patch over to vegetables isn't an option, make it as green as possible by using environmentally friendly ways of keeping it trim:

✔ Keep the grass down using a hand mower instead of a petrol or electric one, thereby saving fuel and reducing pollution. If your lawn is too big, you can get a battery-powered mower that charges using solar power, or use green electricity – there's more information in Chapter 3 on switching to a green energy supplier.

Alternatively, get a goat, which will keep the grass down, fertilise it at the same time, and give you milk.

✔ Leave the grass cuttings on the lawn to feed the soil. If you don't want to leave the cuttings on the lawn, put them on the compost heap.

✔ Use native grass seeds for the lawn as they'll grow better in the British climate.

✔ Resist the temptation to reach for the hosepipe at the first appearance of a brown patch. Once a week is all the watering your lawn needs even in the hottest weather. Over-watering can weaken your lawn by encouraging roots to seek the surface.

✔ If your lawn turned brown in the sun last time you cut it, let your grass grow a little longer and don't cut it so short next time. Longer grass stays greener than a close-mown lawn, is less likely to scorch, and needs less watering.

✔ Dig any weeds out with a trowel or fork rather than using weedkiller.

✔ Leave some of the lawn to grow wild with wild flowers and grasses or plant some trees and shrubs. Those areas will attract wildlife and reduce the amount of effort that goes into caring for the lawn.

All the time, effort, and water you put into looking after the lawn can be producing home-grown fruit and vegetables instead.

Planting native shrubs and plants

The ideal green garden has native plants and shrubs that thrive well in the UK climate. Native plants don't need additional water and can withstand the native bugs and insects, so you don't need toxic chemicals to keep the plants weed and disease free.

Native plants attract native species of butterflies and birds. Grow as many varieties of native plants as possible to support the wildlife in your garden. Grow native plants side by side that naturally ward off each other's pests.

Not all plants native to the UK grow in all parts of the UK. Talk to your local garden centre about the native plants that grow best in the climate and soil where you live. Other sources of information on native gardens include _Organic Gardening Magazine_ at www.organicgardening.com and Garden Organic, the national charity for organic growing, at www.gardenorganic.org.uk.

The plant you think is a weed may be just a wild plant. Maybe you don't want it in your nicely cultivated flowerbed but if it's a native plant, you can encourage it to grow in another part of your garden. For information on how to build up wildflower gardens and save native species try Plantlife International at www.plantlife.org.uk.

Encouraging wildlife

If you feel you can't go green in the garden by growing fruit and vegetables, you can still make a big contribution by creating an environment that attracts and supports wildlife. Many once very common species of garden birds, insects like bees and butterflies, mammals, and amphibians are now thin on the ground due to changes in farming methods and disappearing hedgerows. By offering them an area where they can make homes, feed, and breed safely without danger from pesticides and other chemicals, you help their numbers to recover.

What you plant has an impact on the kinds of wildlife that choose to live in your garden. Think carefully about the species you want and grow the appropriate plants to attract that species. If you grow the wrong plants you may attract unwanted species like ants, wasps, and moles into the garden or they may make it impossible for other plants to survive. If you use pesticides to control weeds other species in the ecosystem may be adversely affected.

Make your garden as varied as possible to attract as many species as possible:

- ✔ **Plants** like roses, honeysuckle, and lavender each attract different insects like bees and butterflies.

- ✔ **A woodpile or a wildflower patch** encourages another set of garden dwellers. You might find frogs amongst the woodpile if it's damp, and if it's big enough to offer a safe place a fox might move in.

- ✔ **A pond** – created from an old bath or basin – draws everything from dragonflies and frogs to birds and snails.

- ✔ **Hedges** are great for attracting birds and insects and providing space for small animals to make their homes. Grow as many different hedge plants as possible together in your hedge as each different plant attracts different species.

- ✔ **Trees and shrubs** that produce fruit, berries, and seeds are sources of food for your furry and feathered friends.

Try A Small Wildlife Garden at www.asmallwildlifegarden.co.uk for ideas and inspiration. The Wildlife Trust (www.wildlifetrusts.org) also has suggestions and information about attracting wildlife to your garden.

Bird and bug boxes, and nut and seed feeders all attract wildlife too.

Designing Ecofriendly Outside Space

Everyone can have a garden of some sort – from the window box on the tiny balcony or window ledge to the community garden shared by the whole neighbourhood; from the allotment hired from the local council to your private garden attached to your semi in the suburbs.

Think carefully about what you want from the space you have. Even if you only have room for a few small pots, you have a choice of growing flowers or herbs. With more space, you can opt for shrubs, bushes, trees, flowers, fruit, vegetables, or a mixture of all sorts. In a bigger garden, you may want a patio, pond, or pool.

Before you start digging and planting think about the time you'll have to spend on working on your patch, what kind of soil you have, the sorts of plants that can grow in that soil, and about the light coming onto those plants. Local garden centres are good at giving advice on the conditions plants need in order to flourish.

Pooling resources

If you fly over certain areas of the UK, particularly the south of England, you may be amazed how many swimming pools you see in private gardens.

Think carefully about the impact on the environment before installing a pool. It takes a lot of water to fill a pool and each time you empty and refill it you use good-quality tap water. If you treat the pool with chemicals such as chlorine to keep it clean and hygienic those chemicals get released into the drains each time you empty the pool. Heating a pool uses up a lot of energy as does pumping it dry. Not only wildlife but children can drown in swimming pools that aren't kept covered. Go green and save yourself time, worry, and money, and use the space to grow vegetables instead.

If you want a water feature in your garden go for ones that use solar power rather than mains electricity and don't use chemicals to keep it clean. A pond attracts wildlife like insects and frogs.

Sketch out the space and where you want to put all the vital ingredients – most importantly, your compost heap or bin (see the section earlier in this chapter on 'Giving Your Waste a New Lease of Life'). The following list sets forth some of the items you may want to include in your design and the issues to consider:

- **Decking and patios:** Think carefully about the impact on the environment of any surface you put down for your seating area. Check with the retailer before you buy that wood for decking or slabs for the patio come from renewable, sustainable – or at least recycled and recyclable – sources.

  Keep in mind that if you concrete over part of your garden to make a patio, water will run off that area and may cause drainage problems on other parts of the garden.

- **Furnishings:** If your garden is another room in your home, it needs some kind of furniture. If you opt for wooden tables and chairs make sure that the wood is from sustainable sources and not made from tropical hardwood. Wooden furniture needs to be treated to stop it rotting when it's left out in the rain. Often the treatment involves toxic chemicals, so make sure that the furniture you buy uses non-toxic preservatives such as linseed oil. Buy wooden furniture that has the Forest Stewardship Council's stamp on it, certifying that it's made from wood from sustainable, responsibly managed forests. You can find out more from the Web site at www.fsc.org.

  Check that plastic furniture is made from recycled plastic. Metal garden furniture is likely to be the least green option as it's more likely to be made from new materials.

- **Lighting:** Candles are very effective in the garden. Put them into glass containers to shield them from wind and rain. You can make your own lanterns from glass bottles.

  The other green alternative is to use solar-powered bulbs that use the power of the sun to build up energy, which then later is released to light your garden.

- **Outside cookers:** Make sure that you use the greenest material possible for your barbecue. Check that the charcoal comes from renewable wood. Don't buy barbecue material treated to make it light easily: It's likely to have an oil- or petrol-based fuel in it which won't do much good for the environment or for your food.

✔ **Outside heaters:** Gardens or yards are often used as extra rooms. Patio heaters are popular so that you can stay out later into the evening and for more of the year, but pleasant as heating the outdoors may be, burning gas or using electricity not only pushes up your bills but adds to the carbon dioxide you're releasing into the atmosphere. Think long and hard before you opt for one of these heaters. They aren't environmentally friendly.

If you do decide to buy a patio heater don't leave it on when you're not using it, and make sure that if you're heating outside, your lights and heat are turned off inside to reduce your energy use as far as possible.

✔ **Plants:** When it comes to deciding what to grow in the garden it's impossible to generalise. You can go for trees, shrubs, fruit, vegetables, pot plants, lawn, or flowers depending on how much space you've got, how much sunlight your garden gets, what the soil is like, how much rainfall your area gets, how much time you have to spend working in the garden – the variables are almost endless. Design your garden to be as energy-efficient as possible, require as little water as possible in dry areas, and provide the best possible habitat for wildlife. The Royal Horticultural Society is a good source of information at www.rhs.org.uk, as is Sue Fisher, Michael MacCackey, and Bill Marken's *Gardening For Dummies* (Wiley).

✔ **Water features:** Most gardens aren't big enough for pools and ponds (see the sidebar 'Pooling Resources') but if you have room for a small water feature like a fountain or a tub, think carefully. Anything that needs electricity to make it function isn't as green as an alternative that can be powered by the sun. Take care that children and wildlife won't be harmed, avoid using chemicals in the water, and provide shelter for any frogs or toads that find their way into your garden.

Leave space to have a drying line for your clothes or for a clothes rack so that you can cut down on the amount of electricity you use running the tumble dryer.

Chapter 6

Waste Not, Want Not: Minimising Your Rubbish

*T*he more you buy, the more of the world's resources you use up and the more waste you generate. Increased consumption equals increased waste.

The best way to deal with the problem is to stop generating waste, but the idea of *zero waste* (explained in the section 'Aiming for zero waste', later in this chapter) is the Holy Grail and a long way off. If you want to be green, work on reducing the amount of waste you generate and try to stop the waste you do generate ending up in landfill sites or incinerators. Zero waste is the ideal – reduced waste is realistic.

The three Rs – reducing, reusing, and recycling – are the key to dealing with waste. This chapter discusses ways of doing all three and the pros and cons involved. There are two other Rs (repairing and regifting) and a C for composting that you may find useful to add to that list.

Wasting Your Life Away

More than 400 million tons of waste are generated every year in the UK and about 25 million tons come from domestic households like yours. The latest government survey found that on average every adult in the UK throws away their own weight in rubbish every seven weeks. Most of that material can be recycled. The UK is the second worst country in Europe when it comes to recycling.

However, the amount of waste that you can see and touch is only part of the equation. For every item you buy there's hidden waste: Processing raw materials such as wood or metal ores produces waste, just as manufacturing items creates waste.

Add to that the amount of energy used all the way along the chain, through to transporting materials and finished goods, and every product costs the earth a lot more than what ends up in your rubbish bin.

You can't go through life not creating any waste, but you can cut down on the total waste generated.

Aiming for zero waste

Ideally, to live the green life as an individual, you reduce your waste to zero. That means that by reducing the goods you buy and the packaging you bring home, recycling, composting, repairing, and reusing, you throw nothing at all into a rubbish bin to be carted off to landfill. Realistically it's difficult to achieve. It requires vigilance and determination to turn your home into a zero waste area.

Governments have a bigger task to reduce waste on a national scale and some have been working on the idea for years. It started in Australia in 1996 when Canberra adopted a zero-waste policy with the target of achieving the goal by 2010. Other countries and areas followed the Australian lead including New Zealand. In the UK a few local authorities are signing up to the idea.

More intensive recycling targets are part of the way to achieve zero waste but manufacturers have to cut down on potential waste such as non-recyclable packaging and design goods with long shelf-lives which are unlikely to need replacing.

Getting rid of your rubbish

You get rid of your household rubbish in several ways:

- ✔ By putting it out for the local authority waste management teams to take away
- ✔ By putting it out for their special recycling collections
- ✔ By taking some of it to the local civic amenity collection point yourself
- ✔ By arranging for the local authority to make a special trip to collect something bulky that you can't dispose of in any other way

Right now about three quarters of your household waste goes into a landfill site, a tenth is incinerated, and the rest is recycled or made into compost.

Experts in waste management say that as much as two-thirds of total household waste can be recycled and as much as two-thirds (overlapping to some extent with the waste that can be recycled) can be composted (Chapter 5 talks about composting). There's no need for any waste to go to landfill sites or be incinerated. But there's nowhere near enough composting or recycling going on to achieve that ideal result.

The government has set green disposal targets. Recycling has to increase to a third of all household rubbish by 2015. More money must be spent on collecting rubbish for recycling and in processing that rubbish. That may mean less money for collecting and processing the non-recyclable rubbish. You will have to reduce the total amount of waste you produce and recycle more of the rest.

Landfilling versus incinerating

The majority of domestic waste ends up in landfill sites – big holes in the earth hidden away on the edge of cities and towns – to rot away over the next few hundred years.

Modern landfill sites are well managed – the holes in the earth are lined and capped to stop toxic chemicals from the degrading rubbish leaking into the surrounding earth and polluting nearby water sources. Systems are built in to capture escaping gases and liquids. Older sites were simply covered with earth and the rubbish left to its own devices. The problem with landfill is that suitable sites are becoming scarce and there is some hazardous waste that can't go in landfill.

A much smaller proportion of your rubbish is burned in big incinerators. Older incinerators are major sources of air pollution as they pump environmentally damaging greenhouse gases into the atmosphere. Newer plants use up-to-date technology that makes them much cleaner and less damaging to the environment. The energy released by burning the rubbish is often used to generate electricity. However, the burning process creates toxic ash.

A debate about whether to build more incinerators has been sparked by the shortage of suitable landfill sites. Public opinion is against incinerators and no one wants one near them. They are expensive to build and only one has been built in the UK in the past ten years.

Cutting Down Waste with the Three Rs (and More)

Until you have a picture of what waste you're generating and how, you can't start to reduce it effectively. One way to get a picture of your rubbish habits is to save a week's worth. Dumping everything in a closed top bin as you go along, or putting a bag of rubbish outside every few days for collection, allows you to take an 'out of sight, out of mind' approach to your own waste. When you see how the rubbish has accumulated you start to see how to reduce it.

Reducing

The best way to reduce waste is to reduce what you buy. Only buy what you really need and will use – be it food, clothes, or electrical appliances. What you're likely to discover once you've looked at the rubbish that you generate in a week is that most of it is packaging – bottles, cans, and plastic wrappers.

Buy less if you can. If you can't buy less, buy a version that has the least possible packaging. If something you need comes pre-packed, look for minimal packaging, or look for products with recyclable packaging. You can also use shops that sell loose items.

Buy fresh food that doesn't come pre-packed. If you buy in the supermarket put your fruit and vegetables directly into the trolley without putting it first into a plastic bag or bring your own bags to reuse.

If some of your waste comes from plastic containers that can't be recycled, next time buy alternative versions in glass or other recyclable containers.

You can go further and take the packaging off before you leave shops and leave it there for them to deal with. Alternatively, send the packaging back to the manufacturers telling them why you won't be buying their product again. Shops and manufacturers will start to get the message if heavily packaged items or products in non-recyclable packaging become less popular. Help them to understand by telling them why you're buying one brand instead of another.

It takes a bit of time to shop around for the least wasteful packaging but you'll see a difference in the amount of rubbish you throw away.

The big debate about a plastic bag tax

If you're an average shopper you use around 300 plastic carrier bags from shops and supermarkets each year. Billions are handed out every year and most of them end their days cluttering up landfill sites and taking hundreds of years to disappear.

In Ireland a tax was put on each plastic carrier bag in 2002. Since then the number of bags used has dropped by 90 per cent. Members of the Scottish Parliament are debating whether to do the same. The problem is what shoppers use to replace carrier bags.

Most supermarkets offer thicker plastic 'bags for life'. They tick all the green boxes: you cut down the number of plastic carrier bags you use; you reuse the bags for life again and again; and eventually they're recycled. But some people use them just once, and put rubbish in them or put them in the bin. Plus, because they're made of thicker plastic they take more space to transport.

Paper bags are greener than plastic bags, can be reused, and recycled or composted. But they're thicker than fine plastic carrier bags so, as with bags for life, they cost the environment more to transport – more fuel and energy creating more emissions.

Plastic carrier bags are handy for putting out the rubbish. You can use large refuse sacks instead – but again they're thicker and harder to transport. Only some of them are made from recycled material and most end up in landfill sites.

If you reduce the number of plastic carrier bags you use don't use more of the alternatives. The best thing for the environment is to switch to canvas bags or baskets that will last for years.

Packaging is not all bad. It may protect the goods so that they can be transported without damage and to maximise the amount of a particular product that can be packed into a container. Sometimes the packaging is there so that fewer containers have to be used and therefore fewer lorries are needed to transport an order. The firms themselves may be thinking primarily of how to cut their transport and damage costs but being greener as a result.

Take your own canvas bags or shopping basket with you so you don't need to accept plastic carrier bags – or reuse carrier bags from previous shopping trips. Use paper bags instead of plastic, when you need to choose.

You have to dispose of some items at the ends of their lives. Aerosol cans, for example, can't be reused or recycled. But you can choose alternatives to buying cleaning products and toiletries in aerosol cans. Chapter 4 has information about natural products you can use instead and there are ecofriendly alternatives in the shops.

Reusing

Reusing and recycling can have a bit of an overlap. *Reusing* is a sort of recycling and *recycling* is reprocessing something so that the materials can be reused.

The aim is to use things for as long as possible, for as many different uses as possible, or by as many people as possible, before they have to be sent for recycling or disposed of in a landfill site. Reusing cuts down the need to buy new.

Put items that can be reused without recycling or composting together in a pile.

Most things have more than one use and you can reuse some items yourself:

- ✔ Reuse printer paper used on one side in your printer for scribbling paper. (You may scribble more than you realize: grocery lists, hand-drawn maps to show your significant other how to get somewhere, or even the rough draft of that novel you're still writing.)

- ✔ Use wrapping paper and gift bags again. Cut down cards to make gift tags. (You can even make a wonderful joke or legacy card amongst your family members and friends by reusing the same birthday card over and over and simply encouraging one another to keep passing it on to the next person who has a birthday – no apologies, just cross out the last giver's name and add on your own best wishes for many happy returns and returns and returns.)

- ✔ Line recycling boxes, drawers, and cat litter trays with newspapers, magazines, and junk mail. (Doesn't your cat deserve the posh images from that upscale museum catalogue?)

- ✔ Alter clothes into more fashionable models (see Chapter 8 for tips) and cultivate your own vintage look by contributing to and shopping at second-hand clothing boutiques.

- ✔ Turn ruined CDs into coasters or sun-catching hanging mobiles.

- ✔ Convert king-sized sheets worn in the middle into a single sheet or a few cot sheets.

If you can't reuse something, someone else may. Old computers, mobile phones, electrical appliances, and furniture may all be of use to someone else. Someone else may be able to make good use of good-quality clothing even when you've had enough of it. If you have items you think may be reusable, but you want them out of your home, try charity shops, private waste collectors – scrap metal dealers or rag and bone firms – friends and family, and work colleagues. You can find a home for most items that aren't of use to you any longer. The trend for buying cheap items, as in the case of clothes and shoes, does nothing to reduce the amount of waste. Instead, buy good-quality items that last and that you can keep using. Cheaper fashion items have less of an appeal as they go out of date, but don't throw them away. Use them for dusters, floor cloths, or to wash the car.

Repairing

Sometimes items are broken or have stopped doing the job they're meant to do. Life may be too short to darn a sock, but a chair with a broken leg or ripped upholstery, a defunct kettle, or an iffy toaster may have years of life left with a bit of tender loving repair. Try having an item repaired rather than throwing it away and buying a new one.

Reusing car tyres

Car tyres pose a big problem for the environment. They don't break down and can't be burned because of the toxic gases they give off. As they sit in piles the earth underneath them becomes contaminated by their toxins and chemicals. If they've reached the point of no return, there are a whole variety of uses they can be put to:

✔ Some can be recycled as retread tyres and used again on cars.

✔ They make great rubber bumpers for boats and for children's play equipment.

✔ You'll find them used for mouse mats, pencil cases, and notebook covers.

✔ Broken down into rubber granules they can be used in surfacing playgrounds and artificial sports pitches.

✔ They can be made into mats and tiles in the carpet industry. Several carpeting companies are using recycled tyres as a major component of the eco-carpets they produce.

✔ Broken down into a fine powder they are used to reduce the noise of road surfaces.

✔ They can be roof tiles and structural supports in eco-buildings.

Garages with the Tyre Industry Council Responsible Recycler Scheme logo are certified to collect tyres and you can be assured that the tyres will be reused and recycled according to the rules. Find more information on the Tyre Industry Council's Web site at www.tyre safety.co.uk.

If you can't repair things yourself find someone who can. The repair industry has found a new lease of life. You can find thousands of furniture restoration businesses, clothing alteration and repair services, shoe repairers, upholsterers, electronic appliances repair firms, and even toy hospitals. The Yellow Pages and recommendations from friends and family can furnish you with some contacts. Ask for references if the item is valuable.

Neighbours and friends may have the skills you need. If you belong to a Local Exchange Trading Scheme (see Chapter 9) other members may have the necessary skills.

Another option is to give items away to an individual or a charity that can repair and reuse them. See the section 'Choosing Not to Throw it All Away', later in this chapter, for suggestions). Apply the principle that what's junk to one person may be useful to someone else, and pass it on repaired or not.

Recycling

If all else fails, recycle. *Recycling* involves collecting goods that have reached the end of their lives and processing them, their parts, or some of their parts, into the raw materials from which new goods can be made.

Recycling isn't as green as reducing and reusing because the process takes energy and emits greenhouse gases such as carbon dioxide just as during the production of new goods. For example, glass can be recycled and come back as bottles but it has to go through a manufacturing process to get there and that uses energy. Ideally that energy is generated using renewable sources such as wind, wave, and solar power so that the recycling process is completely green.

Recycling will become more important as the percentage of waste recycled increases to meet the government's targets. The government has set targets for manufacturers to produce more goods that can be recycled or stripped down into components that can be reused or recycled. It has also set targets for the percentage of waste that has to be recycled: A third of all household waste should be recycled by 2015. You can find out more information about what those targets mean for your household from www.wasteonline.org.uk, the Web site of the charity Waste Watch, which is dedicated to the reduction, reuse, and recycling of household waste.

Recycling versus new production

Recycling reduces the amount of material that ends up in landfill sites and reduces the need to extract natural resources from the earth to make new goods – through mining, for example. In theory the materials involved can keep going round the recycling circle.

Recycling is greener than producing new goods from scratch. Recycling of steel, aluminium, copper, lead, paper, and plastics saves between 65 per cent and 95 per cent of the energy it takes to produce new goods from these materials.

Recycling has led to the design and manufacture of new goods that are more easily recycled when they reach the end of their lives. It is also leading to the design of goods that have longer life spans, because they can be upgraded and added to, rather than just recycled.

Recycling what you can

Some local authorities have well-established schemes for recycling. You may be asked to put all your material for recycling – bottles, food and drinks cans, paper, newspapers and magazines, cardboard, and recyclable plastics – into one bin separate from the rest of your household rubbish. Or you may be asked to separate each type of recyclable material out into separate boxes for collection.

If your council has no organised collection of recyclable waste, you are likely to have access to civic amenity facilities where you can take your recyclables.

If you aren't sure what to do, and you want to recycle more, talk to your local authority at the local council offices. You can find more information at www.recyclenow.com, the Web site run by the Waste Resources Action Programme (WRAP) which is funded by the government to help increase awareness of the problems of dealing with waste in the UK.

Not everything can be recycled yet, but you should be able to find recycling facilities for these five main categories of household waste:

- **Paper:** Most paper can be recycled, including newspapers, cardboard, packaging, magazines, and wrapping paper. Most paper can be made into compost too, so if you have a garden you have a choice of recycling or composting.

  Some recycling facilities take paper products such as milk and juice cartons. Others won't. Cartons are made of cardboard sandwiched between very thin layers of plastic – so some of the material can be recycled and some can't. Check with your local authority.

- **Plastics:** Most plastics are recyclable but recycling rates are low because of the lack of facilities. Most local authorities provide bins for – or collect – soft drinks bottles and bottles used for milk, juice, and body-care products. These usually have a Plastic Identification Code of 1 or 2 (see the next paragraph). In some areas you can recycle other sorts of plastic like plumbing pipes and garden hoses.

  Each plastic product has a Plastic Identification Code – a triangle with the number 1, 2, 3, 4, 5, 6, or 7 inside it. Some of the higher-number plastics can be recycled but there are no facilities available for them.

Check with your local authority which plastics it will take for recycling and buy only those numbers from the shops if you can. If the local authority doesn't accept plastics for recycling try to reduce the ones you buy and reuse those you have if possible.

You can find more information on plastic recycling at www.recoup.org, the Web site of an industry group working for the efficient recycling of plastics.

✔ **Glass:** Most household glass can be recycled. Glass makes up only about 7 per cent of the household rubbish in the UK because there are so many plastic bottles and containers in use. Glass is easier to recycle than plastic, so if your local authority doesn't recycle plastic buy the product you need in a glass bottle or jar if there's one available.

Recycled glass has a whole variety of uses. If you look in many holes by the road or along the street you'll see they're being filled with a mixture of sand and green crushed glass.

Glass items like car windscreens, cooking dishes, and light bulbs will probably have to be taken to a civil amenity recycling facility. They can't go in most recycling bins or collections.

✔ **Metals:** Metal food and drink cans made from aluminium or steel can be recycled. For some reason, when it comes to recycling, cans get forgotten about and end up in the rubbish bin. Aluminium cans in particular are very valuable in terms of recycling material. You can recycle your used aluminium foil too.

✔ **Textiles:** Most local authorities don't have collections for textiles like clothes but some do provide big textiles and clothes (and shoes) recycling bins in supermarket car parks and their own civic amenity sites. The best way to recycle textiles is to take them to charity shops and what they can't use they can sell on to private firms dealing in textiles.

Arguing against recycling

It's hard to come up with arguments why recycling isn't green but as your taxes are paying for the recycling revolution there are a couple of points to think about:

✔ Collecting material for recycling and sending it to independent recycling plants costs local authorities up to five times more than sending it to a landfill site. This reduces the budget for other local services your council provides.

✔ Adding together all the energy costs – of transporting materials and putting them through reprocessing, in some cases more energy is need for recycling than for manufacturing from raw materials.

Paint can't strictly be recycled but it's worth a mention. There are 414 million litres of paint sold in the UK each year of which about a fifth is never used and ends up in landfill sites after months hardening in the garden shed. You can enable someone else to use that valuable resource by donating it to one of the 50 or so Community RePaint schemes around the UK. The paint is sorted and passed on free of charge to charities, community groups, and voluntary organisations for use by good causes or individuals in need. Find out more and about how you can set up another Community RePaint scheme in your area at www.communityrepaint.org.uk.

When you buy anything ask the retailer if there's a scheme for recycling the old one. Find more information on www.wasteonline.org.uk, the Web site dedicated to reducing, reusing, and recycling.

Completing the circle

There's little point in the government throwing its weight behind recycling as a major green initiative if the goods produced by the recycling process languish in warehouses and no one buys or uses them. Buy recycled goods if you can – because they are greener than non-recycled goods. The more demand you create for recycled goods the more of them will be produced and fewer equivalents made from new, precious raw materials will be needed.

The principles of reducing and reusing still apply to recycled goods. Demand that they don't come with wasteful packaging. Reuse them for as long as possible. Just because they're recycled doesn't mean you should buy what you don't need.

Regifting

Regifting – giving gifts you've received to someone else as a gift – isn't for everyone. You may think that it's very rude to give away something given to you by one friend or family member to someone else as a gift.

If your friends and family are trying to be greener they'll understand and start doing it too.

Regifting ticks all the green boxes:

- ✔ You aren't buying new goods, so you're subscribing to the principle of reducing waste and the amount of energy used to produce new products.

- ✔ You're reusing something. You're giving something to someone who will make use of it instead of it ending up in a landfill site.

- ✔ You're preventing recycling so you avoid using up energy to reprocess the item.

Disposing of Electronic Goods (Understanding WEEE)

Many of the items you buy have electronic parts. Every year around a million tons of *waste electronic and electrical equipment* (WEEE) – including things like digital watches, fridges, televisions, computers, mobile phones, and toys – are thrown out in the UK. Around 2 million televisions are thrown out each year and almost as many computers.

Because there's so much WEEE, and it includes so many different products, all made up of different materials, disposing of it greenly is difficult.

If all these waste electronic and electrical items end up in landfill sites or being burned in incinerators, valuable resources go up in smoke or are buried in the ground. To replace all those televisions, computers, fridges, and so on means starting again – mining new raw materials and using valuable water and energy to manufacture and transport new items for the shops. These processes also cause damage to the environment in terms of emissions of greenhouse gases.

Much of the WEEE you throw away can be recycled and all that waste prevented. There are still few places that take, or collect, household electrical equipment for reuse or recycling, but that must change. Under the WEEE Regulations, which should come in April 2007, WEEE will have to be kept separate from other general household rubbish and treated, the hazardous substances removed, and as many of the parts and materials as possible recycled rather than sent to landfill sites.

You won't be banned from dumping WEEE in your bin but there will be a network of collection points for WEEE and you will find it easier to recycle your old equipment. Manufacturers and importers of goods will be responsible for their disposal and the collection points will include facilities in shops where you can take old items back and better local authority civic amenity sites.

In the meantime not-for-profit organisations refurbish white goods and computers and pass them on to schools and charities at a reduced cost. If you have a big item to get rid of, like a fridge, your local authority will have to arrange to collect it – for a fee – or you can take it to your local civic amenity site for disposal free of charge. Alternatively, ask the firm delivering your new one if they will take the old one away.

Mounting up – the mobile phone mountain

There are millions of mobile phones in use in the UK and about 20 million in drawers unused. Reduce the number of mobile phones in circulation by refusing the next time you're offered a new model as a free upgrade by your service provider. If you'd prefer not to do that, give your old model to a friend or relative, who can use it with their own SIM card, rather than buying a new phone. The same goes for phone chargers and batteries.

Some parts of mobile phones contain toxic materials so you need to dispose of your old phones properly. Don't put them in the rubbish to end up in a landfill site.

Most mobile phone shops take old phones back. Charities such as Oxfam (www. oxfam.org.uk/what_you_can_do/recycle), Action Aid (www.action aidrecycling.org.uk), CRUMP – Campaign to Recycle Unwanted Mobile Phones (www.childadvocacyinternational.co.uk), and Against Breast Cancer (www.aabc.org.uk) collect mobile phones. They then repair and sell them, or send them to countries in Africa where there's a poor landline service. Other big electrical store chains have recycling facilities for mobile phones (for charities) through the Fonebak scheme – call 01708 684000.

Scheming to get rid of computers

About a fifth of unwanted computers in the UK are recycled, which means four-fifths end up in landfill sites or are incinerated. As almost 2 million new computers were sold in just three months in the middle of 2006, that means an awful lot of unwanted computers – full of valuable materials and resources – are dumped.

The problem is that it's hard to know what to do with a computer that you no longer use – so out it goes with the general household rubbish.

There's a big chance that the computer you want rid of can be upgraded with a larger hard drive and additional memory capacity, so many of the original parts can go on being used indefinitely – so don't dump it.

If you really don't want to give it desk space any more, give it or sell it to someone who can use it. Some firms buy and sell computers to refurbish and sell on or for spare parts. Hewlett Packard will take back any make of computer from business customers. There are also community projects and not-for-profit organisations that collect computers for reuse projects – in schools, charities, and less-well-off households, or in developing countries (take a look at Computer Aid International's Web site at `www.computeraid.org`). Waste Watch has a list of companies and projects listed by geographical area around the UK that want your old computer. You can find all the details on the Web site `www.wasteonline.org.uk`.

Choosing Not to Throw It All Away

If you can't reuse something, no one you know wants it, and you can't recycle it, you may still have alternatives to throwing it out. You can give things away or sell them if you have access to potential customers. Someone out there will want it.

The only limiting factors are how much someone is willing to pay and whether it's economically viable and green to have the item posted or delivered to that person's home.

If something has to be transported by road or air for long distances, you have to consider the carbon emissions (see Chapter 1).

Deciding what others may want

Sit down and start working out what's lying around your home that other people could use. Some of the most popular second-hand items include:

- **Books, magazines, and CDs:** There's a huge market for these and they can go on and on being reused. Sort out a storage system, if you have room, that allows you to add an item to the correct box each time you finish with something. When a box is full offer it to your local second-hand book or music shop and if you don't get a sale, offer it to the charity shop.

- **Clothes:** Used and vintage clothes are fashionable. Most street markets have several stalls of these clothes and they're popular over the Internet. Go through your wardrobe and drawers and sort out things to give away, swap, sell, or to go for rags. You may be able to reuse some for washing floors.

- **Computers and printers:** A computer or printer that's no longer up to date enough for your needs is sure to be of use to someone else. If you have one to get rid of see the previous section, 'Scheming to get rid of computers'.

- ✔ **Furniture:** All sorts of home clearance firms buy furniture; auctions sell antiques and less valuable furniture and household items; and charities often want furniture of all sorts to help poorer families furnish homes.

- ✔ **Household Items:** Car boot sales, garage sales, jumble sales, indoor markets, church fetes, street stalls, and auctions are places for private individuals to sell unwanted items and they're never short of interested potential customers. If there are no events going on where you can set up a stall, have your own sale. The rules are simply that you must only sell what belongs to you and that the items must be as you describe them.

Giving it away

Giving things away free may appeal to your green ideals more than selling your unwanted items. In terms of being green, offering your used goods to another person reduces waste and fits in with the idea of reusing as much as possible.

Contributing to sweet charity

If you feel that it would fit your green ideals better to give things away to people who have more need of them than you do, rather than sell them, you can donate just about anything.

Make sure that anything you do give is in good condition, usable, clean, and not a problem for the person receiving it. Don't be tempted to dump your unwanted, dirty, broken tat on a charity's doorstep and put them to the expense of disposing of it.

Following are a few organisations always on the look out for gifts in good condition:

- ✔ **The Furniture Reuse Network** supports charities and community organisations and you can find out more from its Web site at www.frn.org.uk. The FRN can also take electronic goods and reprocess them according to the WEEE rules – see the earlier section 'Disposing of Electronic Goods (Understanding WEEE)'.

- ✔ **CREATE UK** (www.createuk.com) repairs and refurbishes household appliances, such as fridges, cookers, and washing machines, and sells them at reasonable prices. It also provides training and work for people who are at a disadvantage in the labour market.

- ✔ **The National Wood Recycling Project** (www.communitywood recycling.org.uk) collects all sorts of wood from different organisations with the aim of reusing that wood and cutting wood waste.

- ✔ **The Bike Station** (www.thebikestation.org.uk) is a community project in Edinburgh which repairs and refurbishes donated bikes. The Web site has more information on this and similar projects around the UK.

- ✔ **Cartridges4Charity** (www.cartridges4charity.co.uk) collects printer cartridges and sells them back to manufacturers for reuse, with the profits going to charity. Many charities collect cartridges too, directly.

- ✔ **Book Aid International** (www.bookaid.org) works in 18 countries in sub-Saharan Africa and Palestine, providing over half a million books and journals each year to libraries, hospitals, refugee camps, and schools.

You can find similar organisations in your area. Your library or Citizens' Advice Bureau – details of which you will find in your local phone book – will know how to contact them. Check with each organisation before you take items to them that they really do want and have room for them. Some may pick up your goods.

Freecycling your unwanted goods

Freecycling is a way of giving your unwanted possessions away for free to other freecyclers who will make good use of them. Freecycling takes the principals of reducing, reusing, and recycling into cyber space. It enables community members who want to find a new home for something, whether it be a chair, a fax machine, or piano, to send an e-mail offering it to members of a local freecycling group. If you want to take up an offer you respond by e-mail. The rule is that everything offered must be free, legal, and appropriate for all ages. There's more on Freecycling in Chapter 17.

There are around 2 million freecycling members around the world – all hoping to get rid of unwanted goods or find wanted goods – in what's basically an Internet swap shop. They are members of around 3,500 local freecycle communities.

Selling and Buying in the Real World

Buying and selling second-hand goods is a hobby for some people, a business for others, and an occasional pastime for the rest. If you like to hunt for second-hand treasures or you have something to sell there are plenty of choices.

- ✔ **Pawnbrokers and second-hand dealers** are much more sophisticated than they used to be and you can find plenty in most areas, including firms such as Cash Converters.

- ✔ **Second-hand book and music shops** are very popular. Trade in your unwanted books and CDs for others in the shop, sell them for cash, or leave them on a sale or return basis.

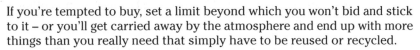

- ✔ **Antique shops** are an option for some items. You may be quite surprised at how much you can get for that old painting that's been sitting in the back of the garage for years.

- ✔ **Auction houses** are generally set up to sell antiques, jewellery, used cars, unwanted office and domestic furniture, and larger household items. You can set a reserve on an item you want to sell and take it home again if it doesn't make that much.

    If you're tempted to buy, set a limit beyond which you won't bid and stick to it – or you'll get carried away by the atmosphere and end up with more things than you really need that simply have to be reused or recycled.

- ✔ **Classified ads** in the local weekly newspaper or the free advertising papers were the places for advertising your goods or picking up a used bargain long before the Internet, and they're still going strong.

Holding a garage sale

If you have a lot of unwanted stuff to sell and it's too big, or there's too much to sell at a car boot sale or to take to a second-hand shop, a sale at home – in the garden or the garage – is an option. You must do some preparation and planning to get the best results:

- ✔ Contact your local council or check its Web site to see if you need any permits to hold a garage sale. There may be issues with some of the items you are thinking of selling, especially food.

- ✔ Check that some friends or family are willing to help – maybe putting up some of their own items for sale, setting up on the day, or selling to customers.

- ✔ Make sure that you have enough space – whether it be in a garage, the front lawn, or the driveway, to display everything you want to sell to its best advantage and to protect it from the elements.

- ✔ Fix the date for a Saturday or Sunday and start as early and finish as late as possible so that you have the chance of getting the maximum number of customers.

- ✔ Advertise by putting signs up on poles and walls around your neighbourhood, putting ads in the local free papers, and by placing posters or leaflets in local stores and community centres.

- ✔ Price your goods – decide what you'd like to get for each item and put a price sticker on it showing a slightly higher price. Customers typically want to haggle for a lower price than is on the label.

Make sure that you have plenty of cash and small change, and plenty of refreshments for yourself and your potential customers.

Buying and selling online

The Internet has made buying and selling used goods much easier. The success of Internet auction sites has shown that selling things that you don't need any more can be quite profitable. The Internet increases the number of potential customers for your goods. You're more likely to get a better price than in your local second-hand shop or through a garage sale. But remember that potential buyers are also likely to find other similar items to choose from.

The best thing about Internet auction sites, from a green lifestyle perspective, is that they make it easier to heed the three Rs – especially the reusing option. You can sell just about anything through the Internet and if you get little response from would-be buyers you know that there's little demand for your used goods.

TECHNICAL STUFF

Selling second-hand goods on eBay

Based on eBay's own advice, here's how to be an eBay seller – there's much more information at www.ebay.co.uk or in *eBay.co.uk For Dummies* (Wiley):

✔ **Getting started:** Register as an eBay seller and create a seller's account. It's free. You get an e-mail with your user account and password information and you use that to log in every time you access the site. You're encouraged to set up an account with eBay's preferred payment system PayPal (www.paypal.com). Buyers can use PayPal for free but sellers may need to pay a small fee just like they would if they set up an account with a credit card company.

✔ **Getting your product ready for sale:** Inspect the item and note any flaws, wear, or damage. Take a picture of it with a digital camera that can be loaded onto eBay's Web site. Write a description with information about the condition, colour, brand, product type, model, size, and style of the item. Get a feel for a starting auction price by again looking at the prices for similar products. Weigh your product so eBay can calculate approximate shipping costs for you.

✔ **List for auction or sale:** List all the information you've gathered. There's a small fee for listing an item for auction. Once your item page has been submitted, the auction automatically starts.

✔ **Complete the sale:** At the end of a successful sale you get an e-mail that includes your buyer's shipping address and payment method. Once you receive an online payment confirmation from PayPal, or a cheque or money order from your buyer, you ship your item.

From the point of view of being green, shopping on the Internet can reduce the number of car trips made to the shops. However, you have to calculate in the amount of freight traffic, both in the air and on the road, that results from increased online shopping.

There are 56 Internet auction sites registered in the UK. You can find the full list at www.auctionlotwatch.co.uk. eBay is the largest of the Internet auction sites with around 4,000 categories of goods for sale. Amazon now provides a portal for buying and selling your own goods through Amazon Auctions. Others include QXL auctions, EBID Auctions, OK2Bid Auctions, and OneWayUK Auctions.

Internet auction sites don't sell anything. You do your own buying and selling – the sites provide the space for you to set up your stall and sell your stuff.

There is the thrill of taking part in an online auction with people from around the world. As a seller, there's always that possibility that your product may make a nice little profit because the market that you are selling to is potentially huge. As a buyer, there is always that possibility that you'll land a bargain.

The credibility and security of the site is important. Choose a reputable auction site. The more you buy and sell successfully on a particular site, the better reputation you will get in the *community*. If you use eBay everyone who buys on the site knows the past selling history of the person they're buying from. Any issues of being sold a dud product have been greatly reduced through eBay's community ranking system.

Be careful you're not ripped off. You have very little protection if you send money and the goods don't arrive, or you send goods and the money doesn't arrive. Internet sales are based on trust. Private sellers aren't covered by the same rules as professional traders. If you are sent faulty goods, or they turn out not to be as they were described on the site, you may not get your money back. There's more information on the Web site of the advice charity Citizens' Advice at www.citizensadvice.org.uk.

By bringing a global community of buyers and sellers together, Internet auction sites generate reuse on a huge scale. By selling on to someone else, you are maximising the potential lifetime value of your goods before they're finally recycled or disposed of in the waste system.

Buying things locally makes your shopping even greener – because the things you buy or sell don't have to travel for long distances using up valuable energy and creating damaging emissions.

Part III
Green Shopping

'Edmund's very green-minded – he's obsessed with feeding the soil whilst protecting our birdlife.'

In this part . . .

You can only reduce the number of products you buy in the shops up to a point, so buy the greenest possible options. Part of the problem about trying to lead a greener lifestyle is that thinking on what is the greenest, most environmentally friendly, product isn't always consistent.

Sometimes you have to work out your own priorities, gather as much information about the goods you're buying and take your pick. In this part I give you some information that helps you make those choices. It can make shopping quite a lengthy process but at least you have the satisfaction of knowing you checked out the facts rather than just threw yet another environmentally damaging product into your trolley.

Chapter 7

Living to Eat or Eating to Live?

*H*ere's one way to make an omelette and salad: Use the tomatoes you bought from your neighbour who grows things organically, grate some of that local handmade cheese you bought at the wholefood deli, beat up those free-range eggs, chop the lettuce you bought at your local farmers' market last Saturday, and add some fresh herbs from your own garden.

If you could make every meal from ingredients like that you'd know where your food was coming from, how it had been produced, what chemicals, if any, had been used in its production, and how far it had travelled. You would also have a fair idea how the people involved in the process – from the planters and pickers to the farmers themselves – had been treated and paid, and what kind of conditions the hens that produced the eggs and the cows that gave the milk for the cheese lived in.

All these are issues to consider as you decide on a greener lifestyle.

One problem is that it isn't always possible to buy every item of food you want locally so it can be difficult to know where it's come from and what's gone into its production. Another is that food produced locally and organically can be more expensive than the alternatives you buy from the supermarkets.

And yet another problem is that there is so much conflicting advice and information around about whether organic food is better for you than non-organic food; whether you should be worried about too much salt and sugar; and about additives and genetically modified ingredients.

Some scientists argue that the only green and sustainable way to produce food is to stop using pesticides that damage the environment and go organic; others say that without the use of pesticides and genetic modification the planet can't feed all the 6.5 billion people living on it at the minute, never mind the 9 billion plus who are predicted to be populating the earth's surface by 2050.

Appreciating What Eating Green Means

Choosing what to eat is one of the most important and sometimes the most difficult green decisions you have to make. Table 7-1 sets forth the key components of eating green and questions you can ask to determine whether the item meets green eating standards.

Table 7-1	Green Eating Components and Standards	
Component	**Questions to Determine whether the Food Meets ...**	**... Green Eating Watermark**
Ingredients	How many additives like colouring, sweeteners, and emulsifiers are in the food? Are any ingredients GM?	Fresh, seasonal, organic with as few additives as possible.
Production methods	How was this produced and did anyone or any animal suffer to get it to my plate?	Organically produced, locally, and in season with high standards ofanimal welfare or Fairtrade products.
Transportation methods	How did this get from the field to me?	Bought from the local farmer or farmers' market travelling as few miles as possible.
Total cost	How much did it really cost, not just in terms of price, but in terms of impact on the planet and its inhabitants?	As small an impact as possible on the planet, environment, and animal welfare while giving producers a fair deal.

Read the arguments, read the labels, and decide what's most important to you – I discuss the issues and leave the decisions up to you!

One way of ensuring that you're eating foods produced in a green way is to buy locally produced organic food. Being organic implies that most of the unsustainable food production processes have been avoided – the 'Farming organically' section, later in this chapter, explains more about organic food production.

Some scientists advise that if you buy locally produced foodstuff – especially from within 12 miles of your home – you do more for the environment than buying organic. So, if you follow the 'shop locally and eat organically if possible' philosophy, you're well on the way to adopting a sustainable diet.

The packing your food comes in is also a green issue. The food itself may be organically produced but if it arrives on the shelves in non-recyclable tin or plastic containers, then it's not as green as it could be. Imported organic food usually has more packaging to protect it on its travels.

If there are no labels on the food or no information displayed about it – which can be the case in smaller shops and fruit and veg sections of bigger shops – here's a few tips to help you make the greenest food choices:

- ✔ Eat organic fruit and vegetables in season – they're more likely to have been grown locally. Those fruits and vegetables on the shelf that you know aren't in season are likely to have been imported or brought by road from the other end of the country.

- ✔ Avoid 'exotic' foods. Some foods and ingredients, such as coffee, grapes, and mangoes, just can't be grown locally; the UK simply doesn't have the climate for them. Check what does grow around where you live and make the most of it. You'll be supporting your local growers.

- ✔ Check out the companies near you that produce, package, and transport things like bread, rice, milk, and so on. If you buy those brands you'll be cutting down on the miles your food travels.

All supermarkets have ranges of organic food but don't forget the small organic stores that are supplied by businesses specialising in organic foods; local farmers' markets; and your local organic farms, which often have their own farm shops. The small specialist businesses will be able to give you more help and information about the food you're buying.

Checking Ingredients and Methods

Do you know exactly what went into your body at dinner time? You may think that you had a simple sandwich but there may have been more to it than just wheat flour and cheese. Lots of chemicals and other additives go into the regular food production process and many of these compromise your ability to live a green life.

Here are some food production issues to think about:

- **Additives:** Most packaged foods you see on supermarket shelves contain additives that help preserve, add flavour, and alter the colour of food. Many additives are chemically generated and some food scientists believe that they can be a source of an increasing number of food allergies.

- **Antibiotics and hormones:** Much mass-produced meat contains drugs used to speed up the growth of animals and increase production, and to stop them from getting sick. Some scientists think that humans ingesting these drugs through eating meat may become less immune to viruses and that the drugs contribute to obesity in some people.

- **Genetic engineering:** The process of transferring genes from one plant or animal to another in order to improve the quality and production of food is controversial. Some scientists, environmental organisations, and food safety campaigners argue that the technology has not been properly tested while others are convinced there's no danger from the technology and the food produced this way is safe to eat. There's more on Genetic Modification later in this chapter in the section 'Getting the gist of genetically modified food'.

- **Farming methods:** Rearing animals and poultry in cages and factory-like buildings produces many more greenhouse gas emissions, chemicals, pollutants, and diseases than more organic and natural styles of farming. The sidebar 'The life and times of a factory farm chicken' in this chapter illustrates why people are concerned about farming methods.

These methods of food production are actually relatively new – your grandparents (or possibly great-grandparents, depending on how old you are), and everyone before them didn't buy pre-packed frozen meals or convenience foods, or fruits and greens sprayed with chemicals and grown in soils supported by fertilisers, let alone animal products pumped with hormones and antibiotics. Back then, farmers had no choice but to follow sustainable practices in order to get the most from their land.

When buying food, read the labels (see the section 'Reading the Label', later in this chapter) or check the manufacturer's Web site to see if the food is produced in the way you feel is acceptable to you.

Explaining organic

You could be forgiven for thinking it should be quite easy to explain exactly what is and isn't organic food. But, as with so much to do with food, it's actually quite tricky. Hundreds of organisations around the world give certificates to say that products are organic and each has slightly different criteria by which it makes its judgements.

In the UK, farmers have to meet the European Union (EU) definition of organic. Basically, the EU controls the use of pesticides, artificial fertilisers, and chemicals, and mandates that animals be reared without the use of antibiotics and hormones where possible (if antibiotics are necessary on the advice of a vet to avoid an animal suffering, they have to be given).

Buying organic food produced in the UK doesn't guarantee that it is pesticide free. However, instead of the 450 pesticides that can be used in conventional farming, organic standards allow only 2 which are not chemically produced unless the farmer has permission to use others from the government's Department for Environment, Food, and Rural Affairs (DEFRA).

For more information, take a look at the DEFRA Web site at `www.defra. gov.uk/farm/organic` or at the Soil Association Web site at `www. soilassociation.org`. The Soil Association is one of the organisations in the UK that can certify that a food is organic and you can find its logo on many UK-produced organic products in the shops.

You may decide you want to eat organic food because it's produced by greener methods, or because you feel that eating food grown using pesticides must be bad for your health, but scientists haven't come to any agreement so far about whether or not organic food is safer and more nutritious than the non-organic equivalents. A study from the Danish Institute of Agricultural Research suggests that organically produced milk may be healthier than conventionally produced milk because it has higher levels of vitamin E, omega 3, and antioxidants which help fight infections. However the content of the milk produced by any cow depends on the feed she was given, so most scientists argue that more research still needs to be done.

Buying organic

Organic food used to be the preserve of 'hippies' and 'tree huggers' who 'knitted their own yoghurt', but that's no longer the case. People choose organic food because they think that it tastes better, they believe that it's safer and more nutritious, and better for the environment and for animal welfare.

However, there are still arguments over whether organic food is any better for you than the conventionally produced alternatives. You must look at the evidence available and make up your own mind. What isn't disputed is that conventional and especially intensive farming methods are damaging to the environment.

Organic food is much more plentiful than it used to be and more in demand so prices have come down. Ten years ago organic food was very hard to get but now all the big food retailers sell organic fruit, vegetables, and meat as well as processed food like bread and biscuits. UK shoppers buy around ten times as much organic food as ten years ago.

Farming organically

Organic farming is much friendlier for the earth and the local economy than mass-produced products. Organic farming of fruits, vegetables, and grains uses traditional methods of ploughing and rotating the soil, which results in better fertility for long-term continual growth, rather than relying on chemical pesticides and fertilisers to get high yields. Farming in a more traditional way also reduces the likelihood that chemicals run into nearby rivers, streams, and the water table below. In turn, you're less likely to be eating any chemicals used to keep bugs at bay and the soil fertile.

Comparing organic to non-organic

When you start looking at labels you'll find it very interesting comparing the types of ingredients in an organically produced food compared to a normal off-the-shelf product. Honestly – you will! Peanut butter, for example, is one of the most popular foods and can be one of the most simply produced foods on the market:

✔ Ingredients in organically produced peanut butter: 100 per cent organically grown peanuts.

✔ Ingredients in brand-produced peanut butter: 95 per cent imported and local peanuts, 5 per cent canola oil (with antioxidants E319 and 320, and antifoam (E900).

Some organic foods are still more expensive than the non-organic versions partly because they aren't grown on such a big scale but if you think about the whole cost – such as having to clean up rivers because of pesticides leaking into them – and the welfare of the animals involved, you may decide that it's worth paying a little extra.

The same environmentally friendly farming can be applied to the production of meat, eggs, milk, and other animal products. Organic meat is produced from animals raised in the fields without chemicals or drugs.

It takes time to convert to organic farming mainly because it takes time for all the existing pesticides and fertilisers to disappear from the soil.

When applying for organic status, farmers must meet and adhere to a set of nationally agreed standards listed by the UK Register of Organic Food Standards (UKROFS). Use of these standards provides transparency and credibility for the industry and is designed to protect consumers against deception and fraud. The register was set up by agriculture ministers in 1987 and you can find more information from the Department for Environment, Food and Rural Affairs (DEFRA) at www.defra.gov.uk.

Farmers who want to convert to organic farming or who want to be accredited as organic farmers must have their farms inspected. The inspector tells them what steps they have to take to comply with the rules. When inspectors are happy that those steps have been taken, the farmer gets the necessary certificate.

It takes two years from when the application goes in to convert arable and horticultural land to organic. During the first year of the conversion period crops grown on that land have to be sold as non-organic. Crops sold in the second year are sold with the label 'Produced under conversion to organic farming'. After that, crops can be sold as organic. The conversion period is different for other types of farming such as animal farming and fruit growing.

Raising organic animals

On the animal front, organic farmers and producers can confine animals – they need to give them access to outdoors but they don't actually have to let them go out. Confinement is a particular issue when buying poultry – there's a big difference between free-range in contained sheds or cages and free-range on pasture. You can find this information on the label on packaged goods.

Compare the organic approach of farming animals to the factory farm method, which stuffs animals in cages and pens and pumps them with drugs (see the sidebar 'The life and times of a factory farm chicken' for more details). Factory farming concentrates many animals in one limited space, which results in an overflow of animal waste on each farm. Most factory farms apply lots of water and chemicals to assist in removing the waste, which can lead to chemicals leaching into the soil and the water table. The organic approach may be a lot slower and less productive, but it produces cleaner and healthier animals. It doesn't take long for the land on which factory farming takes place to become contaminated and unhealthy for the animals living on it.

The life and times of a factory farm chicken

You only have to look at how chickens are treated on a factory farm to understand how viruses — such as a strain of bird flu — may evolve and why eating meat can be a health hazard, not to mention the welfare issues related to treating animals with much more compassion. The US Animal Welfare Institute (on the Web at www.awionline.org) gives an insight into how chickens are reared. Here's a summary:

✔ Many hens born and raised on a factory farm can live their whole lives crammed inside cages next to other chickens, never having seen anything outside the cage in which they're housed.

✔ Most hens raised on a factory farm have never walked, never stretched their wings, never laid a nest, and never foraged for food.

✔ Because of their desire to move around, the hens can become aggressive and peck at the other chickens around them, causing injury and disease. To avoid that, many hens' beaks are cut off when they're born.

✔ At the end of a laying cycle, hens naturally shed feathers. To force moulting artificially and to promote an additional laying cycle, hens are deprived of food and water for up to two weeks. When production of eggs finally drops off, the hens are killed — they've served their purpose.

✔ Just as many male chickens as females are born. On some farms the male chicks are thrown alive into bins, leaving them to suffocate and die.

✔ Broilers — chickens raised for meat — spend relatively short lives in sheds with hundreds or even thousands of other birds. They're fed with growth hormones so that they grow quickly, which makes them predisposed to disease and physical abnormalities. Many of these birds die of heart attacks, dehydration, or starvation because they can't even stand or walk to feeders.

Farming methods like this have evolved to meet the ever-growing demand for meat. Organic meat production is slower – animals have room to move and so fewer animals can be produced from the same amount of land.

A green populace needs to eat less meat to get better-quality meat and good levels of animal welfare.

Free-range meats and eggs – where the animals and hens have been allowed to roam – are much more likely to have less total fat and fewer calories than their factory farm cousins because the animals haven't been artificially fattened. They're also much less likely to carry bacteria like E.coli.

Getting the gist of genetically modified food

Genetically modified (GM) foods contain ingredients that have been modified by altering their biological characteristics using genetic material and proteins from other sources.

Many scientists are concerned that genetically modified foods (or *GMOs – genetically modified organisms* – as they're also called) may be harmful to the environment and to human health. The worry is that altering the genetic make-up of a species poses the risk of mutating viruses, and the fear that cancers and abnormal animal and plant life may evolve as a result. However, as many scientists support GM food as are against it. They argue that there's no proof that problems have been caused by genetic modification and, as long as the process is strictly controlled, any effects can be controlled by science.

The food and agricultural industries are so interested in GM food because it promises to overcome some of the difficulties facing large-scale farming. Food that can be modified to withstand higher doses of herbicides and pesticides or to produce toxins in the plant or seed to kill insects saves industrial farmers millions of pounds.

The GM process also allows additional vitamins and extra taste to be added and even makes foods last longer than they normally would. Using the process can allow producers to produce more food and prevent food shortages, hunger, and disease around the world.

So far consumers aren't keen on the idea of GM and experts who are against using the process say that it isn't the answer to feeding the world's ever-growing population – that there is enough food and its distribution just needs to be managed better.

Most GM crops are grown in Canada, America, Argentina, and China. None are grown in the UK. Any firm that wants to grow GM crops in the UK has to go through a lengthy approval process but the government has outlined plans that it says would protect conventional crops should GM crops be grown here in the future. Those plans were proposed in July 2006 and anyone interested in the issue was given until 20 October 2006 to express their views. At the time of writing no one knows what the outcome will be.

You may be eating GM ingredients in your food and not know it. In EU countries, if a food such as flour, oil, or glucose syrup contains or consists of GMOs, or ingredients produced from GMOs, the label has to say so. If a GM product is sold 'loose', information must be displayed immediately next to the food to show that it's GM. Products produced with GM technology (cheese produced with GM enzymes, for example) don't have to be labelled nor do products such as meat, milk, and eggs from animals fed on GM animal feed. Any intentional use of GM ingredients at any level must be labelled. But there is no need for small amounts of GM ingredients accidentally present in a food to be labelled.

Some of the foods currently subject to genetic modification include:

- ✔ **Soya beans:** Soya is currently one of the main sources of genetically modified ingredients in food, and can found in everything from chocolate to crisps, margarine to mayonnaise, and biscuits to bread.

- ✔ **Canola:** Canola oil comes from certain types of rape plants. GM canola may be used for oils used in potato chips and animal feed.

- ✔ **Corn:** GM corn is mainly used as cattle feed but is also found in all sorts of packaged food, such as breakfast cereal, bread, corn chips, confectionary, and gravy mixes.

- ✔ **Milk:** Cows in the US and some other countries are being injected with a genetically engineered growth hormone to increase milk production. Some imported products such as cheese may contain this hormone.

No fresh GM food is on sale in the UK. When you eat out the restaurant has to tell you if it has used any GM ingredients. Because of public opposition in the UK to GM, most restaurants don't dare use GM foods.

For more information on GM foods, try the Food Standards Agency Web site at www.food.gov.uk and the Food and Drink Federation Web site at www.foodfuture.org.uk. If you want to know more about the campaigns against GM food visit the Friends of the Earth Web site at www.foe.co.uk or Greenpeace at www.greenpeace.org.uk.

Reading the Label

Buying food is confusing. For a start there seems to be endless choice. Who needs all those breakfast cereals and different brands of beans to choose from! But most confusing of all is the advice on what's good and bad for you. One week you're to buy foods that are low in cholesterol, saturated fats, sugars, and salt, but high in calcium and antioxidants, and the next week there seems to be yet another list of ingredients you should actively pursue or avoid at all costs. It's impossible to keep up!

Reading the labels is important because labels are the only source of information about the nutritional content of the food you buy. Labels show you, for example, the percentage of the different ingredients and the presence of potential allergens in foods.

There are strict rules on what can and can't be said by manufacturers on food labels. For example, a food can't claim to be 'reduced calorie' unless it is much lower in calories than the usual version of the same food.

When buying a product, find out if it has arrived on the shelf from an organic or sustainable production process by checking out the following information on the label:

✔ **Ingredients list:** Understanding the ingredients and their nutrients gives you an excellent feel for the quality of your food. Heavily processed food is likely to have plenty of added salt to assist in preservation and taste and several chemicals for flavouring and colouring, whereas naturally prepared foods are usually low in added salt, sugar, and saturated fats, for example.

You'll be amazed at how many chemicals are added to your food once you start looking – so much so that most of them are officially numbered so the manufacturer can list them on the tin or packet. You can get more information on the regulations about food labelling from the Food Standards Agency at www.foodstandards.gov.uk or at www.eatwell.gov.uk/foodlabels.

If a food is labelled 'organic' that means it has been certified as organic by one of the certification bodies – usually the Soil Association. Being labelled 'organic' doesn't mean that every ingredient in a product is organic – just 95 per cent of them. If less than 95 per cent of the ingredients are organic, the word organic can be used only on the ingredients list – not on the product itself.

✔ **Genetically modified information:** By law, manufacturers must say on the label whether a food has been modified genetically. For more information on why that matters, see the previous section, 'Getting the gist of genetically modified food'.

✔ **Animals used:** Some animals and fish are protected species due to their near extinction from being over-farmed or culled. Check the label to make sure that your food doesn't use protected animals; tuna is one to watch out for – The Marine Conservation Society says all commercially fished species of tuna are now endangered. Some tuna fishing uses nets that can trap and kill dolphins. If you want to eat tuna the greenest option is line-caught tuna. There's more information from the Marine Conservation Society at www.mcsuk.org.

✔ **Country of origin:** The label tells you the country the food comes from; British produce carries a red tractor logo.

Tracking Your Food Back to Its Source

'Where does my food come from?' is really two questions. One is to do with how the food was produced and the other is about where on the earth it travelled from, how it travelled, how long it took to get to you, and how long it was in storage before it got into the shops. If you want to be sure that your food is as green as possible you need the answers to both of these questions.

The fast pace of modern life leads to less cooking at home and more reliance on convenience foods that can be unwrapped and put straight in the oven. If you buy ready meals you are less likely to know what's in them and where the ingredients came from than if you prepare a meal from scratch with fresh, raw ingredients.

You may also like to have some information about the employment practices of the country of origin when deciding whether or not to buy certain foods. If you want to live a truly green and ethical lifestyle you'll avoid food from countries that exploit workers or have poor records on human rights. Knowing what you want to buy, and from where, can take a lot of research. Not everyone makes the same decisions and you also have to bear in mind that if you decide not to buy produce from a particular country you may be helping to make life more difficult for the farmers, workers, and producers rather than the country's government.

Eating local produce

Despite all the arguments about what food is best in terms of health, there does seem to be agreement that from an environmental point of view it's best to buy local produce. If you go to the supermarket you'll find fruit and vegetables from Spain, South Africa, and New Zealand, and meat from Argentina and Brazil – stuff that's flown thousands of miles. Where is all the local produce?

The supermarkets are always trying to entice you with cheaper prices and so they buy from suppliers who supply them with what they need: what customers want at the right price. It may be cheaper to buy from abroad and fly goods in from Africa rather than buy them from Kent. Fruit, vegetables, and other favourite foods are increasingly imported into the UK from around the world. This not only reduces access to locally produced food but increases the amount of fossil fuels burned (and pollution generated) to transport the goods.

The supermarkets say that they are giving their customers what they want – avocados all year round at low prices, for example. Whether or not that's the case, when avocados are available all year round at low prices, it's easy to develop a taste for them.

If you want to do the best for the environment by eating local produce you may have to stop buying all those exotic treats that you've come to know and love, and go back to eating what local producers can produce at particular times of the year. That also means getting back into the kitchen and cooking again.

Eating what's in season

If you eat according to the UK growing seasons, you enjoy winter vegetables such as parsnips and swede, and summer vegetables such as garden peas and lettuce. If you shop in the supermarket or the bigger greengrocers' shops you can find just about every kind of fruit or vegetable all year round. You don't have to think about what's in season because you can have anything you want when you want it – but you won't have a green tongue, so to speak.

If you buy only local produce to cut down on the impact on the environment of food travelling round the globe, you may also want to eat only seasonal produce too.

Local producers can grow food out of season but that usually means using artificial heating and lighting, and growing fruit and vegetables under polythene or in poly tunnels to stimulate growth in artificial conditions. It can be just as damaging to the environment for a grower in Kent to grow tomatoes out of season in this way as to transport them in from Spain.

Locally produced, seasonal food can be organically produced more readily than out of season food. Quite apart from the environment and health considerations of eating this way, there's the added pleasure of rediscovering particular foods each year. When the season is over you can look forward to tasting it again next year, instead of becoming used to it all year round and taking it for granted.

Cutting down the food miles

At the heart of all the arguments for eating locally grown, seasonal produce is the need to cut down on what have become known as food miles. *Food Miles* is the distance – often thousands of miles – that food travels from where it's produced to get to your plate. The transportation (by air, truck, or car) results in carbon emissions. Nearly half of our food is imported from abroad and over half of the organic food for sale in the UK is imported.

Food retailers say that customers want exotic foods from around the world. Maybe consumers want them because the retailers provide them but part of the reason may be that people travel more widely and experience different foods from different countries that they then want to be able to buy when they've returned home. Whatever the reason, there are now more than 40,000 different food products available in the bigger supermarkets and many of them have travelled thousands of miles and are responsible for about a fifth of the carbon dioxide emissions the UK produces.

Food flying thousands of miles to the UK from other countries is just part of the food miles problem. Even British produce can travel many hundreds of miles before it gets to your plate. The retailers buy from producers and often transport the food by road to big packaging plants; from there to huge storage facilities; on again to distribution centres; and finally to the shops from where you drive it home. To cut down on those miles, you have to buy locally rather than just buy items with the British produce tractor on the label.

Food that travels and spends time in storage has fewer nutrients than locally produced food. The sooner after it's been picked or harvested you eat something the more nutritious it is. Ideally the best food is that eaten within a day of coming off the tree.

Another dilemma for you to consider is what to choose if you have to decide between organic potatoes from New Zealand and non-organic ones from Cyprus. Do you go for the organic on the grounds that you don't agree with the use of pesticides in farming, or do you go for the non-organic on the grounds that they've travelled fewer food miles and are responsible for fewer damaging greenhouse gas emissions? Many scientists think that buying locally produced food is more important for the environment than buying organic. The decision is far from simple but don't be put off. If you are making decisions that are making your lifestyle greener than it was you are doing something to help rather than nothing.

Eating Animals

If you ask many schoolchildren where bacon comes from they will tell you 'the supermarket'. The process of breeding, rearing, feeding, and eventually killing pigs and other animals for food is something many of them know nothing about. Why should they? They live in towns and cities where they may never come across anything to do with farming. If you want to know what you're eating you need to know what kind of farming methods are used to get the meat you eat from the farmyard to your plate.

Being a 'green' meat-eater

If you lust for a lamb shank and pine for a pork chop you can still be greener. Meat can be, and is, produced in the same organic and sustainable way that many fruits and vegetables are farmed. You can cut down your impact on the planet's resources by reducing the amount of meat you eat, and choosing 'green' meat wherever possible.

Look for meats that have been *pasture raised* or *grass fed*, indicating that the animals were raised outdoors on pasture and that their diet consisted of grasses and hay – a much more natural and environmentally supportive process than feeding them on grain.

Some animals (especially chickens and pigs) are fed some grains to ensure that they get the nutrients they need, but the grains themselves can be organically grown.

Check what is meant by what it says on the labels:

- ✔ **Free-range:** Check the labelling or a company's Web site to find out whether the chicken or pig has been raised on pasture or simply uncaged in an enclosed free-range shed.

- ✔ **Natural:** Labels may refer to beef and lamb, in particular, being produced naturally but this only means that it may not have any artificial colours, artificial flavours, preservatives, or other artificial ingredients – not that they've led the life of Riley outside, gambolling in the fields.

- ✔ **Lean:** Buying lean meat may be healthier but it's not any more sustainable than fatty meat. The only difference between lean meat and non-lean meat is that the fat has been taken out.

Some countries that don't have large meat-producing industries, or are worried about local meat being infected (particularly in Asia and Europe), import their meat from 'safe' countries, such as Australia. The energy required to transport that meat is huge.

A meat-eater can be just as sustainable with their eating habits, although the range of sustainable and organically prepared meats may not yet equal the range of vegetarian food available. You find less organic meat in your local supermarket compared to the increasing range of organically produced fruit and vegetables, tofu products, and other non-dairy delights now available. Don't forget the other options for buying meat. Locally produced meat is more likely to have been raised organically and even if it isn't the advantage of being truly local is that it's greener than imported meat that's travelled thousands of food miles.

If you're finding it hard to get organic meat, ask your local butcher's shop or butcher in the supermarket if they can supply you with some organic and sustainable options – increased demand increases supply. The environment will be better off and your local supermarket or butcher will have a guaranteed customer.

Fishing for sustainable varieties

Buying fish brings with it a whole other range of ethical issues. The world's fish stocks are dwindling. That means that fishermen have to go farther afield, into deeper waters to bring home their catch. Fish are being taken from the sea younger, so further depleting stocks as there are fewer breeding fish in the sea. Fishing in deeper waters means greater use of dragnets which catch endangered species as well as fish for the shops. Only 3 per cent of the world's fish stocks are underexploited. At the same time, demand for fish is growing. It has doubled in the last 30 years and is predicted to go on growing.

One answer has been to farm fish such as salmon. Intensive farming methods have resulted in the same sorts of problems faced in animal farming. The use of chemicals, antibiotics, and disinfectants to protect the fish from disease has led to worries about toxins and cancer-causing chemicals in the fish you eat and there are concerns about escaping fish carrying contamination into wild fish stocks. And all this at a time when nutritionists advise eating more fish for the benefits of the omega 3 oils which help to lower the risk of heart disease.

There are quotas in place in the European Union which set out the amount of fish that can be taken from the various fishing grounds by each country. That has done a lot to conserve EU fish stocks but EU fishermen are going into African waters to meet demand.

When you go shopping for fish you need to think about:

- ✔ **Whether the fish you want to buy is from sustainable stock:** This means the fish are replacing themselves at the same rate as they're being fished. Cod, for example, used to live up to 40 years and grow to six feet but now the stocks are so depleted most of the fish caught are less than two years old and haven't bred replacement fish. People are advised not to buy cod to allow stocks to build up again.

- ✔ **Whether the fish is farmed or wild:** If you're prepared to buy farmed varieties you may want to know that they've been organically reared.

- ✔ **How the fish was caught:** Catching fish by line doesn't cause further damage to the marine environment, but net fishing can do a huge amount of environmental damage. For example, fishing for tuna with nets can and does kill dolphins. Fishing for prawns results in other unwanted species being caught and thrown back into the sea dead. Many of the prawns in the shops are farmed.

Buy fish from a good fish shop where the staff know how the fish were caught, where farmed fish come from, and how they were farmed. Check out the fish facts from the Marine Conservation Society Website at www.fishonline.org or from the Marine Stewardship Council Web site at www.msc.org.

Eating Vegetables

Vegetarians (not the fish and free-range chicken-eating variety, but real non-meat-eating vegetarians) become vegetarians and even *vegans* (no dairy or other animal by-products at all) for a purpose. Many become vegetarian for health reasons or philosophical reasons or both. More vegetarians tend to make green lifestyle choices than not.

When you ask people why they choose to be vegetarians, you often find they're protesting against the meat industry's production methods. Others give up meat in favour of vegetarianism because they're alarmed by health issues, such as:

✔ **Mad cow disease:** This killer disease reared its ugly head on a wide scale in the mid-1990s. Found in cows and later in human form, it's not a virus or bacteria, but a *prion,* which is an infectious protein that causes dementia and possible death in those infected. The sale of beef went down significantly when the disease became prevalent in certain parts of the world including the UK.

✔ **Toxicity:** Artificial hormones, steroids, and other chemicals injected or fed to animals to make them grow faster and bigger are foreign to the body and may lead to vital organs breaking down.

✔ **Bacteria:** The antibiotics pumped into animals can result in them resisting strains of bacteria like E. coli. Overuse of antibiotics may mean you're in with a greater chance of buying meat with undetectable forms of bacteria in it.

✔ **Saturated fats:** Many meats are high in these fats which can cause obesity. In intensive factory farming methods, animals are fed grain (soya beans and maize) rather than grazing out in the fields, which results in high acidity levels in the animal's digestion system, which can cause an increase of sickness in the animal at the time it's slaughtered for eating.

While some vegetarians don't eat meat for health reasons, others are also concerned about the resources that go into the production of meat. Grain feeding animals in a factory farm uses up a lot of resources. Lots of power is used for lighting and machinery and it takes a lot of water to flush away effluent. Even though many farmers keep their cattle and sheep out in the fields, at times when there's not enough grass, their diets are often supplemented with grain.

The Global Resource Action Center for the Environment in the US states that beef cattle must each consume about 3.6 kilograms of grain in order to yield just under half a kilogram of meat. A typical grain-fed animal consumes approximately 1,200 kilograms of grain by the time it's ready for market. Add into the equation that it takes up to 100,000 litres of water to produce one kilo of meat and you can see that meat production is hard on the environment.

In the West and in the United States in particular people eat a lot of meat. Three-quarters of the grain grown around the world is used in meat production. That amount of grain would feed many, many more people if it wasn't fed to animals. It takes about 24 acres of land to keep an American fed and about 1 acre to feed an Indian.

One of the big issues for vegetarians is GM – see the previous section on 'Getting the gist of genetically modified food'. Many vegetarian products on the shelves, like tofu and textured vegetable protein (TVP), are based on soya beans, and much of the soya now grown is genetically modified.

If you want to be a greener vegetarian, here are some foods that are more likely to help you do so:

- **Non-GM canola, corn, and soya:** Scrutinise the label – many companies now proudly identify that they're a non-GM food.

- **Nuts:** Buy locally produced nuts that have been organically grown if possible.

- **Local organic fruit and vegetables:** Pick them up at your local farmers' markets or farm shops.

- **Tea and coffee:** Look for fair trade varieties. See the section later in this chapter on 'Understanding the Fair Trade Arguments'.

- **Chocolate:** Go for chocolate that is made from organic cocoa and is locally produced or fair trade (vegans may prefer to buy organic soya-based chocolate).

- **Beer and wine:** Shop for alcohol that uses organically grown and locally produced ingredients, and buy from local breweries and (even in the UK!) wineries.

Vegetarians are more likely to think 'green', but eating a vegetarian or vegan diet doesn't guarantee that you're ecofriendly. If the fruit and vegetables you eat are grown locally and/or organically, that's great, but if they're travelling thousands of food miles and using litres of pesticides you may be no greener than anyone else. Although a vegetarian's choices mainly revolve around food and, more recently, clothing and accessories, vegetarians still turn on the lights at night, waste water, and produce rubbish.

Choosing Where to Buy Your Food

The choice of food retailers is almost as great as the choice of food products. The sections here help you make the freshest picks.

Buying from the supermarket

Because most people have little time to shop, supermarkets are the convenient option. You can get everything under one roof and do a big shop every so often so you don't have to make too many visits. They entice you in with buy-one-get-one-free offers, loss leaders, loyalty cards, and the promise of low prices. It's worth getting your calculator out though and doing an experiment to see if your shopping really is cheaper than elsewhere and factor in the quality of the food you're buying as well as the shelf price.

Organic food is generally still a bit more expensive than conventional items, but prices are coming down as more organic producers come on stream – which means demand is increasing too. The entrance of the big supermarket chains into the organic food market – as a result of increasing demand for organic food – is driving supplies, and because they have huge buying power they can keep prices down.

You're now more likely to be able to find a greater variety of well-labelled, organically produced foods in large supermarkets than in some local greengrocers' shops or your local corner store. Have a look in the fruit and vegetable, health food, breakfast cereal, and tinned products sections; these sections tend to have the majority of the organic food on offer.

Beware big business barging in

Because of concerns for animal welfare and the possibility that eating food produced using pesticides and other chemicals may cause health problems, the demand for organic food has increased to such an extent that big businesses are interested in its money-making potential. When that happens you have to take into account the impact that big business has on local businesses such as butchers and greengrocers.

Big supermarkets have been blamed for putting small competitors out of business and accused of forcing producers and suppliers to cut their profits in order to push down prices while keeping the supermarket profit margins high. Big businesses have greater buying power than small competitors but they also transport food farther to storage and distribution facilities – increasing factory and transport emissions and reducing the nutritional value of the stored food.

When big business becomes involved in the sale of organic food, you lose most of the benefits of buying locally produced and seasonal produce.

Although the big supermarkets generally offer cheaper and a larger range of organic products, many lack the character and ethics that your local speciality organic food shop, co-op, or local market provides.

You may be less concerned about buying organic foods than about getting locally grown foods. The supermarkets tend to treat food grown in the UK as locally produced. Even if a lamb starts its life in a farm a mile away from you it will travel to storage and distribution centres miles from home and will have travelled a large distance before it gets back to your supermarket. Check with the shop how local 'local' is.

Thinking outside the supermarket

A surprisingly large number of smaller speciality shops and co-ops sell organic and/or local products. Some shops only sell organically produced and labelled food, whereas others combine organic food with health food, vitamin and mineral supplies, and other wellbeing and fitness-related products.

These suppliers are popping up everywhere in cities and towns and are increasingly moving into many large shopping centres, such is the demand for organic food lines.

Meeting the grower at your local farmers' market

Farmers' markets have increased in popularity in the last few years. Farmers and their employees go to towns and suburban locations throughout the big cities, perhaps one day a week, to set up their stalls and sell their wares. They cater to locals interested in buying fresh, cheap, organic, local produce, and tourists interested in learning a bit about what is grown and eaten in the region.

You're able to sample and buy local fruit and vegetables that are in season, and talk to the grower about their produce – they're usually passionate about the things they grow – so that you know exactly what you're getting and eating. You can find details of local farmers' markets at www.farmersmarkets.net.

Not all the produce at a farmers' market is certified organic. Some farmers use conventional methods, some may be going through the certification process to convert to organic (see the section earlier in this chapter – 'Explaining organic'), and others are keen vegetable gardeners with green fingers.

Getting to know the local farmer

If there isn't a local farmers' market there will be a farmer somewhere not too far away from you who sells their produce straight from the farm or has their own farm shop – unless you live right in the middle of a big city. If you get to know that farmer you'll know what's about to be in season, how it's produced, and when it will be on sale, and you'll probably get cookery tips too. Some farmers even deliver to established regular customers.

The produce may be a bit more expensive from a farm shop as the farmer won't be selling the kind of volumes of produce that allow them to cut prices. If you have to drive to get there and back you have to think about the fuel you're using and the impact of that on the environment when you're working out how green an option shopping this way is.

Boxing clever

You can join a box scheme and have your fresh fruit and vegetables delivered. There are hundreds of them up and down the UK. You get a delivery regularly, usually of local produce that's in season. In lean periods when there's not much being harvested on the local farms, some of what is delivered is imported. Many of the schemes are certified organic by the Soil Association. There's more information on their Web site at www. soilassociation.org.

Some schemes are run by big companies that deliver just about anything and travel miles. If you choose a local one you'll cut down on the distance your food travels.

Picking your own

Getting to know the local farmers and shopping directly from farms has the added advantage of providing a fun day out for all the family. Local farmers often have days when you can go and pick your own fruit – usually strawberries and raspberries, but there may be a whole range of pick-your-own opportunities in your part of the country.

If you pick your own fruit and vegetables you know whether they're organically grown or not, you know that they're local, you're not contributing to any damage to the environment from machinery being used to do the picking, you won't have a lot of waste from packaging, and you'll get the maximum possible nutrients from the produce because you're using it straight away. You'll have kept the children amused for a day and given them an insight into where their food comes from and how it's produced. Just don't let them eat too many berries or they'll be sick on the way home!

Growing your own

If you have the time, energy, space, money to buy seeds and plants, and green fingers, the greenest option of the lot is to grow some of your food yourself using organic methods. That ticks all the green, ecofriendly, sustainable boxes.

If you haven't got space of your own for growing fruit and vegetables there may be allotments near you. Call you local council for information or contact the National Society for Allotment and Leisure Gardeners on 01536 266576 or take a look at their Web site at www.nsalg.org.uk.

When you've started to harvest enough produce you can sell it at the farmers' market but remember that if you want to sell produce as organic you have to have the correct certification. See the section 'Explaining organic', earlier in this chapter. There's more information on being green in the garden in Chapter 5.

Eating out

When you go out for a meal you're usually at the mercy of the chef when it comes to green principles. Many chefs though make a point of buying only truly local and/or organic produce. If you want to be sure of what you're getting call the restaurant ahead of booking and ask about the ingredients they use. Good restaurants won't mind and if more customers demand greener restaurant meals, chefs and managers will get the message.

Restaurants have to warn you if any of their ingredients are genetically modified and many have banned GM from their menus because of public hostility. There are plenty of vegetarian restaurants and even if you're usually a meat-eater you may decide to have vegetarian meals out as the ingredients are more likely to be locally produced and organic.

Understanding Fair Trade Arguments

Fairtrade is a trading scheme that works to make sure that producers in the developing world get fair prices for what they produce and that they have reasonable working conditions and fair terms of trade with the firms they supply. The idea of Fairtrade is that more of the money you pay goes to the producers who can then pay their workers better and invest more in their businesses. It's a trading partnership that aims at sustainable development for excluded and disadvantaged producers and does this by providing better trading conditions and by raising awareness and campaigning.

In UK shops and supermarkets you can find a range of goods with the Fairtrade logo on them. There are around 300 on the list, including tea, coffee, chocolate, bananas, herbs and spices, flowers, cotton, and footballs, and the list is growing as the scheme extends its reach. You can even find cafes that trade on the fact that the coffee they sell is Fairtrade.

The Fairtrade label allows you to be sure that the products it appears on meet the Fairtrade standards and contribute to the development of disadvantaged producers and workers. By buying Fairtrade goods you are saying – 'I'm willing to pay a bit more because it matters to me how the producers are treated'. The scheme aims to make sure that:

✔ Producers are paid a fair price that covers their production and living costs so that they have some security, that they have long-term contracts so they can plan ahead, and that their business is sustainable.

✔ The extra you pay goes towards other aspects of the producers' welfare, such as education.

✔ Producers and workers are allowed to join unions and other organisations that can protect their rights and ensure that they have fair working conditions.

✔ No child labour is used.

✔ Production methods are environmentally friendly and pesticide free.

You'll find more information about fair trade on the Fairtrade Foundation Web site at www.fairtrade.org.uk.

The Fairtrade label from the Fairtrade Foundation doesn't appear on things like clothes and craft goods but you can buy clothes and craft goods that have been traded in a similar fair way. Charity shops such as Oxfam (see the Web site at www.oxfam.org.uk) and shops run by the British Association for Fair Trade Shops – its Web site is at www.bafts.org.uk – have similar schemes where they make sure the goods they buy and sell have been traded using similar principles to the Fairtrade scheme.

One of the UK's main fair trade organisations which buys and sells a whole range of fairly traded non-food products is Traidcraft. You can find out more at www.traidcraft.org.uk. These schemes are run on the same lines as the Fairtrade label scheme.

Now you have another factor to take into consideration when you deciding what to buy. Do you go for the organic item that's travelled thousands of miles; the local equivalent that is non-organic, or the Fairtrade version from somewhere in between. Being green is about weighing up the pros and cons and deciding what is most important to you.

Chapter 8

Wearing It Well

· ·

· ·

*E*very season the shops fill up with new clothes. Winter coats, short and swinging last year, are long and dragging along the pavements this year. Wedges and platform soles are *so* last year – this year's shoes are flat and bright. As the trends change, last season's must-have items look so unappealing and dowdy. The magazines are full of the latest, hottest, most up-to-date fashions and consumers feel obliged to keep up if at all possible.

The insatiable appetite for clothes puts pressure on the textile industry to supply enough material to cater for the demand. The clothing industry's response has been to encourage the use of new synthetic materials as well as mass producing natural materials such as cotton. It has also taken advantage of skills available in the developing world to produce clothes cheaply. Prices have fallen dramatically over the past ten years and as a result clothes are now disposable. Shoppers buy cheap clothes, frequently and in greater quantities, get bored with them before they wear out, and dump them.

However, a growing number of clothing and textile retailers sell fashionable, green, ecofriendly clothes. And a growing number of concerned shoppers are buying them. Green consumers are also repairing, reusing, and recycling as a way of reducing the amount of clothing that has to be produced. Buying this way can help reduce the negative impact on the environment currently being created by the global clothing industry.

Dressing Green

The only real answer to being greener when it comes to clothes is to buy fewer, better-quality items, use them for longer, repair and recycle them, and make sure that what you do buy comes from as naturally produced materials as possible – like organic cotton – grown without the use of pesticides and other chemicals which often contaminate water supplies in cotton growing areas.

The basic principles of green living as applied to clothes are reuse, repair, and recycle. Don't throw anything out before you've got every ounce of wear out of it by repairing and reusing. When you can no longer do that think about whether it's still fit for someone else to wear so that it can be recycled. By repairing, reusing, and recycling you're doing the most important thing, which is reducing the amount of clothing you're buying in the first place, which in turn reduces the amount that has to be produced.

If you simply can't use the item any longer and there's no life left in it, but the material was organically produced and the fabric wasn't dyed or treated with chemicals, you may be able to put it on the compost heap and help to recycle some nutrients back into the soil.

One of the most effective methods of reducing the demand for clothes is to keep all the items currently in people's wardrobes in circulation for much longer than they usually are. Whether it be by handing them on to other people or charities, trading them over the Internet, or keeping them for yourself, you can ensure that these clothes can continue wearing on to reduce the demand for new supplies.

Last but not least, think about regifting. We've all been given those jumpers we wouldn't be seen in under any circumstances but there may be someone you know who'd like the items you don't. Regifting is green because it cuts down the amount you buy and the amount being produced. Give an unwanted clothing item as a present instead of buying another one.

The four main green issues to consider when it comes to choosing clothes are:

- ✔ **Impact on workers:** Buying clothes produced by people on low wages who have no union representation and benefits isn't green. The workers are being exploited and aren't making enough to feed their families and are banned from an organisation that can help them fight for the same rights as the people who can afford to wear their products.

- ✔ **Impact on local economy:** Losing local textile companies that relocate overseas can be devastating to the UK economy.

✔ **Impact of production methods:** Commercial cotton is often farmed using unsustainable, intensive farming practices and synthetic fabrics use chemicals. Persistent environmental pollutants are used in some clothing (such as fabrics with Teflon coating) and in some imported clothes. Check the labels as far as possible and if you're unsure go for the green option – such as organically produced cotton and wool or silk.

✔ **Impact of materials:** You have to count the environmental, social, and economic impact of using skins and other animal by-products from declining animal populations. Other materials like rayon and viscose are man-made from wood pulp treated with chemicals. If you want to avoid the chemicals go for greener natural and organically produced materials.

Following the Thread of Where Your Clothes Are Made Overseas

It's estimated that around half of clothes sold in the UK are imported from overseas from countries such as Bangladesh, China, Fiji, India, Pakistan, Madagascar, Mexico, and Turkey. Some of these items are made by people who are poorly paid and working in poor conditions. Some are made with the help of child labour. These practices keep the manufacturing prices down and makes the clothes cheaper in UK shops.

Buying something made in the UK is no guarantee that the people who made it have been treated well and within the laws of this country. There are sweat-shops in various towns and cities where people work in poor conditions and don't get paid the minimum wage. Many don't complain because they fear they'll lose their jobs and whatever income they do have, or because they don't have the right paperwork to allow them to stay and work in the UK.

By using lower-paid workers in other countries or using sweatshop labour in the UK, companies can keep the prices of their goods down and still make a profit. Their overhead costs are low compared to companies that use factory labour on reasonable wages. That makes it difficult for more responsible manufacturers to compete, so they close or they too move their manufacturing process abroad. All that means fewer employment opportunities in the textile industry at home.

Exploited workers face dehumanising conditions, including the following:

✔ **No legal protection:** Some workers aren't recognised as workers and, in some countries, the factories they work in are not recognised as work-places. Workers therefore have no right to complain about their lot and the workplaces operate in an unhealthy and unsafe environment.

✔ **No trade union:** This can be a result of the worker not being officially recognised or the wages being so low that they cannot afford the union fee.

✔ **Low wages:** Worker pay is extremely low, making it difficult or impossible for workers to support themselves and their families.

Workers have no access to the opportunities available within the wider community because of their lack of status, low wages, and long hours.

Organisations that campaign against textile and clothing companies setting up in the developing countries say that you should ask the retailers about how their clothes were manufactured before you buy. You can get more information from the campaign group No Sweat at www.nosweat.org.uk and from the Clean Clothes Campaign which aims to improve working conditions in the global garment industry – www.cleanclothes.org.

You could argue that the cheaper clothes and shoes are, the more shoppers buy, and the more jobs there are available for people overseas who wouldn't have those jobs otherwise. Boycotting certain brands can put that firm out of business and leave workers without a source of income. Many charities working in developing countries advise you not to boycott goods unless the workers themselves want a boycott.

Some organisations are working with suppliers and producers overseas to make sure that they get as fair a deal as possible:

✔ Producers and workers are allowed to join unions and other organisations that can protect their rights and ensure that they have fair working conditions.

✔ Workers have fair wages and conditions and can afford to feed their families.

✔ Child labour isn't used.

✔ Production methods are environmentally friendly and pesticide free.

If you want to know that the producers and workers who made your clothes were fairly treated buy from charity shops such as Oxfam shops (see the Web site at www.oxfam.org.uk) and fair-trade shops run by the British Association for Fair Trade Shops – www.bafts.org.uk. Traidcraft is the UK's main fair-trade organization and sells a whole range of fair-trade goods. You can find out more at www.traidcraft.org.uk. You generally pay a bit more for fairly traded goods but you may feel it's worth the difference.

There is also a similar fair-trade scheme for food producers – run by the Fairtrade Foundation. Fairtrade products carry the Fairtrade logo and apart from food the logo can be awarded to Fairtrade cotton, with which many fairly traded clothes will be made. There's more about the Fairtrade scheme in Chapter 7.

Some global companies and charities that sell clothes are also registered by the International Fair Trade Association (IFTA). You can get more information from `www.ifat.org`.

Living in a Material World

Look at the labels attached to the clothes you're thinking of buying. The information on the label gives you an idea of how green the clothes are. It tells you where the clothes are made and what they're made of and therefore gives you clues as to how green the production process is likely to be.

Natural fibres, such as cotton, that come from plants and animals are preferred. Synthetic fibres created by a process that includes the use of chemicals are to be avoided. Synthetic fibres are usually cheaper than their natural competitors – both in quality and cost.

Wearing green materials

Despite reservations about the ethical and green credentials of some of the materials used by the clothing industry, the number of sustainable clothing materials available is increasing. These include the following:

- **Hemp** is one of the greenest crops because it's resistant to pests and so doesn't need chemicals to maintain its quality. It's easy to grow in large quantities and enriches the soil when in the ground, both of which are big plus points.

- **Linen** is made from flax, which is resistant to pests and grows more easily than cotton.

- **Organically grown cotton and wool** isn't genetically modified (in cotton's case), uses natural fertilisers and pesticides, and traditional farming practices.

- **Recycled materials** are also a green choice. For example, clothes and shoes for outdoor use (especially in wet weather) can be made using recycled polyester, rubber, and even car tyres.

- **Silk** is made from the saliva produced by the larvae of several species of moth, commonly called silkworms but really caterpillars. It's a sustainable source of material but it takes thousands of larvae to produce a silk tie and some people prefer to avoid it because it can't be produced without the death of a living creature.

Linking clothes and oil

About 25 thousand barrels of oil a day are used to manufacture materials many of which are used to make clothes. Oil is a non-renewable resource and the petrochemical industry can cause serious pollution. The resulting materials aren't biodegradable and large quantities of greenhouse gases are emitted in the production process.

The most popular synthetic materials – nylon and polyester – are made from petrochemicals. Processing petrochemicals into small fibres uses a large amount of oil and energy and emits greenhouse gases. Manufacturing polyester also uses a large amount of water.

Because of the move away from the use of fur in the fashion industry, fake fur has become popular. Up to four barrels of oil can go into the manufacture of a jacket. Think carefully before you buy fake fur – the real thing is sustainable as long as the animals aren't from an endangered species but the fake alternative is not. If you don't want to buy real fur you may well decide not to buy either.

Synthetic fabrics take a long time to break down in landfill sites. If you want to be green, avoid any clothes that have these types of materials in them, no matter how much of a bargain they may appear to be in the shops.

Knowing that natural doesn't necessarily mean green

Just because the two most popular natural fibres come from plants (cotton) and animals (wool) doesn't mean they're green. Like food, it's best if natural fibres come from an organic farming process, whether it's from a cotton field or from a sheep's back.

Cotton is one of the most natural fibres on earth but it is also one of the crops that uses most pesticide. Traditionally grown cotton uses about a quarter of all the pesticides used in the world. Chemicals are used because cotton plants can be easily affected by insects and fungus.

Pesticides can create health problems for those who work on cotton farms. The World Health Organisation estimates that 3 million people are poisoned by pesticides each year and of those around 20,000 die. Pesticides also contaminate ground and surface water. They're not good for the long-term health of the soil either. The Pesticide Action Network of North America (www.panna.org) suggests that pesticide residue stays in the cotton fabric after is has been manufactured and may pose a health risk for cotton workers too.

It takes about 20,000 litres of water to make a cotton T-shirt and if you add in the dyes used and the amount of energy to process the raw cotton into fabric it doesn't add up to a very 'green' fabric. The manufacture of most clothing materials involves the use of huge quantities of water and that can lead to problems for human populations in dry regions where water is in short supply. It's very difficult to know how much water each individual item of clothing might have absorbed but research into the country where it's made gives you information on the abundance and quality of the water supply.

Wool obviously comes from sheep and you don't usually associate pesticides with animals, but they're used to maintain the quality of wool. Sheep dip, the chemical concoction sheep are dipped into to kill parasites, contains organophosphates, which scientists now know are a major cause of excessive tiredness, headaches, poor concentration, and mood changes in humans exposed to it, not to mention the effect on the sheep that are dipped into it.

The animal welfare charity People for the Ethical Treatment of Animals (PETA) is also concerned about sheep being mistreated, because animals can be herded together in a factory farm type situation, to produce as much wool in the shortest time possible.

Synthetic and chemical products are sometimes added to cotton and wool clothing products, including colour dyes and bleach. There is also an increasing number of poly-cotton products on the market, also referred to as *permanent press, no wrinkle, no ironing needed,* and *crease-resistant* products – all using chemicals.

Buy clothes made from organic cotton and wool. The materials are grown and processed without the use of toxic chemicals.

Debating leather versus non-leather

Some people refuse to eat food produced from animals and some of those also refuse to wear clothes made from animal products such as leather, fur, reptile skins, and even wool. The main reasons are that they feel that:

- ✔ Animal-based products involve the premature death or injury of an animal, so are therefore inherently cruel.

- ✔ The global demand for some animal-based products is greater than supply so the animals themselves are in danger of disappearing.

- ✔ Modern methods of manufacturing leather goods in factories use similar high levels of energy that other mass-produced products use, whereas the true green way to make leather is using natural dyes and drying skins in the sun.

It's quite hard to find green alternatives to leather and fur. The increasing number of cruelty-free and vegetarian clothing stores that sell alternative products are made of vinyl, PVC, and other chemically produced materials that have major impacts on the environment – use big quantities of oil, water, and energy, and produce high emissions of greenhouse gases.

Making a decision about what to buy is about weighing up the pros and cons and deciding what's most important to you. The best way to be green is to buy less! See the next section, 'Buying Green Clothing', for more info.

Buying Green Clothing

When you're deciding where to buy your clothes ask yourself:

- ✔ Has the product been produced locally so that it supports the local economy and doesn't need as much fuel to transport it to the shops?
- ✔ Has the product been manufactured and produced by a company known as an ethical operator?
- ✔ Has the product been made using sustainable clothing materials, such as organic cotton, hemp, linen, or recycled materials, using non-toxic colours and dyes?

If you can answer yes to each of these questions then you are buying some of the greenest clothes around.

The more packaging and plastic bags you bring home with your new clothes the more of the world's resources you're using up and the more waste you're helping to create. Buy clothes without packaging and bring your own reusable shopping bag to the store.

You can find plenty of Web sites selling green clothes by typing 'eco-fashion' into a search engine. As a starting point, the following online sites tick the green boxes:

- ✔ American Apparel (www.americanapparel.co.uk) promotes itself as paying the highest wages in the US garment industry, as well as selling several sustainable edition lines made from organic cotton.
- ✔ Patagonia (www.patagonia.com) is a global sports apparel company that offers organic cotton products as well as fleeces made from recycled plastics.
- ✔ Ecomall (www.ecomall.com) is one of the most extensive directories of sustainable US retailers. Click on 'clothing' to find a list of sustainable clothing choices.

- People Tree offers Fair Trade and ecological fashion at `www.people tree.co.uk`.
- Howies (`www.howies.co.uk`) offers clothes from recycled cotton and denim.
- Spirit of Nature (`www.spiritofnature.co.uk`) sells baby clothes and organic clothes made from organic raw materials such as hemp, silk, and cotton.
- Terra Plana sells shoes made from vegetable tanned leather at `www.terraplana.com`.
- The Hemp Trading Company offers clothes made from hemp at `www.thtc.co.uk`.

The UK Ethical Consumer Research Association scores companies and products on their ethical and environmental impact, coming up with an Ethiscore out of 20. The higher the score a company has, the more ethical and 'green' it is. All sorts of issues are taken into account when coming up with the score, from use of chemicals to the treatment of workers. The scheme applies not just to clothing but everything you may want to buy. Take a look at their Web site `www.ethiscore.org` – a subscription and payment-based site with a few free pages available for some products, including trainers.

If you want to buy alternatives to leather, try:

- Vegetarian Shoes UK – `www.vegetarian-shoes.co.uk`
- Moo Shoes (Vegan Shoes NYC) – `www.mooshoes.com`
- Alternative Outfitters, US – `www.alternativeoutfitters.com`
- PETA (People for Ethical Treatment of Animals) Mall – `www.petamall.com`
- Vegan of Light, US – `www.cafepress.com/veganoflight`
- Glamourpuss, Sydney – `www.glamourpuss.com.au`
- Vegan Store – `www.veganstore.co.uk`
- Vegan Wares, Melbourne – `www.veganwares.com`

Yearning for Vintage Clothes

One way to reduce the number of new clothes you cause to be manufactured is to buy clothes from the past. Lots of good-quality clothes in market stalls and second-hand, vintage, and charity shops fit the bill for something different. The retailers are trying to get in on the act by producing designs that look like they're old but they're not likely to be made from the greenest of materials so the older versions are better from an environmental point of view.

The great thing about becoming a vintage clothes convert is that it fits quite nicely within the three Rs model of reducing, reusing, and recycling. Even though many vintage clothes are made from unsustainable materials, at least keeping these clothes in the supply and demand loop reduces the demand for manufacturers to supply a new stock of unsustainable clothes – and keeps that groovy 1970s polyester shirt out of the landfill a while longer.

Raid your older relatives' wardrobes. There may be all sorts of gems there that no longer fit their owners but that you can remodel or alter to fit you.

DIY clothing tips

About.com offers great advice on caring for clothing and salvaging old clothes at `http://frugalliving.about.com/od/caringforclothing`. I picked out some of the more sustainable tips for clothing care:

✔ Avoid using a clothes dryer and dry your clothes naturally. Constantly drying clothes in a machine shrinks the clothes and wears them out very quickly. Actually, washing as often as the population tends to do doesn't help either – wash only when you need to and only when you have a full load.

✔ Wash thick clothes like socks and pullovers inside out – it revitalises them.

✔ Use lukewarm or cold water in your wash to help retain the shape and colour of your clothes, especially those made from cotton.

✔ Pre-treat stains immediately – it makes it easier for the stain to come out in the wash. Rubbing some normal bathroom or basin soap on the stain and scrubbing the stain with your hands is as effective a measure as anything.

If you know the difference between a sewing machine and a tailor, you can extend the life of some garments using these tips:

✔ Turn worn collars by taking the collar off carefully, turning it around and stitching it back on.

✔ Convert long trousers into shorts (especially for kids who get holes in the knees) by cutting off the legs just before the knee and sewing a hem.

✔ Use patches either on top or behind holes in your clothes to keep the garment together for longer. Sew-on patches are much more effective than iron-on patches.

✔ Re-jig clothes that are just too far gone as cooking aprons, cleaning cloths, washers, dusting rags, shoe polishers, and anything else where you have an application for a rag inside the home. And make sure that you save any buttons, zips, elastic, or trims for use in repairing other clothes.

These are all common sense approaches that your grandparents employed as second nature because there wasn't so much money around for new clothes. Now they're part of a greener lifestyle – but life's still too short to darn socks!

As with any fashion, what vintage clothes are in demand changes with the seasons and the other designs around on the high street. Most shoppers like to mix and match their vintage buys with current fashion items.

Good clothes bought today will last long enough to be the vintage buys of the future. If you buy fewer, better-quality items instead of many cheaper items you'll be helping to reduce the amount of clothing produced in the long run.

A quick search of the Internet shows you that there is a growing number of vintage clothes retailers on the Net. The only trouble is working out which ones are selling authentic used clothes and which ones are selling clothes made to look like vintage clothes.

Try charity shops and markets, and online auction sites. Enter 'vintage fashion' on a search engine and you'll find dozens of shops – some of which may be in your area.

When you go looking for vintage clothes take along any you'd like to get rid of. You may be able to sell them to the same shop you buy from or arrange a trade-in.

Disposing of Clothing

Most clothes no longer in fashion end up in the household waste and go from there to landfill sites. Despite the proliferation of charity shops, only around a fifth of old clothes are donated to charity – either directly to the shops or through one of the increasing numbers of clothes banks springing up alongside glass and paper recycling facilities. Many items that go to clothes banks are bought by private companies that give the designated charity a donation and sell the clothes on to developing countries.

You may feel pleased that clothes you've finished with get a second life in another country where people can't afford to follow fashion, but often these clothes are unsuitable for the climate or culture of the country they end up in. Plus, by sending these cast-offs abroad the textile industries of those countries can be seriously undercut and destroyed – forcing local manufacturers to close down.

In the meantime, the clothes that don't get to other countries or recycled through charity shops are degrading in landfill sites. Some – like tights and other items made with high proportions of nylon – can take hundreds of years to break down and disappear, and toxic chemicals that were used in the production can leach out into the soil and nearby water sources. The UK is also running out of space for landfill.

Chapter 9

Banking on Your Ethics

*I*t isn't only at home, in the garden, while shopping, and travelling that you can lead a green lifestyle. What you do with your money can affect the planet and its people, and you can invest in such as way as to make sure you do no harm and possibly even do some good. Investing and saving in financial products that claim to benefit the planet and other people is usually called ethical investing.

What matters to some people and to them is ethical will differ from what others feel is ethical. Some savers may want to avoid any products that harm the environment but won't necessarily decide to boycott a company that doesn't pay its workers well. Other savers may be more concerned about how a firm treats it producers and employees than about any damage it causes the environment. It's up to you to decide where your own priorities lie and make your money decisions accordingly.

Making Your Money Greener

Your money has power. You can choose to buy only the green and ethical products such as those mentioned throughout this book, and as consumer demand for these products grows, more producers switch to green production methods, putting more green products on the shelves. A happy by-product is that cost comes down, bringing green products within the financial reach of more people.

You have power too by choosing carefully what *not* to spend your money on – by boycotting goods, services, and products you believe are doing harm to the planet or to the people involved in the manufacturing and production processes. If enough consumers boycott a product, the firm selling it may be forced to change its practices to benefit the planet and the people involved in the production.

Although the managers of your bank, building society, pension fund, or investment fund invest and handle your money for you, you have the choice of simply letting them get on with it and taking no interest in where your money is invested or you can be quite clear about the types of investments you want your money used for. If you take the first approach your money may be invested in firms that harm the environment or treat producers unfairly; if you take the second approach you can make sure that it is invested in companies that protect the environment or their workers. The choice is yours. Think carefully about what you do and do not want your money used for and take ethical financial advice.

By all means, take the time to review your banking, savings, and investment accounts. Do an audit to find out what exactly your money is currently invested in and how ethical those funds and companies are. And if they're not green enough to suit you, move your money to a place or product that is.

Considering Ethical Accounts

One way to use your money ethically is to keep it in green accounts. You can talk to your branch about a green account as you would about any other savings or current account. Ask about their codes of business ethics and social and environmental policies.

Keep in mind that some banks may offer the odd ethically sound account but ignore green and ethical issues in the rest of their business dealings. You want to know that your bank is behaving ethically as well as using your money ethically.

Some banks and building societies are waking up to the fact that their savers are concerned about the planet and the good of the people, creatures, and plants living on it. If your own bank or building society can't give you a green version of the kind of account you're looking for, whether that's a cash account where you can take money out of an ATM (Automated Telling Machine) or an ISA (Individual Savings Account), move your money to one that can. Make it clear that you are moving your money because you want a green account.

Building societies are mutual organisations run for the good of the members rather than for the benefit of shareholders, so your building society is less likely than banks are to invest in firms that trade in arms or in countries run by oppressive regimes.

Apart from the high street names, you can try the places in the following list for green accounts:

- The **Co-operative Bank** has been describing itself as green or ethical for many years. It's part of the co-operative movement in the UK which includes the Co-op shops, insurance, and funeral services.

  The bank's Web site at www.co-operativebank.co.uk has a section called *Ethics in Action*, which describes its policy. That policy includes not lending to firms that damage the environment; are involved in the arms trade, genetic modification, or animal testing; or have a poor record in human rights and employment practices.

- **Smile** is the Internet banking arm of the Co-operative Bank and if you open particular accounts with Smile it makes a donation to charity. You can find more information at www.smile.co.uk.

- **Triodos Bank** describes itself as one of Europe's leading ethical banks and guarantees that your money will be used to finance only businesses and charities that benefit people and the environment. For example, opening a *Wildlife Saver Account* helps protect some of the UK's wildlife habitats.

  In the UK, Triodos has links with The Soil Association and Friends of the Earth among other green organisations. You can find more information about how it all works on the bank's Web site at www.triodos.co.uk.

- The **Ecology Building Society** uses money invested in it to fund mortgages on energy-efficient homes, green renovation and green enterprises that have low impact on the environment. Its own headquarters is built from straw bales with photovoltaic panels and a turf roof – all earth-friendly, energy-conserving materials. You can see pictures on the Web site at www.ecology.co.uk, where you can find information on the various projects it's involved in.

Because they're listed here doesn't mean that I'm recommending these institutions; I'm just offering them as places that can give you an idea of how green banking works.

It's also worth thinking about some of the Islamic accounts available through the Islamic Bank of Britain, or high street banks like Lloyds TSB. There's more on how these work in the upcoming section 'Taking the interest out of banking'.

Ethical or green banking is growing in popularity and so more accounts will come on stream. As with any other kind of accounts, shop around to get the one that best suits both your banking needs and your ethical concerns.

Because green ethics are not always black and white choices and implementation of green investing varies with each banking institution, you may find that you need to prioritise what matters most to you about a green account. After investigating your options, for example, you may realise you want to work with a particular institution because even if it doesn't measure up on every front, it is committed to change and gives you an opportunity to have a voice in those coming changes.

Investing in Ethical Financial Products

People just like you currently have around £4 billion invested in the ethical market in the UK. These investment funds operate on the principle of not investing money in any enterprise that would harm the environment, people around the world, or animals and wildlife – and some actively encourage progressive green companies. The idea is that the money you deposit with the institution is invested only in green firms.

Most financial institutions offer a few ethical or green investments, pensions, life insurance, and savings, and some also offer green mortgages, which are explained in 'Borrowing for Green Homes', later in this chapter. As demand for green and ethical products grows, more and more are becoming available.

These investments are called SRIs (Socially Responsible Investments) or Ethical Investments.

Pay attention to where the money you put into any investment fund goes and how it's being used. For example, if you invest in an ethical unit trust, your money is pooled with that of other investors and used to buy shares in companies that have a good track record of looking after their employees and the environment. As in a standard unit trust, you make money as the values of the shares grow.

You can choose to invest in light green or dark green funds. The greener the fund, the stricter the rules governing what that fund can be invested in and the more green the companies invested in – for example, a fund where the only rule is that it won't invest in firms involved in animal testing isn't as green as one which won't invest in firms involved in animal testing or companies that produce harmful pesticides.

The Ethical Investment Research Service (EIRIS) is a charity that provides independent research into the behaviour of thousands of different companies. The Web site at www.eiris.org has a directory of ethical investment advisers and a frequently asked questions section that gives you useful information on ethical investment. You can check with it to see how green companies are before you decide whether or not you want your money invested in their operations.

Greening your pension

The most likely way for most people to invest is through their pension funds. Some of these have ethical policies and some don't, but trustees for UK company pension funds have to tell you whether yours has such a policy and if so what it is. Ask for a copy of the *Statement of Investment Principles* relating to your fund and find out what the ethical, social, or environmental considerations are.

You can have an influence on how your pension fund invests your money and can transfer your pension contributions to one of the socially responsible funds.

If you don't belong to a company pension scheme and are setting up your own stakeholder pension or personal pension plan, shop around for a fund that meets your ethical principles, but be warned that there aren't as many to choose from as with regular pension funds. Try the big pension providers and take advice from an independent financial adviser who specialises in ethical investments.

Get good financial advice before making any decision about where to put your money.

Staking your money on ethical stocks

If you hold company shares directly, ask those companies about their business ethics and find out if they produce a social or environmental report.

You can invest in ethical index funds on an ethical exchange, and by buying shares and investing in companies with strong corporate social responsibility, you can encourage and support them. Another way to make businesses greener is to buy shares in companies that need to change so that you can attempt to have your voice heard and influence the company's behaviour through shareholder meetings and your voting rights.

The *FTSE4Good* is a stock market index listing firms that have particularly ethical trading policies. Some investment funds track that index – so if the value of the shares in the index as a whole goes up your investment is worth more. *Ethex* is an ethical stock exchange where investors can buy and sell shares in ethical companies such as Fairtrade companies, explained in the upcoming 'Looking at lending practices' section.

The value of your investments can go up or down – there are no guarantees. Even if a company's shares have done well in the past that doesn't mean its share values will continue to go up in future. You're taking a gamble so don't gamble with money you can't afford to lose. That goes for any stock market investment – ethical or not. And ethical investments don't always give you as good a return as non-ethical ones. Shares in companies that manufacture drugs, tobacco, and arms often perform better. You may have to pay for your green principles.

If you want to invest in ethical companies through the stock market take advice from a stockbroker who understands the ethical markets. There's information on how to get in touch with one in the upcoming section 'Finding Green Financial Advice'.

Investing in insurance

You can even find ethical insurance policies if you look hard enough. Talk to your current insurance provider, and shop around by calling other companies, enlisting the services of an insurance broker, or contacting the Ethical Investment Research Service (EIRIS). There's more information on its Web site at www.eiris.org.

An ethical insurance firm may fund environmental or animal welfare projects. One example for pet lovers is Animal Friends Insurance (www.animal friends.org.uk), a not-for-profit organisation that uses any money it makes to help animals in need around the world. Examples of some of the projects it has helped are The Gambia Horse and Donkey Trust, the Born Free foundation, and The Philippine Dog Rescue, as well as various projects in the UK.

Choosing an Ethical Institution

When it comes to investing your money you have to decide which financial institutions and products match up to your own standards on what's green or ethical. You may want to save through a mainstream high street organisation and be more interested in the countries it invests in than whether or not it deals with firms that use child labour, or you may prefer a lender that doesn't deal with firms that pollute or damage the environment. You may want to shun the big banks and building societies in favour of the kinds of organisations that offer special investments to people with particular faiths and beliefs or that invest at a local level. Shop around, ask what each organisation's ethical or green policy is, and consider all the alternatives before coming to your decision.

Looking at lending practices

The biggest impact any bank or building society makes is through its lending policy. If it doesn't have an ethical lending policy it may lend to businesses that trade arms, harm the environment, and exploit workers.

Even if you don't have any savings and simply need a bank to have your salary paid into and to pay your bills from, be sure you're happy with that bank's lending policies. If not, move your account and tell your bank why. If you have savings, choose a bank or building society that won't lend them to any organisations you disapprove of.

An example of an ethical lending organisation is Shared Interest (www.shared-interest.com), a co-operative lending society that aims to reduce poverty in the world by providing fair and just financial services. It pools your investment with money from other savers to facilitate fair-trade practices in which producers are paid a fair amount for their labour and products. (Chapter 7 talks in detail about this.)

Shared Interest works with fair-trade businesses all over the world, both producers and buyers, providing credit so that producers get paid in advance and can therefore afford to produce their goods and make a better living for themselves and their families.

Taking the interest out of banking

Whether or not you're Muslim you may find that the ethics of Islamic banking suit your needs. Basically the charging and paying out of interest on accounts and investments is forbidden. You make money on your savings because they're put to work in real transactions. Your money is used to buy a real stake in a company and as that company makes money you get a share of the profits. The companies invested in have to conform to Islamic beliefs, so you're assured that you won't invest in firms that produce tobacco, alcohol, or pornography, for example.

If you borrow to buy a home, the bank buys the home for you, and you pay rent to the bank each month plus a bit extra to buy a share of the property. Gradually you own more and more of the home until it's all yours.

You can't get an overdraft on a current account or receive interest through an Islamic bank.

Islamic financial products are mainly available through the Islamic Bank of Britain but other high street banks are getting in on the act with their own versions. Lloyds TSB has an Islamic current account and Islamic mortgage in England and Wales, and is launching an Islamic student account. HSBC bank offers Islamic home insurance policies and there are more Islamic accounts coming on stream from other banks. Shop around as with any other account to find the one that suits you best.

Banking on an alternative

Banks and building societies aren't the only places for your money. *Credit unions* are financial co-operatives owned and controlled by their members. They offer savings and great-value loans plus they are local, more likely to follow ethical guidelines, and know what their members want.

Members of each credit union have some sort of *common bond* which determines who can join it. They may work for the same company, live in the same area, or belong to the same club, church, or trade union. Members save at least a certain amount regularly and once you have more than the threshold in the credit union, you can apply for a loan. Credit unions usually offer a cheaper rate than a bank loan and there are no hidden charges or penalties for repaying the loan early.

The idea of credit unions is people helping other people. If someone's in debt, the credit union may be able to give him or her a loan to help that person get out of debt. Credit unions can help when banks can't or won't. You may find that you can borrow from your credit union to adapt your home to be more green.

There are almost 400 credit unions in the UK with around 400,000 members in total, holding about £380 million in savings with another £350 million out on loan. The Association of British Credit Unions Ltd (ABCUL) is the main trade association for credit unions and there's information, including how to start one up, the rules for running one, and a list of existing credit unions on the Web site at www.abcul.org.

Borrowing for Green Homes

If you want to build a green home, buy and renovate a derelict building to become a green home, or to adapt your own home to be more green, the chances are you'll need a *mortgage* – a loan secured against the property concerned.

Few high street lenders are geared specifically to deal with green projects but many are willing to lend money to buy, build, or renovate a property as you like. Be patient and shop around. Talk to your own lender and if there are objections and obstacles try to negotiate. Lenders are always concerned about the degree of risk they're taking and whether they'll get their money back if you can't keep up the repayments. Talk to a mortgage broker about where to try for a loan if you draw a blank.

You may be able to negotiate a staged loan so that the lender agrees to give you a certain amount of money in total but releases proportions of the total when various stages of the work are complete.

Applying for a green mortgage

Another option is a loan from a lender that offers green mortgages – loans specifically geared for green buildings. A *green mortgage* is a loan given on a home built or renovated in such a way that it reduces the negative impact it and its occupants have on the environment. Usually a green mortgage is granted only for a home that's green itself.

Although interest in all things green is gradually reaching the high street, only three lenders at the time of writing offer green mortgages: the Co-operative Bank (www.co-operativebank.co.uk), the Norwich & Peterborough Building Society (www.npbs.co.uk), and the Ecology Building Society (www.ecology.co.uk). All three lenders support reforestation schemes, so when you take out mortgages with them, you're helping the environment. However, they all have different criteria on who they will lend to and the types of buildings they will lend on. Most lenders will not work with businesses that are known to pollute or damage the environment in any way. The lenders that offer green mortgages often contribute to charities that support the environment or that look after the welfare of people who need help.

If you want to borrow a green mortgage try the British Insurance Brokers' Association at www.biba.org.uk or on 0870 950 1790.

Your green mortgage may cost you more than an ordinary mortgage in terms of interest charged.

In some cases when you take on a green mortgage the lender does an audit of the energy efficiency of your home to monitor your household emissions and energy usage. You can benefit from the knowledge that you are causing less damage to the environment, and you can save money on your electricity and gas bills!

You may be able to remortgage your home through a green mortgage if you can convince the lender that your home is green enough or that you will make it green enough.

Getting loans for green conversions

Chapter 3 talks about some of the steps you can take to produce some of the energy your home uses by harnessing solar or wind power, or adding solar panels. That chapter also points you towards some of the grants available to help you finance these modifications. However, those grants are unlikely to cover all the costs.

If you need to borrow more money to top up any grant, try borrowing from your bank or building society. The three financial institutions which offer green mortgages (mentioned in the preceding section) may be able to lend for your home improvement, but you may be also able to convince some of the high street lenders to lend for that purpose even though they don't specifically offer green loans.

Renovating old properties to green properties

Renovating old properties such as barns, lighthouses, or other derelict buildings to make homes is very green. You are using existing sites and in most cases some existing building materials. Lenders of green mortgages (see the previous section 'Applying for a Green Mortgage') – the Ecology Building Society in particular – are very keen on projects that get derelict properties back into use. They see it as a form of recycling. Talk to your own bank or building society about the possibility of a loan for this kind of work and if they turn you down, try the main green lenders.

Doing Without Cash

Money may make the world go round but it isn't always necessary. You can make things happen without cash and as a result become involved in community-based projects that are more sustainable, ethically sound, and greener than relying on money.

Trading in LETS (Local Exchange Trading Systems or Schemes)

LETS are local networks in which people exchange all kinds of goods and services with one another. No money changes hands. LETS are based in local communities and use alternative currencies to the pound. For example, if your skill is in furniture making and you make a table for someone, you get a certain number points in whatever your scheme's currency is called. You can then use some of those points to pay someone to do some babysitting for you. Schemes like this encourage less buying of new products and more sharing so they make less impact on the environment.

There are hundreds of LETS schemes around the UK. You can get information on how schemes work in more detail and how to set one up in your area from www.letslinkuk.net.

Sharing in time banks

TimeBank is a scheme whereby local people volunteer to share their time and skills. Instead of giving money, use your skills to do something for someone else and deposit your time in the bank. You can then make a withdrawal from the time bank when you need someone to spend time doing something for you. A timekeeper adds up the time spent and matches people up to help as they need it – and no payments change hands.

Everyone's time is equal: one hour of time earns one time credit to spend when needed regardless of what you spend that hour doing.

You can get more information from TimeBank UK (www.timebank.org.uk), the national charity that links and supports time banks across the country by providing inspiration, guidance, and practical help. TimeBank appeals to people who know that their time and skills are in demand but just don't know what to do about it or where to start.

Giving Ethically

If you want to give away some of your hard-earned income, thousands of charities are only too eager to accept it. Choose your charity carefully to match your environmental, ethical, and green priorities. You can give to local housing projects or to clean-water projects in remote parts of the world. Whatever your principles, there's sure to be a charity to match.

You may want to do some research by calling a charity's head office to find out how much of the money you give ends up invested in the project you've picked and how much goes in administration.

Below you'll find some of the many different ways to give and to make sure that the money arrives in the right place.

- ✔ **Charity greetings cards** are very popular as you don't have to make any regular commitment to giving. You'll find them in the charity's own shops or at Christmas in branches of supermarkets, department stores, special Christmas shops, and newsagents.

- ✔ **Affinity or charity credit cards** give a small percentage of your spending – usually around a quarter of 1 per cent – to charity.

  For example, The Royal Bank of Scotland offers customers the option to support the Royal National Lifeboats Institute or the Woodland Trust. Customers of the Bank of Scotland can donate to Mencap, Cancer Research UK (Scotland), or the Scottish Society for the Prevention of Cruelty to Animals, and Nationwide's card benefits Comic Relief.

  Charity and affinity cards often charge you a higher rate of interest on your spending than conventional credit cards.

- ✔ A **direct debit scheme** transfers the amount you designate from your bank account to the charity of your choice each month.

  You can also give through work. Your donation is taken directly from your salary and paid straight to the charity. And because you don't pay tax on that amount, it's tax-efficient as well.

When it comes to giving gifts to friends and relatives you can be green about that too. Chapter 9 offers some thoughts on the kinds of green presents you can buy if you want to give someone something they can use. The other way of giving green gifts is to give money to a project or to buy something in your friend's name that is used to benefit someone in need elsewhere in the world.

Over recent years there's been a big increase in that kind of ethical giving. You can give money for a goat, donkey, chickens, sheep, trees, guide dogs, wheelchairs, bicycles, school equipment, and water filters. The charity running the scheme gives you a card or certificate showing that the money has been given on behalf of your family member or friend, and you give that person the card showing what's been donated in their name.

A gift of this sort ticks all the boxes – it helps someone, is green, doesn't damage the environment, and there's no need to fret for weeks about what to buy someone. It's appropriate for nearly every occasion: holidays, birthdays, weddings, graduations, and so on. And there's no wasteful wrapping paper either!

Finding Green Financial Advice

Get investment advice from a financial adviser who specialises in socially responsible investment (SRI). Specialist advisers offer all the services of a mainstream adviser, but can also advise you on aligning your financial plans with your values and beliefs.

The Ethical Investment Association is a group of financial advisers from around the UK who promote ethical and socially responsible investment, and have agreed to a code of conduct. Their Web site at www.ethicalinvestment.org.uk has a list of members as well as information on ethical investments.

If you're looking for an Independent Financial Adviser (IFA) in your area to advise you on green investments, the Association of Independent Financial Advisers is on 020 7628 1287 or www.unbiased.co.uk. EIRIS – the Ethical Investment Research Service – also has a directory of ethical investment advisers on its Web site at www.eiris.org. It can also give you details of IFAs who can act as brokers. If you want to invest in green stocks and shares ask your financial adviser whether he or she can help or can recommend a stockbroker who understands the green markets, or contact the Association of Private Client Investment Managers and Stockbrokers, APCIMS, on 020 7247 7080 or at www.apcims.co.uk.

Part IV
Thinking Green Outside the Home

'... and this little piggy walked
all the way to school.'

In this part . . .

1t's not only in the home that you can be greener. Green living is about changing the way you and other people think and changing their habits.

A whole range of green projects goes on in schools from recycling to growing vegetables for the school canteens, from walking buses where parents take turns to walk dozens of children to and from the school gates, to worm farms. When children are involved they spread green thinking into their own communities. At work adults are more set in their ways. It can be more difficult to get them walking or cycling to work or the station and using public transport. Think about it. If your office is buying paper it might as well be recycled paper and if you take waste bins out and put recycling bins into the workplace recycling becomes second nature. This part deals with spreading the green word to classmates and colleagues.

Chapter 10

Implementing Ideas for a Greener Working Environment

*L*ike most people, you want the firm you work for to be more environmentally aware but even if you're green at home you may do very little in the workplace to protect the environment. Part of the problem is that workplace systems are set up by the time you get there and getting those systems changed can take so long you forget you ever suggested it. You may feel that you don't have enough control to effect change. This chapter is here to say that you can make a difference, so don't give up.

Your employer may have to abide by laws on the environment. Things like the handling of effluent, storing and disposing of chemicals, and dealing with packaging are subject to regulations, depending on the size and type of business. The government's business advice service and the Environment Agency both have details. You can check out their websites on www.businesslink.gov.uk and www.environment-agency.gov.uk. But the best businesses think ahead. As tighter regulations come into force they are already following the best practice, with policies on carbon emissions and carbon offsetting (see Chapter 1) already in place. You can help make that happen.

Simply talking to your work colleagues about green issues and how to reduce the impact you make on the planet can bear fruit. Get together with workmates and look at ways to change things and then go to the boss with your suggestions. Being green can cut business costs and if you present it as a cost-cutting exercise from the beginning you may well get the boss on side.

Of course, if you telecommute or work for yourself, you have control over how green you are in your own workspace. If you have to go into an office to work, take your green principles with you and work on making them part of the work culture.

Convincing Your Company to Change Its Ways

Ask not what your company can do for you but what you can do for your company! Greening your workplace just takes someone – you! – to monitor the waste that goes on in your workplace, come up with the solutions, and talk to the powers that be about the best ways to change things. You may find you've added to your workload because you get the job of implementing the changes, but at least you'll know that you're doing your bit.

Change has to come with commitment from the top, so get the bosses on your side, keeping in mind that employers don't want you to go to them with problems – only solutions. Your bosses may not have the time or knowledge to get to grips with any shortcomings in the greenness of the building and workspace and may welcome your help.

Companies are now more willing to make changes because they know that they can make savings in energy costs and improve productivity from their staff. And in truth, most changes don't involve spending a lot of money and can even save the business money.

Suggest that someone from one of the following organisations comes in to your workplace and recommends how to improve it.

- ✔ The Green Business Network offers support to businesses putting green policies in place – www.greenbusinessnetwork.org.uk.
- ✔ Envirowise is a government organisation that advises businesses on minimising waste at work – www.envirowise.gov.uk.
- ✔ WRAP, the Waste & Resources Action Programme, funded by the government, can also help – www.wrap.org.uk.

Being green means looking after people as well as the environment. Getting known as a green firm can be attractive to potential employees. In times of skills shortages, being green may give your company the edge in attracting the best staff.

Damaging the planet from the office

Most people are responsible for far more carbon emissions while they're at work than when they're at home:

✔ Nearly a tenth of all greenhouse gas emissions are produced by the commercial property in towns and cities. And these emissions are growing at the fastest rate of any sector.

✔ Heating and air conditioning systems pump the majority of greenhouse gas emissions from offices into the atmosphere and use up vast amounts of electricity.

✔ Many buildings aren't designed to reduce the amount of heat and air conditioning they use and are built from materials that don't come from renewable sources.

✔ Office buildings have an insatiable appetite for electricity to power lighting, air conditioning, computers, printers, and photocopiers. Equipment can be left on 24 hours a day, seven-days a week – even when there's no one working there.

✔ Offices consume vast amounts of paper. Even with more offices recycling a large amount of paper, waste still goes to landfill sites or incinerators.

✔ Apart from paper there's all the other waste including equipment of all sorts, especially computers. Companies regularly upgrade their equipment to be competitive.

✔ Many of the traffic jams in towns and cities are full of people trying to get to work – wasting time and polluting the atmosphere.

Making Your Office Greener

To make your workplace greener, you use the same green principles and methods as you do at home. Chapters 3 and 4 offer dozens of tips that you can apply to the workplace:

✔ Set up a complete recycling system – for bottles, cans, photocopier cartridges, and plastic. Reuse anything that can be reused, such as CDs, and recycle the rest.

✔ Recycle paper. This happens in most offices, but you can push to get the best possible use out of it by using both sides of paper to print on and using scrap paper to leave each other notes instead of buying those sticky note pads.

✔ Make sure that all equipment is turned off at the end of the day rather than left on standby. Last person out turns out the lights, or get an electrician to put them on a timer that switches them off when there's been no movement in a room for a certain amount of time.

✔ Change your electricity supplier to one that provides green electricity generated from a renewable source. Chapter 3 has more details.

✔ Sort out the kitchen with a fridge and a kettle instead of the flashy drinks machine that uses cartridges and polystyrene cups. Recycle polystyrene cups – Save a Cup at `www.save-a-cup.co.uk` collects them and has them recycled into stationery that you can buy back for the office.

✔ Campaign for office coffee and tea to come from Fairtrade and organic producers.

✔ Give everyone their own mug and remind them to save electricity by not boiling up more water in the kettle than they need each time.

✔ Keep tap water in bottles in the fridge rather than using a vast supply of plastic containers that have to be delivered and collected.

✔ Offices are often too hot so turn the thermostat down and ask people to wear sweaters or jackets rather than heating the place up to the temperature for shirt sleeves.

✔ Change the air conditioning unit to fans which are quieter and use less energy. Direct them where the cooling power is needed rather than reducing the temperature of areas that don't need it. Keep the blinds down when the sun is blazing through the windows.

Talk to your local authority about the recycling facilities it offers, over and above the domestic bottle and paper bins, and ask if there are any grants available for taking energy efficiency measures.

Encouraging green travel

Set up a car-sharing scheme so that employees can make arrangements to travel in and home with each other. In addition, set aside space in the car park for secure parking for bikes and ask the boss for a shower and lockers so that people can cycle in.

Look carefully at the amount of travelling people do in the business. Get a videoconferencing facility and cut down on travelling to meetings. If you do have to travel, change from planes to trains. Using public transport such as trains and buses means that your journeys are responsible for fewer carbon emissions than using a car and flying is the most environmentally damaging way to travel – there's more information in Chapters 12 and 14. When you take into account the time for check-in, security checks, and collecting baggage you may find there's little difference in terms of time taken out of the working day.

Greening the building itself

Having taken stock of all the things that are easily sorted out in the office, turn your attention to the building itself and see what you can do to make it more energy efficient – it will be money well spent in the long run.

Actions to take include:

- ✓ Switch to highly rated energy-efficient appliances.
- ✓ Make sure that heating and air conditioning systems are regularly serviced and have timers fitted so that they're in use only when people are in the office.
- ✓ Install water-saving taps, showerheads, and dual flush toilets.
- ✓ Install screens and shutters on windows to block out direct sun during summer and reduce the need for air conditioning, and to let sun and light in during winter. Both these steps can reduce energy costs – less electricity is used to cool the premises in summer and to heat the premises in winter.
- ✓ Invest in furniture made from natural or recycled materials and paint and equip the office with as many non-toxic materials as possible (natural paints, less plastic, floorboards rather than carpet, and so on). CABE (the Commission for Architecture and the Built Environment) has information on its Web site at www.cabe.org.uk.

People are likely to respond to these changes positively if they feel they're being made for the good of the planet rather than just as an inconvenient cost-cutting exercise. Get them involved. Make someone responsible for each aspect of the firm's green policy.

Check the rate of illness in the building. If it is generally high it may have something to do with the poor air circulation in the building. A better working environment cuts absence due to sickness.

Buying greener

You buy green goods for your home (about which there's more in Chapter 4) and you can extend that principle to the workplace. There's little point in being green enough to recycle paper but buying paper that isn't produced from recycled materials.

Encourage your bosses to buy from green suppliers selling green products for office necessities such as paper.

Before going out and buying new, apply the green basics of reusing, repairing, and recycling, whether you're buying a new piece of machinery, paper, loo roll, or paint.

- ✔ Check whether the business already has something that would do the job.
- ✔ Hire what you need instead of buying new.
- ✔ Look for a version that has as much recycled material in it as possible.
- ✔ Go for an option with as little packaging as possible.
- ✔ Buy the most energy-efficient product you can find that will last as long as possible.
- ✔ Make sure that equipment can be serviced and repaired so that it has as long a life span as possible.
- ✔ Think about disposal issues – consider what happens when the item is used up, no longer needed, or can no longer be repaired.

Buy from local companies to reduce the number of miles goods have to be transported and therefore the amount of fuel it takes to get them to your workplace.

Word spreads in the business world and the more demand there is from companies for green products the more there are for sale and prices come down. As your firm is going greener it buys from suppliers that are going greener too and in order to get your business the green ethos will spread.

Being green means being fair to people as well as the environment so when you buy green products remember to be fair about paying your suppliers on time.

Going paperless

Back in the 1970s, there was excitement about the office of the future, where technology would improve to such an extent that no one would need to use paper. If you look around your office today you'll probably find reams of paper waiting to be used for photocopying and printing; piles of used paper in the printers – printed off and forgotten about; a full recycling bin; shelves with files full of paper; and desks piled high with papers relating to work in hand. Internet and e-mail don't seem to have helped reduce the paper used.

People send e-mails and then print them off so that they have a paper trail, or e-mail reports and send out hard copies. The more advanced the technology the more demand there seems to be for paper. The more people are able to exchange information, the greater demand for paper.

From a green perspective, reducing the amount of paper you use is a priority. Paper is originally produced from trees, which are a declining natural resource, and much of it goes to waste. That means not only the wood is wasted but the chemicals and energy that went into processing the paper.

More paper is being recycled than ever before but the process of recycling paper uses energy – which is saved if less paper is used. Not to mention the amount of steel saved, as you don't need paper clips!

Even though the idea of the completely paperless office seems to be fairly unrealistic, technology allows you to greatly reduce the amount of paper you use at work. The younger you are the more comfortable you're likely to be with reading information on your computer screen, hand-held computer, and even mobile phone. The more you use a computer, the more likely you are to edit material without printing it off and using a pen. The more you trust the technology, the less likely you are to have a paper filing system to back up your computer filing systems. Use the technology – forget the paper:

- ✔ E-mail and Internet access is a necessity, with advances in technology also enabling people and companies to combine e-mail with fax and voice-mail retrieval.

- ✔ Portable and mobile PCs, laptops, and hand-helds are great for down-loading documents and reading or working on wherever you are and are just as portable as paper.

- ✔ Scanners are great for getting images onto a network or computer so that documents can be exchanged electronically and copied into reports.

- ✔ Online storage systems enable centralised electronic information management on a network that everyone in the company can access. These help replace hard-copy filing systems.

- ✔ Make sure that people have remote access to the company network so they can work from home or another remote location without taking a heap of documents home with them.

- ✔ Make the next printer one that can print on both sides of a sheet so you can reduce your paper use even further.

If you can't go paperless, buy recycled paper from local businesses to cut down the energy used producing new paper, and save trees and fuel in transportation.

Telecommuting Cuts More Than Petrol Costs

Telecommuting is a system in which employees or contractors connect to work via a computer from home or another remote location, thus reducing that person's need to commute to work – hence the term *telecommuting*. Companies tend to offer telecommuting on a part-time basis, with employees working from home one or two days a week.

Telecommuting is attractive for a variety of reasons:

✔ You can be more productive, as working from home means you can concentrate better on your job without answering phone calls and dealing with other distractions in your workplace.

✔ You feel trusted by your bosses to get on with it and it gives you the flexibility to look after anyone at home who needs a bit of help during the day – children or elderly parents, for example. As long as your work gets done – on time – you have more control.

✔ Bosses can cut their overheads because they don't have to cater for the needs of all their employees five days a week. If some staff telecommute several days a week, the bosses can reduce the number of desks, the size of the office, the amount of stationery, and the amount of parking.

✔ Telecommuting gives a greater range of people job opportunities. If you are the principal carer for children or other relatives or can't physically travel to work, telecommuting may allow you to become part of the workforce again.

If there's no telecommuting in your office, it may be that the bosses haven't thought of it as an option. If you'd like to give it a try come up with a plan as to how it would work and use the arguments in the preceding list to help win them over.

Some jobs and some people are simply not suited to telecommuting. Many jobs require face-to-face contact and some people don't have the discipline and personality to be as productive as they would be in the office.

Reducing transport trips

Telecommuting not only has benefits for the employer and employee but also for the community and the environment. The main selling point from an environmental point of view is that it cuts down the number of home-to-work trips during weekday rush hours. If these trips are normally by car, traffic congestion and air pollution are reduced as well as fuel consumption.

Telecommuting used along with workplace travel plans that encourage use of public transport, walking, and cycling, and car-sharing schemes plus workplace parking restrictions have real potential for getting employees to leave their cars in the garage.

Employers can lend employees cycles and cycling safety equipment and there's no tax or National Insurance to be paid on those perks. More information is available on Her Majesty's Revenue and Customs Web site at www.hmrc.gov.uk/green-transport/travel-plans.

Telecommuting in action

Not everyone can telecommute. Many people have to be on site so as they can be involved in meetings, have access to the right equipment, or serve the public. Even if you have a job suited to telecommuting, you may not have the right home environment. The most suitable candidates for teleworking are employees who produce discreet and generally self-contained pieces of work – project work and policy analysis, research, planning, and writing for instance. Telecommuters need to be able to work without supervision, don't need social interaction with workmates, are self-motivated, and have a trusting relationship with their manager.

If you have the job, personality, and discipline for telecommuting you also need:

- ✔ **The right computer equipment:** It makes it much easier if you have a computer that enables you to access everything at work as if you were there.

- ✔ **A suitable home office environment:** You need a set-up that enables you to separate your home and work life – a separate room with a desk, an office-style chair, good lighting, no outside distractions, and room for office equipment like a printer.

- ✔ **A telecommuting agreement:** You and your boss need to outline your working time, whether you need to log on and off the network at a certain time, at what times you communicate with the office, and whether you can claim any expenses (computer and printing costs, paper, coffee, and so on).

If you're working from home most of the time, you can get left out of the loop. It's one thing avoiding all the office politics but it's less satisfying to miss out on the gossip, spontaneous outings to the pub, and the general praise when all's going well. Make sure that you stick your head around the door often enough so that you don't get forgotten!

Being Ethical as Well as Green

Being green is about protecting the environment *and* behaving ethically. Behaving ethically is about taking personal responsibility for your actions and making sure that they don't have a negative impact on the environment and the people around you and with whom you deal. When at work, that means not doing anything that's unfair to your fellow workers, customers, suppliers, and the community in which you work.

Businesses have become much more aware of the importance of ethical behaviour over the past few years. Employers have to be sure to treat their employees fairly by complying with a whole raft of employment legislation – you have to be paid at least the minimum wage, be given at least 20 days' holiday a year, and may not be sacked unfairly, for example. Your boss has to make sure that you are given a safe and healthy working environment.

In turn, you have to make sure that you don't bully your colleagues, discriminate against them because of their race or gender among other things, and that you don't behave negligently and cause them injury. Not all workplaces, employers, or employees manage to behave completely ethically all the time of course, but moving towards a greener lifestyle makes people more aware of the consequences of their actions.

Whether it's because firms are beginning to realise the business benefits of appearing to behave ethically, or that they believe in embracing the green ethos, many are beginning to take their role in the wider community more seriously too, embracing what's called *corporate social responsibility*. Corporate social responsibility is about what a business does, over and above what it has to do to comply with the law, to make sure that the operation of that business doesn't do any harm and benefits everyone around it and involved in it. You can help your bosses come up with corporate social responsibility policies for the company. There's lots of information available from the government Web site at www.csr.gov.uk or from the government's small business support service Business Link at www.businesslink.gov.uk.

Firms can encourage other businesses – such as their suppliers – to be greener, more ethical, and act in a socially responsible way. Persuade your bosses to deal with suppliers with green policies. The word soon spreads, awareness is raised, and attitudes and habits change for the better.

When you're thinking about improving your workplace by making it more green, consider the other ethical aspects too.

The business you work for is part of the local community it has its offices or factories in. There are neighbours, schools, other businesses, community projects, environmental and conservation projects, hospitals, and all the other infrastructure around it that forms the community. A truly green business makes sure that its actions don't damage that community and in some way benefit it.

If the wider community benefits from that business, the residents will be loyal to the business and the business will benefit too.

There are many different ways of contributing, some of which cost very little:

- Donate old computers to schools or community, voluntary, or charity projects.
- Send used toner cartridges to charities like Oxfam (www.oxfam.org.uk) or an organisation like www.cartridges4charity.co.uk which collects them on behalf of charities.
- Do a deal with a local charity instead of cluttering up landfill sites if the business regularly dumps products that aren't perfect.
- Ask your boss if you can spend some time away from the workplace on a voluntary basis working with a local community project.
- Set up a scheme in which someone from your workplace goes to local schools to talk to older children about business and getting into work.
- Offer local young people work experience.
- Ask employers to offer staff more flexible working hours so that they can look after relatives or do some voluntary work.

As well as contributing to the local community you may want to get your firm to look at supporting charities and organisations helping communities in other parts of the world.

Running your own green business

A green business may be involved in environmental protection but can also be any kind of business that follows green practices. When you set up a business – whether it provides eco-holidays, is an office-based call centre, organic farm, beauty salon, or a building contractor – you can build environmentally friendly policies such as those covered in this chapter.

If you're already running a business, you can't get away with ignoring the green issues. A whole raft of legislation covers how businesses of all sorts must protect the environment.

A government organisation at www.netregs. gov.uk helps you understand what the regulations require you to do on all these issues – such as what business waste can and can't go to landfill sites and what responsibilities you have for making sure that none of your business waste gets into local rivers. The Green Business Network offers support to businesses putting the law into practice – www.greenbusiness network.org.uk.

Business owners and managers often complain about all the red tape involved but when it comes to keeping your business as green as possible you find there are benefits for you as well as the environment. Recycling, energy conservation, energy-efficient office equipment, and water-saving devices all save you money by cutting your bills. Taking preventative measures to protect the environment saves the costs of expensive clean-ups when things go wrong. Getting your employees involved in making the business greener and the office and other workplaces more energy-efficient makes them feel part of the team and motivates them. The messages you send out at work regarding the environment spread and greener workplaces are likely to be healthier and safer so you lose less money through staff being off sick.

Write your green principles into your business plan – including those covered in the rest of this chapter. Keep reviewing them to take account of new technology that can improve things and cut your costs further and make employees responsible for certain aspects of your green policies so the green ethos is part of the work culture.

Chapter 11

Going Green at School

Green living is a hot topic in many schools all around the UK. Lots of primary schools in particular run green projects – a few of which are mentioned later in this chapter in the section 'Getting green ideas from other schools'. At secondary schools green issues are an integral part of citizenship, science, and geography classes. But there's no national policy on whether and how to teach about being green, so what your children learn is usually down to the individual teacher and the enthusiasm of the headteacher. This chapter looks at how you can become involved in making sure that your child's school is as green as possible and influencing its teaching by bringing your ideas to the table.

Most universities run green projects. Some of these aim to raise awareness in local schools and the wider community, some are research projects, and some involve students in working with local people to improve the local environment. If you get to university and find there's no suitable project that you can get involved in, persuade your student's union to appoint a Green Officer and set the ball rolling.

What you do in your own home to live a greener lifestyle can be translated to the school environment and what your children learn at school can be put to good use at home – everyone wins!

Reaching Kids Early

Just as the banks want to get your children to open an account with them – because they usually become customers for life – so you want to get your children interested in green issues as early as possible because they're likely to be committed for life.

Children seem to understand green issues – sometimes better than adults. They can relate to the plight of animals caught up in the havoc caused by human over-indulgence, and to the effects on children of their own age in developing countries. They readily take on board the tips they learn in school about living a greener lifestyle and put them into practice at home. Once children feel that there's something they can do to help other children less well off than themselves or to prevent further suffering to animals, they usually go to it with enthusiasm.

Children like to be able to teach their parents a thing or two as well. Give them the chance to take the lead at home – put them in charge of various aspects of your environmental policy at home and they'll love the role.

When you do something at home to make your life greener explain your reasons to your children but don't force changes on them. Lead by example and they will soon adopt your plans, whereas if you force them to be greener they may rebel.

You don't have to become a paragon of green overnight and you shouldn't expect your children to either. As the saying goes: 'How do you eat an elephant? Bite by bite!' Start with the things that are easiest to change. Every little change counts.

Getting to School

Green education can start before children even get to school. The sections here look at ecofriendly ways to travel to and from school.

Walking to school

Driving the children is a must for people who live too far away to walk or cycle. For other people, driving is just habit born of convenience. If the school is close enough to walk to, leave the car in the garage. Explain to your children that when you do short journeys in the car it doesn't warm up to run most efficiently and therefore those journeys cause most pollution. Walking is the greenest way to travel and does least damage to the environment.

Don't forget to get up a bit earlier in the mornings or the damage will be to your health through the stress of trying to get everyone ready and out of the house on time. Start by walking on mild dry mornings and driving when the weather's less good.

Children love to see their friends so you can talk to the parents of those friends closest to you who go in the same direction to school and join forces. You can then split the task of walking with the group of children to school. If there are enough children in your area going in the same direction, set up a *walking bus* in which the children all walk together with a parent at the front as the driver and a parent at the back. The Web site www.walkingbus.com has all sorts of information about the benefits of walking to school.

Walking isn't just green. It's good exercise and saves you money. You may even get there faster than if you get stuck in the car in congested streets.

When the children are old enough and competent enough on bicycles, let them cycle to school. Think about having them take a cycling proficiency class so that you both feel confident that they can handle themselves in traffic. Go to www.ctc.org.uk for information on the National Standards for Cycling Training. You'll find details of trainers in your area.

If the school is too far away check out the buses. If there's a stop near enough to walk to and a convenient bus, then that's the next best thing to walking or cycling.

Sharing the school run

If you have to use a car to get your children to school, you can cut down on the number of cars all going in the same direction each morning and afternoon by sharing the school run. Organise a group of parents to pick up the number of children that can safely be transported in the smallest car and then take it in turns.

Not only does sharing the school run save fuel, reducing the carbon emissions caused by the cars, but it also saves everyone time and money. Car-sharing also gives you more flexibility as you don't always have to be there to pick up children after school.

Being greener at school – this bit's for the kids!

If you want to do your bit for the planet and you're keen on getting the rest of your school involved, make a list of the things you would like to see change and take it to a teacher. They can help you to introduce your ideas into school, and may be able to register your school with a nationwide environmental scheme, like the Eco-Schools programme which gives you information and a programme to follow to make your school a greener place to work in. You can read all about it at www.eco-schools.org.uk or get some ideas from Friends of the Earth which has a series of 'Mad About' booklets designed for 6-10 year olds. These can be downloaded for free and have colourful posters with useful information and suggestions on how to make a difference.

Other things you can do to be green include:

✔ Find out if you can walk to school, cycle, or get the bus instead of being driven. There may even be a school bus in your area. Taking a bus or a train reduces the amount of carbon getting into the atmosphere but walking or cycling is even better for the environment as there are no carbon emissions involved at all and you get all the exercise you need.

If going by car is the only option ask your friends if their parents would be interested in setting up a car-sharing scheme where you all go to school in the same car instead of a number of different ones.

✔ If you do your bit to save energy and water at home get everyone to do the same things at school and in their own homes. Turn off the lights if you're the last to leave a room for example, and switch off your computer when you've finished with it. Explain to your friends why it's important to save energy and water and persuade your teachers to do their bit too.

✔ On average, each person in the UK gets through 200 kilograms of paper every year. Get everyone including the teachers to use both sides of a piece of paper before they throw it away and make sure that the school is using recycled paper and has a recycling bin for paper that is ready to be thrown away. When you're using a computer, print something out only when you really need to and use the other side of the paper to print on next time.

✔ Set up a recycling scheme for printer cartridges or find out where you can get them refilled. Make sure that your school isn't just putting them in the bin when they run out.

✔ If your school doesn't have recycling bins in the dining hall or canteen, talk to your headteacher about getting some – for cans, bottles, plastics, and paper. You also want waste food to be turned into compost so you need to ask about a bin for that too.

✔ If you drink water from plastic bottles, keep and refill them instead of throwing them away.

Changing the School's Approach from Within

It's all very well sitting on the sidelines complaining that your children's school isn't doing enough for the environment, but sometimes you have to get involved in order to change things. Teachers listen to parents – especially if those parents are offering constructive ideas rather than simply moaning about bad teaching or the treatment of their precious offspring.

As a school governor you have more access to the school, teachers, and pupils than you do just as a parent, and you can influence the thinking of all concerned including the other governors.

You don't need any particular skills or experience to be a school governor. You don't need to be a doctor, teacher, or lawyer to be considered; lorry drivers, builders, and housewives are just as valuable. You don't even need to know anything about the education system; you get governor training and learn on the job.

You can apply to be a parent governor at the school your children attend, but you also can apply to a school where none of your children belong (and even if you don't have any children, you can still become a school governor).

Schools need governors. They can't make decisions unless they have enough and in many parts of the country not enough people come forward to serve. For information on how to put your name forward, go to www.schoolgovernors-oss.co.uk.

Raising awareness of green issues

As a school governor – or even as a concerned parent – you can help the environment by raising awareness of all sorts of green issues.

Ask for an appointment with the headteacher or a teacher your child is keen on to go over your ideas. Keep things very simple and offer to help the teachers and the school rather than demanding that things are changed. Offer to take a class every now and again or to talk to the whole school for ten minutes every so often about green issues. Ask what you can do for them not what they can do for you.

Suggest ideas for making things greener that won't cost the school money. There's likely to be little to spare. Some examples include:

- ✔ Find out who can supply the school with recycled goods like paper and loo roll and offer to negotiate a good deal.
- ✔ Offer to provide recycling and composting bins.
- ✔ Change light bulbs to low-energy ones.
- ✔ Set up car-sharing and walking/bus schemes and provide parents with information on public transport.

Getting advice on energy saving

It's not just the teaching of green issues that's important but the school itself. School buildings generate a huge amount of carbon: Schools are responsible for 15 per cent of the total carbon emissions from all the government buildings, such as hospitals and government offices, in the UK.

You can help reduce carbon emissions by raising awareness of the problems caused by greenhouse gases. (Chapter 2 talks more about greenhouse gases and how to reduce them.)

One practical way to help and to save the school some money is to arrange for an energy expert to come into the school to work out where savings can be made. The Carbon Trust (www.carbontrust.co.uk) advises on how to save energy at all sorts of sites and has an energy saving guide for teachers.

Initiating Green Projects

Schools have a role to play in the wider community and can lead by example. The ultimate goal of greening schools is to get the children involved in projects that help build a greener community. If the school uses renewable energy and recycles and composts food waste, it shows children, parents, and other people in the community green living in action.

The best projects are ones that everyone in the school from the youngest and least academically minded to the brightest and most practically minded can get involved in. Go for a range of projects if possible that allow everyone the chance to play their part.

Getting green ideas from other schools

Schools around the UK are going green in a variety of ways. Here are some examples:

- Kingsmead Primary School in Cheshire was built to be as green as possible and the pupils and teachers have changed the whole school's ethos so that everyone behaves as greenly as they can.

- At Dorothy Stringer High School in East Sussex, pupils and staff converted an unused outbuilding into an 'eco-centre' from where they run all sorts of environmental projects.

- At Nab Wood School in Bingley in Yorkshire a group of pupils launched a Stop Climate Chaos Campaign. They are now working to get their headteacher and governors on board. By the end of the campaign they hope the school will be using renewable energy; have a bike shed so people can cycle to school; have cut its waste to a minimum – possibly with a scheme where ten pence spent on each drink can or bottle is returned when they are recycled; and have someone responsible for the school's environmental policy and the management of it.

- Leigh CE Infant School has been awarded the prestigious 'Green Flag' award by ENCAMS (formerly Tidy Britain) because of its outstanding contribution to the environment by planting bulbs, recycling paper, reusing cut-offs of coloured card, and collecting household rubbish to recycle in school artwork. The next step is for the children to plan a safe outdoor environment including play equipment, new benches, and garden sculptures.

Ideas for projects can come from the things you do at home or from looking at what other schools are doing – check the nearby 'Getting green ideas from other schools' sidebar for some examples and browse the Internet for more suggestions. Don't forget to ask the children for their ideas as well.

The kinds of projects running around the country range from recycling and composting schemes to worm farming and vegetable production for the school canteen, and mentoring schemes where older pupils go into primary schools to teach younger pupils about the environment. The following sections focus on ways to make any school greener.

Digging the pupils' vegetable plot

If the school has any spare ground that can be used to grow things, persuade teachers to agree to a vegetable plot. Students can grow organic vegetables (organic farming is covered in Chapter 7) to use in the school canteen.

The school saves money by producing some of its own food; the children learn about food, organic production, local and seasonal food, and the link between the land and what ends up on their plates; children and teachers benefit from getting exercise outdoors; and everyone is more likely to eat their greens because they are proud of having grown them themselves.

Introducing green school lunches

School lunches are a controversial issue as the government worries about the rising levels of childhood obesity and celebrity chefs try to raise the standard of the food served in schools. If you're concerned about the quality of food your child gets in school try persuading the headteacher and the cooks that the food should be as green as possible. Much seasonal food can be bought locally rather than imported, thereby promoting green living on a number of fronts (turn to Chapter 7 for more on eating green).

School administrators have very little money to spend on school meals so they will be resistant to changes that cost more money. Check with your local suppliers and go to the head teacher with the figures on the best deal you can negotiate. If the school can't go green in terms of food suggest a vegetable garden or give your children green packed lunches.

Visiting the local landfill site

It may seem like a strange way to spend a day out, but taking children to a *landfill site* – basically a big hole in the ground – to see the reality of waste management can have a big impact on their habits. If children can see how much waste is produced in their own small area and get a concept of how waste piles up in all the similar sites around the country they are more likely to see why the UK can't go on managing its waste in that way.

Nearly three-quarters of the waste generated by UK households goes to landfill sites, but the UK is running out of suitable holes in the ground to use for landfill and needs to persuade everyone to reduce the waste they produce and reuse and recycle as much as possible.

Help children identify things that could have been reused, repaired, or recycled. Explain how long it takes various items they see to decompose and what if any toxic chemicals are put into the ground in the process. Then discuss the various other options for getting rid of and reducing the waste to a minimum in the first place. From the landfill site, go to the local authority domestic recycling facility and show the children what happens to the stuff sorted and processed there. Being on site gives children a much clearer picture which they then take home and discuss with parents and friends.

If you can't arrange landfill site visits because your local facility managers can't allow it, or your school's staff feel there are too many health and safety concerns, try the next best thing and think about arranging a visit to

- ✔ Alternative technology centres
- ✔ Community composting schemes
- ✔ Community gardens
- ✔ Urban farms

Other green projects in your area may also be willing to help. You'll find information from your local authority and the Internet. There are also numerous Web sites that the children may find fun and informative; we list some in Chapter 16.

Planting trees

You can plant trees anywhere as long as the owner of the land doesn't object. If the school has no land of its own on which to grow some oxygen-producers, find somewhere else you can plant a few trees that the children can watch grow. Planting trees is an important element of being carbon neutral, as explained in Chapter 1.

People who fly are asked to plant a tree or pay for a tree to be planted so that it can absorb the carbon that is pumped into the atmosphere as a result of that person having made that flight. The same goes for other sorts of travel, and you can attempt to make your whole lifestyle as near to carbon neutral as possible by planting trees or paying towards other carbon offsetting schemes as explained in Chapter 1. Explain the principle to the children and see if you can become involved in a scheme to offset the carbon emissions from some project that has been undertaken at the school where carbon was released into the atmosphere. If you can link a particular event in another part of the world to the planting of the trees, the whole concept of carbon offsetting will be much easier for children to grasp.

Plant fast-growing trees so the children can get the joy and benefit of seeing them grow.

Launching a green prize

Prizes give children incentives to work, and green projects should be no different to any other aspect of school life. If you can afford to present the school with a prize every year, the teachers are hardly likely to refuse your offer. Knowing that there is a green prize raises awareness of green issues among pupils, teachers, and parents.

Be very clear about what the prize is awarded for so that pupils who want to enter the contest know what's expected. The rules may say that the prize goes to the pupil who comes up with the best green project of the year or who writes the best essay on a specific green issue, for example. As with anything in life, the better the prize the more people will want to compete for it.

Making Sure That Your University's Colour Is Green

Many universities have some kinds of green projects on the go, either as research or community schemes involving local people and students. If yours doesn't have anything that you can get involved in or you feel that there are other projects to set up, the best way forward is usually through the Students' Union.

Cambridge University Students' Union, for example, has a Green Officer who co-ordinates the university's green campaign, CUSU Green. The Green Officer represents student opinion within the University to the administrators. The aim is to raise awareness of environmental, ethical, and social justice issues among students and there are recycling, ethical investment, and Fairtrade projects, and a campaign for green energy use. Students are also involved in the Cambridge Green Belt Project helping to promote conservation and to maintain local green open space with the involvement of local people. The aim is to allow people to enjoy and appreciate nature and learn about wildlife without having to venture too far.

As far as your university is concerned, it's possible to have all sorts of projects going on and to forget the basics like conserving energy, recycling and reusing, and cutting down car use. Using the Students' Union to reach students and encourage a change in behaviour is as important as taking the message to the wider community.

Persuading university staff and administrators to put green practices in place – such as ensuring that used paper is recycled and new paper is made from recycled materials, that more cycle parking bays are provided, and using energy-efficient light bulbs – is something else that can be done through representation by the Students' Union. Many of the suggestions about going green in the workplace in Chapter 10 apply to universities too.

Part V
Travelling Without Doing Any More Damage to the Planet

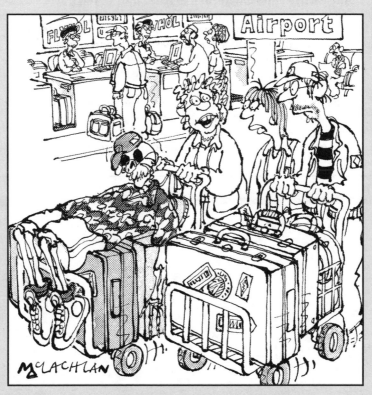

'We went on an eco-tour down the Amazon but unfortunately Brian fell in & the piranhas got him.'

In this part . . .

Travelling – flying in particular – is blamed for a large proportion of the carbon gases that get pumped into the earth's atmosphere. In this part I look at the travel alternatives. Think of the favour you are doing your body when you walk or cycle and the amount of travel costs you save. If you need a car, increasingly environmentally friendly options are available as firms develop more fuel-efficient cars and ones that run on alternative fuels.

This part also looks at the impact on the planet of tourism and offers some suggestions as to how you can become a greener tourist – travelling in ways and to places where the environmental impact will be kept to a minimum.

Chapter 12

Choosing Your Transport Wisely

● ●

In This Chapter

▶ Cutting down on car use

▶ Using other forms of transport

▶ Working out getting to work

▶ Shopping online

▶ Making a difference by taking fewer flights

● ●

*W*hen you were growing up, you probably wondered whether you would ever have your own car – a car that would give you the independence from your parents that you yearned for: to visit your friends; to go to places never seen; or just to get away from it all. Or perhaps you wanted a brand-spanking-new set of wheels to show off in – to show that you were as cool and important as the next person. Not too many of my friends grew up craving to catch the bus or train, or upgrade their push-bike when they got older.

The independence and status that the car has provided has had as much influence on the style and development of our urban areas as has the desire to live in large houses with plenty of space. The flexibility to travel far and wide in our cars has also enabled us to live far from our jobs, shops, schools, friends, and family. As a result, urban sprawl and high car use go hand in hand: We have large, sprawling urban areas because cars let us travel as far as we like. But high levels of car use are synonymous with less desirable characteristics – air pollution, road accidents, reduced health and fitness, and, in some places including rural areas, poor public transport.

Can you maintain your travelling freedom by owning and using a car while ensuring the sustainability of our urban areas? The answer is yes, if you're willing to balance your car use with other transport options.

This chapter discusses some of those options and various initiatives aimed at getting you to leave your car in the garage more often, and also explains some of the more sustainable transport options available.

Reducing Your Reliance on Cars

You may wonder how realistic it is to reduce your driving. You probably use your car at some stage most days, either to get to work, do the shopping, or drop the kids off to childcare or school. But do you need to use it for every trip, every day?

Each person in the UK travels about 7,000 miles a year on average and uses a car for 80 per cent of that travel. A quarter of all car journeys are less than 2 miles and at least a third of those could easily have been made on foot or by bicycle. People in the UK have a real love affair with the car but by just cutting down on the number of miles driven everyone can play a part in making our green and pleasant land more green and pleasant. Imagine better air quality with subsequent reductions in diseases like asthma, fewer deaths and injuries due to traffic accidents, and safer walking and cycling spaces.

There are more than 32 million vehicles on the UK's roads, of which around 26 million are private cars. Those vehicles produce 33 million tons of carbon dioxide each year and are responsible for almost a fifth of the total greenhouse gas emissions in the UK. Reducing the number of cars on the roads, changing the types of fuel used in those cars, and using other types of transport such as buses and trains can cut down the amount of carbon dioxide and other greenhouse gases produced and have a positive impact on our cities and towns.

Paying to drive in London

In February 2003 the mayor of London took drastic action to reduce car use in the centre of the capital. Motorists who drove into the central zone were initially charged a congestion charge of £5. The aim was to make drivers think about whether they needed to drive into the centre or if they could leave their cars outside the zone and travel in by public transport or even walk. Estimates show that congestion fell by about a third when the £5 charge was introduced and that when it was increased to £8 in 2005 congestion fell by a further 5 per cent. The mayor now plans to increase the charge to £10 and extend the scheme to make the congestion charge payable over a much bigger area of the city. Other towns are thinking of following suit. The government is looking at other traffic-charging schemes such as tolls and pay-as-you-drive as ways of forcing reductions in car use.

Cutting down on your car use

Some of the best methods you can adopt to reduce your car use are:

- ✔ **Leaving your car at home for a day:** Use your car to drive to work only four times a week rather than every day of the week – walk, cycle, or use public transport on the fifth day.

- ✔ **Sharing your journey:** How often do you drive somewhere alone and see hundreds of other drivers going in the same direction as you – also alone? Reduce the amount of time you drive alone by organising to drive with a workmate or to take neighbours' children to and from school.

- ✔ **Freeing up some space in the garage:** Sell the second family car and organise to share the remaining car with other family members.

  Especially, get rid of the SUV (Sports Utility Vehicle), 4x4, or four-wheel drive. Whatever you call it, unless you live in the middle of nowhere, you're very unlikely ever to use it as it was meant to be used, and it uses far more fuel than you need for your urban journeys.

- ✔ **Telecommuting:** More flexible working arrangements mean you may be able to work from home by accessing your work network via the Internet. Ask your employer if you can telecommute, or telework, from home one day a week.

- ✔ **Planning your travel:** Consolidate your errands into one big trip rather than making lots of smaller trips. For example, combine your shopping trip with the school run.

Adopting some of these tips greatly reduces the number of cars on the roads and the miles clocked up.

When you use your car, drive as greenly as possible by keeping your car fully serviced and make sure that the tyre pressures are as specified in your handbook – otherwise you use more fuel than necessary. Under-inflated tyres can increase your fuel consumption by as much as 3%. And remember that speed not only kills, it uses more fuel, as does keeping the engine running when you're not moving and revving it at the traffic lights!

If you already have a car you may be able to get a Powershift grant to make it greener. Transport Energy has plenty of tips for reducing fuel consumption on its Web site at www.transportenergy.org.uk, or call 0845 602 1425.

The charity Carplus promotes more responsible use of cars. Their Web site at www.carplus.org.uk offers advice on vehicle choice, alternative fuel technology, minimising car use, car clubs, car sharing, improved driving, journey planning, responsible disposal of cars, and all aspects of how cars are perceived and used in the UK. The government also has a 'Smarter Choices' campaign which promotes everything from car-sharing and the use of public transport, to school, workplace, and individual travel plans that involve less car use. You can get more information from the Department for Transport's Web site at www.dft.gov.uk. As part of the Smarter Choices project Darlington, Peterborough, and Worcester have been given grants to become *sustainable travel demonstration towns* where you can see the difference that using a whole package of Smarter Choices makes.

Helping solve the energy crisis

In cities across the globe, driving a car is a typical person's most air-polluting activity.

One of the greatest benefits of reducing car use is the decreased demand for mining and using fossil fuels. Some commentators argue that fossil fuel reserves have already peaked and we are now using the second half of remaining stores.

The current high fuel prices indicate that supply is not what it used to be; you only need your simple primary school economics to work that out. What you can now be sure of is that oil and gas, like most things that are sourced from the earth, are finite resources that need to be managed much more effectively before they run out.

Given that most of the fossil-generated oil and gas is used by the transport industry, it doesn't take a rocket scientist to work out that reducing use of cars also reduces the need for oil and petrol, thereby decreasing the pressure on ever-dwindling reserves.

Cars that use alternatives to petrol and diesel (discussed in detail in Chapter 13) offer some energy relief, but alternative fuel cars alone can't provide the whole answer for drivers. And, rather than wait for more efficient versions of these cars to be developed, by which time oil and gas reserves may have dwindled even further, environmentalists agree that throttling the addiction to the use of motor vehicles is the way to go. A key part of reducing car usage is to make sure that there are more sustainable transport choices on offer for people and to provide incentives for people to use them.

Yearning to breathe free

Car use is having a huge impact on the environment. The Department of Health figures show that between 12,000 and 24,000 people die early deaths each year as a result of poor air quality. Much of that pollution comes from car exhaust fumes.

According to the Department for Transport, transport is responsible for a quarter of the total greenhouse gas emissions in the UK and about four-fifths of that comes from cars and lorries. Cars are 10 per cent more fuel-efficient than they were in 1997 but there are more of them on the roads.

Greenhouse gases such as carbon dioxide (see Chapter 1 for the full definition of greenhouse gases) aren't the only emissions cars produce. Add into the mix hydrocarbons, nitrogen oxides, and particulate matter and you get the full, unhealthy picture.

A number of these contaminants have been linked to causing cancer, birth defects, brain and nerve damage, and long-term injury to the lungs and breathing passages. Of particular concern are hydrocarbon emissions, which result when fuel molecules in the engine burn only partially. Hydrocarbons are a major component of what we refer to as smog. A number of exhaust hydrocarbons are also toxic, with the potential to cause cancer.

Car emissions are especially unhealthy for the increasing number of asthma sufferers out there. Emissions from cars that cause smog and soot have been proven to worsen asthma and trigger attacks. Some evidence suggests that ozone, which is a main ingredient in smog, and exhaust particles combine to cause asthma in some people. The charity Asthma UK says that there are roughly four times as many cases of asthma recorded now as there were thirty years ago and that much of that is caused by exhaust fumes. You can contact Asthma UK by calling 08457 010203 or find information on their Web site at www.asthma.org.uk.

The combination of all these emissions contributes greatly to the air we breathe and that dirty-looking horizon we often see. No longer do scenes of cyclists in Tokyo wearing masks over their faces and noses provoke awed surprise – that's no longer an uncommon sight in central London and other big UK cities.

The UK target is to reduce carbon emissions by 2012 to 12.5 per cent less than they were in 1990. In order to reach those targets it's clear that emissions from cars have to be cut drastically.

Choosing Sustainable Transport Options

The continued high level of car usage is unsustainable. Walking and cycling, which only require the energy you have in your legs, are very sustainable.

You may agree that it would be nice to reduce your car use but you don't know how to switch to more sustainable transport. Having been brought up on a farm, I realise that if you live in a rural area, lack of public transport may mean the car is your only realistic transport option. But this section is here to tell you how to make use of various forms of sustainable transport, from public transport and car-sharing schemes to human-powered walking and cycling.

Choosing public transport

If you don't need a car as part of your job, think about changing to public transport.

Improving your health with car alternatives

As well as the toxic emissions your car produces, using your car all the time has an adverse effect on your health; the over-reliance on car travel encourages a lazy lifestyle. Why walk when you can drive, right? Well, if you've noticed that your midriff is expanding, think about how many times you could have walked or cycled rather than using your car in the last week. Many of your urban car trips, such as trips to the local park or school or shops, are probably within easy walking or cycling distance, and walking is one of the best ways to lose that spare tyre.

The car can be defined as a non-active form of transport. *Active transport* choices – such as walking and cycling, using buses and trains, or trams and ferries in some parts or the country – can have extremely positive health benefits. If you walk a little bit as part of the journey to and from work you're not only adding valuable exercise to your day, but you're also doing your bit to reduce the cost of maintaining the health system.

As you increase your physical activity, every time you decide not to use your car, you're going a long way to preventing cardiovascular disease and reducing the risk of obesity, adult-onset diabetes, and osteoporosis. And the

recent phenomenon of road rage suggests that psychological benefits are also achieved by not driving your car as much as you do.

People who walk, cycle, or use public transport are on average half a stone lighter than those who use cars to travel everywhere. You'll be doing yourself and everyone else a favour if you cut down your car use.

The laziness involved in driving everywhere is particularly important if children are involved. Children who grow up inactive are more likely to be overweight. Recent government figures show that almost a fifth of 5-year-olds and a third of 15-year-olds in the UK are overweight. Critics say those figures are inaccurate and too high because of the method of measurement but there is clearly a problem.

Apart from the negative health aspects from physical inactivity, children who are accustomed to being driven to school are missing out on important life skills – they may be less motivated to get out and find their own way around; they can be unaccustomed to navigating and feel uncomfortable in public places; they may be less street-wise; and, having less experience in personal road safety, they are at risk of more severe accidents.

People give several standard reasons for not using public transport, but others give just as many reasons why they love it. Those against trains and buses, in particular, refer to safety and security concerns, unreliability, and lack of services near where they live. Advocates for public transport talk about the importance of reducing the negative impact individual travellers in cars have on the environment. Using buses and trains is greener because of the numbers of passengers: the amount of polluting gasses emitted divided by the number of passengers means each individual travelling is responsible for much less pollution than an individual in a car. They also argue that trains and buses are safer and more secure; passengers benefit from becoming part of a community with other passengers, they have time to read the papers, do the crossword, finish off some paperwork, and arrive feeling more relaxed after the trip. Busses and trains have become more reliable and punctual in many parts of the UK because of growing public demand and concern, greater lobbying by passenger groups, and an increasing philosophical support for public transport generally.

Yet another group of travellers is not exactly sure how to use public transport. These people grew up not using buses or trains, and now find making the switch a bit daunting. Never fear: In the age of the Internet you have all the help you need to work out how to use public transport.

Most public transport providers in cities and towns have excellent Web sites that can help you plan your public transport journey. You can find timetable information, maps to show you the route travelled, fare information, ticketing options, and destination information. Just take the details down from the sides of buses or at stations, or call your local authority offices for more information.

Some of the larger transport agencies even provide you with a trip planner that tells you what to do after you leave your home. On these sites, if you enter your address, the address of your destination, and the time you want to leave, you're provided with the quickest transport options, route information, the bus stop or train station to get off at, and even walking routes and distances to your selected destination:

- ✔ The Department for Transport provides door-to-door travel advice at `www.transportdirect.info` for advice on how you can make more of your journeys on public transport.

- ✔ Transport 2000 is the environmental transport organisation. Take a look at the Web site at `www.transport2000.org.uk` for information on green transport options.

In Northern Ireland the public transport buses and trains are all run by Translink with three operating companies – Metro and Ulsterbus operating the buses and NI Railways operating the trains. The aim is to have an integrated public transport system so that passengers can get around the region with as much ease as possible. The Web site at `www.translink.co.uk` has more information about the system and for passengers.

Passing on the numbers for public transport

What about public transport and sustainability? Buses run on diesel and trains use a lot of electrical energy but they still fall into the sustainable category. The reason why is in the numbers. Buses and trains take many more people in the one vehicle or carriage than cars do. Cars can only take up to five people, although they regularly take only one or two. Buses take approximately 60 passengers or 120 if it's a bendy bus. Virgin Trains, one of the UK's big train operating companies, runs a fleet of 334 trains that carry 94,500 passengers each day – an average of 280 passengers per train. Commuter trains run by other operators carry many more passengers depending on their type, how many carriages they have, and the time of day.

Your first step as a public transport novice should be to check your local transport service provider's Web site and see whether you can get from home to work (and other destinations for that matter) by public transport. If you find a service, develop a timetable that gets you to your bus stop or train station on time both going and coming home.

Increasing the number of buses, trains, ferries, and trams and running them as near full as possible reduces traffic congestion and wasted time and money from sitting at traffic lights for half the morning and most of the evening, as well as reducing polluting emissions. All told, using public transport reduces the carbon footprint of your journey (see Chapter 1 for more information on the impact you're having on the environment).

Catching a bus

Around 9 out of every 10 people in the UK live within reasonable walking distance of a bus stop, so you've little excuse for not taking advantage of this option.

In London, buses are the responsibility of Transport for London, which grants licences to private operators. There's more information on the Transport for London Web site at www.transportforlondon.gov.uk or 020 7918 4300.

Elsewhere in the country the buses are run by private firms such as Stagecoach, National Express, and FirstBus; by one of six Passenger Transport Executives in England; or by local authorities. Ask at your local authority offices for information; you can find their details in your local phone directory.

Boarding a train

The trains are run by the train operating companies such as Virgin and Silverlink. Each train operating company produces a passenger's charter which tells you what standards of service you can expect and how to convey any feedback or suggestions you have for improvements. The charters have to be approved by the Rail Regulator from which you can get more information at www.rail-reg.gov.uk or by calling 020 7282 2000. You can get train times and fares from the National Rail Enquiry service on 08457 484950 or online at www.nationalrail.co.uk.

Going for underground services

In London, Transport for London has responsibility for underground train services – see www.transportforlondon.gov.uk or call 020 7918 4300. Underground services outside London are the responsibility of the Passenger Transport Executive for that area. You'll find contact details in the phone book. Glasgow also has an underground service, and places like Nottingham, Sheffield, Manchester, Blackpool, and Dublin have tram services (find more information on www.thetrams.co.uk).

Sharing the driving – and the car!

Car-sharing is becoming increasingly popular in some parts of Europe, and some schemes are already up and running in the UK. Although there are a whole range of differences between various local schemes, car-sharing comes in two basic flavours:

- ✔ **Lift-sharing,** in which a group of employees regularly share a car to and from work. The car used is usually provided by the person whose turn it is to drive that day. In some cases the employer donates the car to the group for use as a car-share.

  If you're looking for someone to share your travel costs with, register at www.liftshare.com to find other people in your vicinity willing to share.

  You don't have to share journeys with someone working for the same firm as you. You can arrange your own car-sharing scheme with people who live near you who travel into the same town or city but work in different companies. You can register with National Carshare at the Web site www.nationalcarshare.co.uk and use its matching services.

  Software is now available to assist companies organising car-sharing groups, based on where people live and what time they want to arrive and leave from work. Various different software firms sell their own versions or create the software to your requirements. Have a look at the

Department for Transport website at www.dft.gov.uk for more information.

✔ **Car clubs,** in which members have access to the club car for short-term hire as and when they need it. A club may be run by a group of people living in the same area or by people working together at the same company. The members share a centrally located car or cars and book them for use by signing up and paying a small fee.

This model of car-sharing works a little bit like a hire-car system, except you share the car only with a small number of members of your club, which means that the car is more than likely to be available at the times you request it.

There are about 40 car clubs around the country with 10,000 members and 400 cars. You can get more information on existing clubs or running a club from Carplus, which is a national charity promoting responsible car use at www.carplus.org.uk.

So, if you find it difficult to use public transport but want to make a sustainable difference to the way you travel, how about trying car-sharing?

The greatest impact that car-sharing has is that it reduces the number of single-passenger trips and therefore the number of cars on the road.

Various towns and cities in the UK such as Cambridge, London, and Edinburgh have tried bike-sharing schemes but most have been unsuccessful because the bikes have gradually been stolen, repainted, and sold. Attempts in France and Germany have worked better, perhaps because there is more of a bike-riding culture there than in the UK.

Why not form a bike-sharing club of your own? Buy a bike with friends and use it in turns; even it you only ride to work once a week you'll still be a greener traveller.

Getting to Work Greenly

The most obvious trip to consider converting from car to other forms of transport is your journey to work. Many initiatives set up to encourage a more balanced approach to car use rely on a major player in society – the workplace.

Talk to your employer about changing your start and finish times so that you can travel on public transport when it isn't so busy. If you're the boss, think about whether you really need all your staff to start work at the same time and especially at the same time as all the other workplaces in that area. If not, institute staggered schedules for your employees. The Government's business advice service Business Link gives information on how to bring flexible working patterns into your business (www.businesslink.gov.uk).

If you don't have reasonable access to public transport from where you live think about driving to the nearest train station or bus stop and leaving your car there. Or, consider the possibility of moving closer to where you work. If that's a realistic option you can then walk or cycle.

Changing your travelling to work habits is beneficial to the environment, your peace of mind, and your wallet. The relative cost savings can be substantial. A non-car user who uses a combination of public transport and taxis over the year, with the odd hire-car thrown in, usually runs up lower bills than someone who buys and runs a car, with its insurance, fuel, and maintenance costs. Imagine the costs for families with two or more cars per family.

If you have to use your car, find out whether you can share driving with someone else travelling the same or a similar route – check the previous section 'Sharing the driving – and the car!' for advice. People park at a pre-agreed location and are picked up by colleagues for the rest of the journey. Informal arrangements like this have led many local authorities to provide official *park and share* areas. You can make a difference.

These legs were made for walking (and pedalling)

The reality is that many people live too far from their work to walk all the way. Or do they? An increasing trend in many cities around the world is for people to live close to their workplace and social attractions, so they walk to work via the many shops and services that exist in inner urban areas.

If the walk to work is too far, walking to a nearby train or bus stop is a much healthier and less expensive transport option than driving.

Cycling is also becoming an increasingly popular mode of transport – largely as a result of many cities and towns investing in good, safe, and direct cycling paths that don't compete with other traffic. In some cases, using a bicycle to get to work may be quicker than dealing with traffic congestion.

The key to cycling to and from work is doing the necessary planning:

- ✔ Make sure that your workplace has good cycle parking and locker facilities, ensuring your peace of mind that no one is going to cycle off with your treasured transport investment.

- ✔ Check that you have accessible showering and changing facilities. If there are no washing facilities at your workplace talk to your boss about the possibility of making them available and why you think they'd make a difference to the work environment as well as the wider environment. Many employers just haven't considered washing facilities a necessity because no one has ever brought up the subject.

- ✔ Research the route you use – look for roads or paths that are well surfaced and wide enough to avoid conflicts with other vehicles.

If you've done all that then what are you waiting for – on your bike!

Sustrans is a charity that promotes sustainable methods of transport. It co-ordinates the 10,000-mile-long National Cycle Network and a number of safe cycling routes, and offers maps showing the safest routes to use. Contact Sustrans at www.sustrans.org.uk or call 0845 113 0065. Cycling England is a national organisation set up by the government to promote more and safer cycling in England, with six towns including Brighton and Lancaster taking the lead by demonstrating best practice. You can find out more from the Cycling England Web site at www.cyclingengland.co.uk.

If you take up cycling to become a greener traveller, don't forget to stay safe. Make sure you have good lights on the bike and wear a helmet, highly visible clothing, and reflecting bands. Motorists need to be able to see you easily in the dark or in poor visibility.

About two-thirds of people in the UK live within cycling distance of a train station but very few of those get to work by train because facilities for bikes at stations and on trains are scarce. Some train operating companies are very strict about the number, size, and type of bike they allow on board and some allow them only on particular trains, if at all. Check out the situation before you travel and lobby hard for more facilities for bikes at stations and on trains.

Making a difference with workplace travel plans

Employers are becoming more interested in encouraging their employees to leave their cars at home.

Many companies have become burdened by employees expecting a car with their salary package. But if businesses can encourage alternatives instead, they can benefit themselves and the environment. Cutting down on the number of company cars means employers need less parking provision and can use the additional floor space for more productive purposes.

Workplace travel plans encourage people to make more sustainable transport choices by offering incentives and choices that encourage employees to reduce their car use. The types of incentives and choices being provided in workplace travel plans include:

- ✔ Public transport fare subsidies and passes – a cheaper alternative for the company and an incentive for employees to choose public transport over operating a car with its fuel, parking, and running costs

- ✔ Personalised travel information and marketing material

- ✔ Better bus stop facilities at the workplace

- ✔ Car park space allocation that favours car sharers

- ✔ Flexitime, homeworking and teleworking – all of which make it possible to leave the car at home some of the time; travel at times of least congestion or use public transport at a more convenient time of day

- ✔ Local area cycling and walking route information

- ✔ Car pool mileage clubs rewarding those who reduce car use

- ✔ Provision of a pool of bikes for use to and from home

- ✔ Provision of low-emission vehicles for staff

- ✔ Public transport service announcements and other real-time information

- ✔ Public transport, walking, and cycling events (breakfasts, lunches, seminars, and so on)

- ✔ Timetables and links to interactive trip planners.

 If your workplace does not have a travel plan in place, ask some of your colleagues to join you in lobbying for one. If you can gather support, go to your manager with a report or some Internet material that outlines the benefits for the company in developing a travel plan. You can get details of how to set up travel plans from the government's Web site at `www.local-transport.dft.gov.uk/travelplans` or from the Association for Commuter Transport at `www.act-uk.com`.

Provide your company with information that promotes the positive benefits of developing a travel plan, such as:

 ✔ Facilitating better relationships between staff and management

 ✔ Improving the ability to retain and attract staff

 ✔ Boosting the company image in the community for adopting sustainable approaches

 ✔ Saving money by subsidising employee public transport rather than providing cars as part of salary packages.

Shopping Till You Drop – from Home

The biggest impact the Internet has on transport is by offering the ability to shop online and curtailing trips to shopping areas. You probably make most shopping trips in your car, especially for groceries, hardware items, and things that can be carried in your car boot. Rather than go to the hassle of finding a parking space in a humongous big-box shopping centre, you can now look to the Internet for many of the goods you don't need to go and see in a shop.

Although the number of commercial deliveries by planes, trains, and courier vehicles may increase with more online shopping, the impact is negated by the reduction in individual car trips people make to the shops to pick up the goods. Increased online shopping may have a negative impact on the economic and social sustainability of urban centres and towns, but this issue is still being debated.

Some of the most popular online shopping categories that reduce individual transport trips include:

 ✔ **Books and music:** Amazon.com was one of the first companies to popularise buying music and books online. The attraction in ordering from home is the greater choice online compared to your local shop. You can even order from overseas companies, but this may not be great for your local economy.

 ✔ **Perishable and non-perishable foods:** Many of the large supermarkets and specialist organic food stores encourage online shopping because of the growing number of people who are Internet savvy, have a set shopping list, and do not have to go to the shop to see what they are buying.

 ✔ **Takeaway food:** Home pizza delivery was one of the first 'dial-up and get it quickly' home delivery services provided to urban areas. Now there are a number of companies offering tasty and culturally varied menus online.

✔ **Home furniture and electronics:** Most large retailers have glossy online catalogues that encourage you to order and have your bulky purchase delivered without you having to lift a finger.

✔ **Anything and everything:** Sites such as eBay, which give people a chance to sell their own goods, have taken a lot of business away from the modern-day pawnbrokers who used to operate in many cities and towns.

Most retail operators now have interactive Web sites that provide picturesque catalogues of their goods and services, which you can browse through to your heart's content.

Go to your favourite online shopping site and follow these steps:

1. Click on a product you like to send it to a virtual shopping cart, where your selection is stored until you're ready to buy.

2. Complete your shopping session by clicking through to the checkout, where your goods are totalled and your additional taxes, shipping, and delivery costs are added to give you an invoice total.

3. Use your credit or debit card to pay for the total cost and provide your address details so that the goods can be sent to you. If the thought of giving your details over the Internet worries you, you could try PayPal. This allows you to pay anyone who has e-mail and an online account number without giving out your card details. You'll find more information at `www.paypal.co.uk`.

4. Receive an e-mail that confirms the goods you have bought, how much they cost, and that your purchase is in the process of being delivered.

Bingo! All from the comfort of your home.

Cutting Down the Air Miles

Wherever you are in the UK, if you look into the sky, it won't be long before you see a plane. Between 3,000 and 4,000 of them are flying over Europe at any given moment. Even with an average of only 100 passengers each that adds up to 400,000 passengers up there now and many more taking off and landing by the time you reach the end of this sentence. About 220 million passengers use UK airports each year. The number using London airports has doubled since 1987 and the number using regional UK airports has gone up three times in the same period. The Government thinks the number could double again by 2030. Air traffic is predicted to go on growing as flights continue to be relatively cheap – bringing air travel within the reach of more and more people.

Add to that the increasing numbers of people from developing countries joining in the travel rush and you begin to see why air travel is a big concern for scientists worried about its effect on the environment. More flights mean more airports, more take-offs and landings, more demand for fuel, and more harmful greenhouse gases pumped out into the atmosphere.

Aircraft are the fastest-growing polluters in the world. In the UK they account for around 6 per cent of the greenhouse gases emitted but because those gases are pumped out at high altitude into the atmosphere they do at least twice the amount of damage caused by emissions from homes and factories. The aircraft manufacturers argue that they're building ever-cleaner, more-efficient engines but even though that's true the rate of growth of air travel outweighs those technological advances.

The bigger planes being built and taking over on some long-haul routes may mean more passengers can travel more often without the need to increase the number of flights but that only works if they fly full. Governments are resisting the idea of taxing aircraft fuel, which would push up ticket prices and make people curtail their travel plans. But while they hesitate, flying has become the most environmentally damaging way to travel.

You can help by cutting down your air travel by taking holidays and short breaks in the UK instead of abroad and looking for greener ways to make journeys you have to make – such as using the train. You can also take steps to neutralise the carbon emitted by the flights you do make – such as paying to have trees planted to absorb the amount of carbon dioxide your flight is responsible for producing. There's more information in Chapter 1.

Chapter 13

Expanding the Green Car Evolution

In This Chapter

▶ Moving on from the internal combustion engine

▶ Using fuels that reduce emissions

▶ Becoming more fuel-efficient

▶ Designing the green car of the future

*T*he car gets blamed for many of our environmental problems – dirty air in towns and cities, urban sprawl, traffic accidents, congestion, and increasing levels of obesity. But it's hard to imagine a life without them. It may be possible to cut down on their use, influence, and impact but, in reality, they're not about to disappear off the roads. Each person in the UK travels about 5,500 miles each a year by car on average – the average car travels 9,000 miles.

Because cars use petrol or diesel and those fuels are produced from oil, a fossil fuel, cars give off carbon emissions as they drive along. Those carbon emissions amount to over a quarter of the carbon pumped out into the earth's atmosphere by the UK. And, that carbon is partly responsible for the climate change that's worrying people concerned about the future of the planet.

This chapter focuses on how you can reduce the negative impact that your car has on the environment through using renewable, cleaner, and less polluting energy sources for powering cars. It also looks at the new generation of greener cars that are being developed and coming to a showroom near you.

Driving Smarter and Greener

People once spent most of their work and social time within their own local community but the invention of the car gave greater mobility. Now some people commute over two hours each way to work and drive long distances to visit families and friends.

The mass production of cars powered by fossil fuels makes cars the most affordable way to stay on the road, which results in more fuel being used producing more greenhouse gases and increasing pollution levels.

The way to reduce the impact your car has on the environment is to cut down car use by walking, cycling, or taking public transport instead, and to use greener fuels to power cars. Just cutting down on your car use makes you greener. There's more in Chapter 12 about cutting down on the use of your car.

If your car runs on unleaded petrol (and you can't afford to invest in a new alternative fuel as described in the next section), you can still reduce your fuel use and therefore your carbon emissions by following these tips:

- ✔ Have your car serviced regularly. Older cars pollute more heavily than newer, better-performing ones and regular servicing can cut that pollution.

- ✔ Reduce your speed and avoid hard accelerating and heavy braking – driving more slowly and smoothly reduces fuel consumption. You use a quarter less fuel at 50 mph than you do at 70 mph.

- ✔ Switch off the engine when you're stationary and don't rev your engine when starting up the car. A car idling gives off 80 percent more pollution than one that's moving. The US Department of Energy says it's more economical and causes less pollution to switch off the engine and start it again if the car will be stationary for 30 seconds or more (there's no equivalent UK research).

- ✔ Travel lightly. Take anything you don't need out of your car to reduce weight, improve your fuel consumption, and reduce emissions.

- ✔ Make sure that your tyres are inflated to the correct pressure because soft tyres increase fuel consumption by as much as 3%.

- ✔ Use your air conditioner and other electrical gadgets only when you need to because they can use up to 10 per cent extra fuel.

- ✔ Avoid driving at peak times because idling in congested traffic wastes fuel.

Consider car-pooling and car-sharing wherever possible and think about buying a car with another person and sharing.

Motorbikes and powered scooters are greener, more fuel-efficient forms of transport (see the 'Two-Wheeling is Greener Than Four' section, later in the chapter).

Fuelling Interest in Alternative Fuels

Not surprisingly, dwindling supplies and rising fuel prices have sparked interest in alternative fuels. Even the Americans have realised that they need to reduce their reliance on oil and petrol.

Several less-polluting, more energy-efficient fuels have less impact than petrol:

- Ultra-low and low-sulphur diesel and *biodiesel,* which is fuel made from vegetable crops such canola, soya, and rape, and from tallow and waste cooking oil.

- Ethanol-based fuels, including Diesohol (15 per cent ethanol and low-sulphur diesel) and hydrated ethanol and unleaded petrol mixed with ethanol (ethyl alcohol). *Ethanol* is a high proof alcohol made mainly from Brazilian sugar cane; the ethanol used in cars also contains poisonous additives.

- Gaseous fuels, including hydrogen (which can be converted to electricity to power hydrogen fuel-cell cars), compressed natural gas (CNG), liquefied natural gas (LNG), liquefied petroleum gas (LPG) as autogas, and LPG as propane gas.

Some alternative fuels can be mixed with traditional petrol and diesel for use in internal combustion engines, so they still produce carbon emissions but much less than straight unmixed petrol or diesel. But as yet there's no mass production of vehicles that run on these alternative fuels available in the UK so those that are available are still more expensive that the ordinary petrol-powered car.

Choosing biofuel and biodiesel

Biofuel is ethanol used as a substitute for petrol. It's usually made from sugar beet, sugar cane, or maize and is widely used in places such as Brazil. In the UK, biofuel is usually mixed with petrol rather than used as a complete substitute for petrol. There's more information in the next section, 'Mixing it up'. Using pure ethanol instead of petrol cuts carbon emissions by about 13 per cent, taking into account the carbon released during the production process and the fact that cars running on ethanol get 70 per cent of the mileage of a petrol car.

Biodiesel is made from various plant oils and is the preferred compromise fuel for diesel engines. Made from vegetable oils or animal fats mixed with an alcohol-like substance like methanol, most biodiesels are currently mixed with regular diesel (usually 20 per cent biodiesel) so as they can be used in current diesel engines without modification. You can put 100 per cent biodiesel in a diesel engine and the engine will work and produce substantially fewer emissions (up to three-quarters of a normal diesel vehicle), but doing so without modifying your car can cause damage to the engine. You may be able to have your own car converted to run on the greener fuels, especially if your current car uses diesel fuel.

The UK aims that biofuel will make up 5 per cent of transport fuels by 2010 and European Union rules say that conventional fuels have to be mixed with biofuels and it aims that they should account for 5.75 per cent of transport fuels by 2010. Demand around the world for biofuel is growing at 25 per cent each year.

Biofuel and biodiesel are often hailed as the perfect clean green fuel. But those oils come from plants that require a lot of land. In some areas, including parts of South America and South-East Asia, natural forests, including tropical rainforests, have been cleared in order to grow crops like maize, sugar, palm trees, and soya that produce the oil to convert to biofuel and biodiesel, pushing prices up.

As demand for biofuel increases, so will the destruction of natural forests unless the fuel manufacturers make sure that the crops used for biofuels are grown in a sustainable way – using quick-growing trees on land that isn't needed for food and doesn't have to be cleared of natural forests.

Various stories are published in the press about drivers running their cars on cooking oil mixed with methanol at home, creating a cheap home-made car fuel. Don't forget you still have to pay fuel duty on this home-made mix!

Mixing it up (your fuel that is)

Ethanol can be used as a fuel for cars. Ethanol is produced by fermenting and distilling crops such as sugar cane, maize, barley, and wheat, or anything else that contains starch or sugar, in a process similar to that for making pure alcohol.

Ethanol is generally mixed with petrol to form a much more environmentally friendly fuel that works in combustion engines. If you want to use pure ethanol and have the choice of switching back to running on petrol should you need to you'll need a flexible fuel vehicle (FFV). You can find an increasing number of FFVs on the market because it takes only a small change to the standard combustion engine equipment.

The most popular fuel mix is 85 per cent ethanol to 15 per cent petrol (called E85). This mix is the most popular compromise alternative fuel at the moment because it doesn't require great changes to the current design and style of cars. An E85 mix greatly reduces greenhouse gas and pollution emissions, although not as much as the other alternative fuels mentioned elsewhere in this section.

Hailing the future of hydrogen

Hydrogen, the simplest of the natural elements, is everywhere – in water, plants, and animals. The US Department of Energy says that hydrogen is the cleanest and most energy efficient of the alternative fuels. Because there are no limits to how much of it can be produced, it could solve the energy supply crisis the planet finds itself in. Hydrogen can be used to power vehicles, the hydrogen being supplied to the fuel cell (which is like a battery). In the fuel cell, a chemical reaction between the hydrogen and oxygen produces electrical energy to power the car and the only by-product is water. The fuel cell – unlike a conventional battery – doesn't go flat so long as the hydrogen and oxygen are supplied to it.

For it to be adapted for use in mass transportation, however, the US government states that the following issues need to be resolved:

✔ The energy levels per litre for hydrogen are not as high as those of petrol (petrol provides up to five times more energy per litre than a hydrogen fuel cell).

✔ No leading manufacturers are producing hydrogen-cell vehicles for sale to the general public (yet).

✔ Building new hydrogen fuel stations with a good geographic spread is a massive undertaking that will entail large costs and much effort – as providing any alternative fuel will.

Some buses in big UK cities, particularly London, already run on hydrogen.

The US government conservatively estimates that it may be between 10 and 20 years before hydrogen vehicles and the infrastructure to support them become widely available although car manufacturers themselves are claiming they could be on the forecourts as soon as 2010. Some well-known Japanese car companies are making big advances in developing new hydrogen-powered vehicles, to such an extent that you may be able to buy a hydrogen cell vehicle from the showroom within five years.

Getting a whiff of natural gas

Compressed natural gas (CNG) is a better option than petrol because it produces fewer harmful emissions. There's a relatively good market for natural gas cars in the US, where it's widely available, but it's not that common in the UK yet. The big issue from a green perspective is that CNG is produced from gas wells in the ground or as a by-product of crude oil production and so doesn't come from a renewable source. But natural gas is also a component of methane, which is produced during the treatment and recycling of sewage, so there is a greener, renewable source of the gas which can be tapped in future.

The downside of using CNG is that it provides about a third of the energy of petrol.

The other gas option is *liquid petroleum gas* (LPG), which is produced as a by-product of natural gas processing and petroleum refining. So, it's not as natural as CNG sourced from wells in the ground, although it has similar clean air benefits.

LPG produces much more energy per litre than CNG (surprisingly not that far below petrol) and the supporting infrastructure needed to make it available to the public is easier to provide. Whereas natural gas is generally piped to a storage area, LPG can be transported in trucks around the countryside – although that increases the transporting costs and adds to the emissions from the transport vehicles.

Focusing on the Cars of the Future

The next car you buy can be greener than the one you drive at the moment. Years of research and investment by companies into powering your car with renewable, clean, and energy-efficient fuel means greener cars coming onto the market. But these new alternative fuel cars don't come cheap. Until they're developed for a larger market, these cars are likely to be a little more expensive than their petrol-powered cousins.

Assessing the extent of the car problem

The car of today – with the internal combustion engine under the bonnet, two seats in the front, room for three in the back, a chassis to protect the driver and passengers, and four rubber tyres – is designed in much the same way as over the past 100 years.

The internal combustion engine is very inefficient when it comes to energy use because:

✔ There are 34 megajoules of energy in every litre of petrol that powers a car's engine, and nearly a third of that energy is lost due to the inefficiency of the engine.

✔ A further 8 per cent is lost in running the engine accessories.

✔ Some 17 per cent is wasted after turning the car on and idling.

✔ In total, 87 per cent of the fuel is used up before the car ever starts travelling along the road.

Greenhouse gases and pollution are produced when fossil fuels like oil are burned, as explained in Chapter 2, and much of the oil pumped out of the earth's crust is processed as petrol and diesel for cars, trucks, buses, and other heavy vehicles.

If you want a new greener car, you can get more information from the Environmental Transport Association, which has a car buyer's guide showing the cleanest, greenest cars on the market. Check it out online at www.eta.co.uk or call 0845 389 1010. If you're not quite ready for a green car yet you can buy a new car that's greener than your old one. Check out the carbon emissions for a whole list of new cars from the Vehicle Certification Agency at www.vcacarfueldata.org.uk.

Finding out what's on the car market

Green cars are available on car forecourts now. If you're planning to make your next car green, check out the specifications – such as fuel consumption and type of fuel used. The government has also introduced 'green' labelling for cars so that you can see from the colour-coded label how environmentally friendly a car is. You can find out more about the Fuel Economy Label at www.direct.gov.uk/EnvironmentAndGreenerLiving/Greenertravel.

Most of the current options use green biofuel mixed with petrol or diesel or can run short distances on electricity before reverting to ordinary fuel. The smaller the engine and the lower the fuel consumption, the greener your car is. The environmental campaign group Friends of the Earth has details on their Web site at www.foe.co.uk of savings you can make by buying a more fuel-efficient car. *What Car?* at www.whatcar.com is a good source of information about the various types of green cars on the market.

Check the details carefully because some so-called green cars produce as much, if not more, carbon dioxide as their petrol and diesel counterparts because they have high fuel consumption.

In London your green car may be exempt from the congestion charges. Electric cars are exempt, but to find out whether your car is, visit www.est.org.uk/ fleet, the Web site of the Energy Saving Trust.

Honing hybrid hysteria

Hybrid is a term used to describe a car with a combustion engine that can also use another type of fuel – usually electricity. Hybrids are increasingly popular with UK drivers, especially in London. The hybrid switches from petrol mode to electric mode when idling or travelling at low speeds, thereby reducing petrol consumption and emissions.

One of the selling points of the hybrid is that the electrical component of the car doesn't need to be refuelled via an electrical socket on the wall – you charge the electric battery every time you press the brakes.

The best known of the hybrids is the Toyota Prius (www.toyota.co.uk), which retails at approximately £17,000. The Honda Civic Hybrid (www.honda. co.uk) is the main competition to the Prius and costs around £15,000. Most of the big car firms have their own hybrid model.

Encouraging electric enthusiasm

Until recently the only electric vehicles on the streets were milk floats, but if it works for milk floats why not ordinary cars? Electric cars produce the lowest levels of greenhouse gases, spewing out no carbon emissions at all. If the electricity comes from renewable power sources such as wind and solar your car is truly green.

The US Department of Energy says that the cost of running and maintaining an electrically powered car is much less than alternatives, especially petrol. Electric cars have fewer moving parts to service and replace, although you have to replace the batteries that store the electrical power every three to six years.

There's a difference of opinion on the sustainability of using electricity to power cars because most of that electricity still comes from oil-fired power stations rather than from renewable sources such as wind farms.

Sparking interest in London

In London, an organisation called GoingGreen (www.goingreen.co.uk) sells the electric-powered G-Wiz, a two-door hatchback with a top speed of approximately 60 kilometres an hour, which is enough for London driving conditions and speed limits. It also has a range of up to 60 kilometres before needing to recharge and costs about £7,000.

The G-Wiz isn't a hybrid and so far there are few recharging ports outside London, so it's only really relevant for Londoners, but the big attraction is that there is no engine, radiator, clutch, gears, exhaust, oil filters, spark plugs, or many of the parts that wear out. And it produces no emissions.

Anyone else in the UK who wants to own a G-Wiz has to rely on recharging at home or – if their employer is really forward-thinking – at work. Have a word with your employer and see if recharging facilities can be arranged – so that you can drive home again!

Some argue that cars running on electricity are unreliable, require constant maintenance, and have limited storage capacities – so they can't run very far without being plugged into an electrical power source. It can take up to six hours to fully recharge the battery from the mains – which isn't much good if you're running late for an important meeting. The infrastructure for recharging is still limited. There aren't many service stations where you can pop in and fill up. The batteries are also heavy and create waste issues due to the lead in them.

Electric cars have the advantage of being small, easily parked, and exempt from congestion charges in London. Many of them are hybrid cars that can run on electricity or be switched to petrol when the battery runs down. There's more on hybrid cars in the preceding 'Honing hybrid hysteria' section.

Electric cars are really still for driving around town on short journeys so you can recharge overnight at home in the garage – but there are increasing numbers on the streets. For more information on the pros and cons of electric vehicles, go to the Environmental Transport Association's Web site www.eta.co.uk.

Holding out for hydrogen

When all the alternatives are weighed up and compared, it appears that a hydrogen-fuelled car is the great green hope. Possibly as a result of seeing the writing on the wall regarding the dwindling supply of oil, most of the world's major car-makers appear to be racing each other to get the first fully fledged hydrogen car on the road.

Honda first introduced its FCX hydrogen fuel-cell car in 1999 and has been trying to get it ready for the market ever since. One of the issues that the company has to resolve is developing a hydrogen tank small enough to fit within the relatively tiny cars that Honda builds but big enough to hold the fuel cell.

Honda is also well advanced in developing prototype hydrogen refuelling stations and a home-based energy station that generates hydrogen from natural gas for use in cars, as well as powering the electricity and hot water in your home.

General Motors, Ford, and Toyota are also in the process of developing fuel-cell prototypes using hydrogen.

Opening to other options

The alternatives to hybrid and electric cars are those that run on compressed natural gas or liquid petroleum gas, as described earlier in the section 'Getting a whiff of natural gas', or on a mixture of biofuel and petrol or diesel. Car manufacturers are working hard to bring out new cars specifically designed to run on these alternative fuels. Check out the possibilities with the Environmental Transport Association at www.eta.co.uk or call 0845 389 1010.

Here are some of the alternative fuel cars on the market:

- Honda have four alternative fuel models: a CNG-powered Honda Civic and three electric/petrol hybrids – a Honda Accord, a Honda Civic, and a Honda Insight.

- Ford have five alternative fuel models: one electric/petrol hybrid and four E85 ethanol powered cars.

- General Motors have six alternative fuel models: one electric/petrol hybrid, one CNG-only-powered engine; one CNG/petrol bi-fuel utility, and four E85 ethanol models.

- Nissan have one E85 ethanol model (Titan).

- Toyota have two electric/petrol hybrids: a Highlander SUV and the Prius.

- Daimler Chrysler have four E85 ethanol models.

Looking into the crystal ball

As demand for green cars increases, more manufacturers will jump on the bandwagon and competition will drive prices down. As congestion charges reach parts of the UK outside London, demand will increase for green cars that qualify for exemptions to the charges. As more outlets become available for refuelling with alternative fuels, more people will buy green cars. As parking problems increase, smaller cars that take up less space and use less fuel will become more popular. It all adds up to less pollution, fewer carbon emissions, and cleaner air.

But greener cars need to go hand in hand with reduced car use to make a real difference. It still takes energy and huge amounts of the planet's resources to produce cars in the first place. If the UK doesn't cut car use and the number of cars on the roads goes on rising overall carbon emissions won't fall, roads will become more congested, and more roads will be built using up valuable land and destroying parts of the countryside.

Two-Wheeling Is Greener Than Four

Mopeds and small motorcycles have really caught on in the cities in recent years – often because they are so much easier to manoeuvre through heavy traffic and to park, but more recently in London because they are exempt from congestion charges. They're well suited to people who don't have to travel too far to work, shop, or meet friends and family or carry around any large, fragile objects.

A motorcycle or scooter running on petrol produces far fewer greenhouse gases than a car. So an increase in moped and bike use and a corresponding decrease in car use would be good news for the environment.

A number of companies make scooters, small motorcycles, and even electric bicycles. Many of the most robust models are powered by petrol, but, just as with cars, you can find an increasing number of electric mopeds and bikes becoming available. Try www.greenconsumerguide.com for more information on green two-wheeled transport options.

The greenest option of all is to walk or ride a bicycle and you have all the benefits of the exercise walking and cycling give you.

Paying the Tolls

The government has to get cars off the roads before streets in the UK become gridlocked with vehicles. One way of doing that is to make driving more expensive so that people choose to use public transport instead. To that end all sorts of road-charging schemes have been springing up around the country and a national one is to be introduced soon.

Avoiding the congestion charges

In London, drivers have to pay £8 or £10 to come into the centre of the city on Monday to Friday between 7 a.m. and 6.30 p.m. apart from public holidays. However, drivers of electric and some alternative-fuel cars are exempt. Visit www.est.org.uk/fleet (the Web site of the Energy Saving Trust) for more information on exemptions.

A few other cities operate similar schemes or are planning similar schemes. If there is one in operation where you live check which types of vehicles are exempt from the charges or can claim discounts.

Pay-as-you-drive schemes in the pipeline

A new pay-as-you-drive scheme is in the pipeline and will be introduced within ten years in England. Cars will be fitted with black boxes that will record how far they drive and drivers will be charged by the mile. They will pay more if they drive at peak travel times.

Transport policy is the responsibility of the Scottish, Welsh, and Northern Ireland parliaments so they will have to make separate decisions on whether or not to implement the scheme.

Taxing times for the gas guzzlers

The Mayor of London has waged war on what he calls gas guzzlers. These are vehicles on the carbon emissions band G – the vehicles that produce the highest carbon emissions such as some Range Rovers, Porsches, and BMWs.

Drivers of band G cars will be charged £25 a day in congestion charges from 2009. People who live inside the congestion charge zone are entitled to a 90 per cent discount on the charges but that will be withdrawn for drivers of band G cars. At the same time cars that have the lowest emissions (in bands A and B) will become exempt from the congestion charges.

Chapter 14

Becoming a Green Tourist

- -

In This Chapter

▶ Examining the impact of tourism

▶ Cutting down the carbon emissions

▶ Getting the most out of your green holiday

▶ Ecotourism do's and don'ts

- -

*T*ourism is one of the biggest industries in the world. Visitors come to the UK and Britons go to every corner of the earth. Holidaymakers travel farther and more often. The no-frills budget airlines allow people to have not just one holiday a year but two or often three.

In days gone by, much of the travelling to and from chosen tourist destinations was done by train and boat. Now travellers want to get there and back faster and as cheaply as possible – so having longer to enjoy staying in a nice hotel at a wonderful resort with every possible attraction and recreation facility built by governments that wanted visitors to bring money and jobs to local areas.

The impact on the environment is felt in terms of the amount of carbon pumped into the atmosphere by flights and the degradation of the areas popular with tourists. Local populations in some parts of the world deeply regret the day the first traveller set foot on their beautiful unspoiled beaches because now they're overrun, overdeveloped, and no longer attractive – any benefits of tourism long since forgotten.

Everyone has a part to play in reducing that negative impact and making sure that the tourist destinations benefit from their visitors. *Eco-*, *ethical*, and *sustainable tourism* have been hailed as the way forward. These types of tourism aim to reduce the negative impact tourists have on the places they visit, to bring financial benefits to local people, and to increase awareness of the local environment and culture. But travellers have different ideas about how best to help local people and environments and preserve them. And as more people opt for environmentally correct holidays, numbers of visitors to ecotourism destinations may grow to the point where they are no longer sustainable.

Adding Up the Cost of Tourism to the Environment

As with anything involving increasing human demand, tourism has an impact. The impact on the environment and local communities from holidays is significant. The World Wildlife Fund (www.wwf.org) says that the impacts of increasing tourism in once remote parts of the world include:

- ✔ Huge developments in coastal areas ruining the local ecosystem, particularly plants and wildlife.

- ✔ Water use for tourism, including hotels, swimming pools, and golf courses in dry regions, greatly reducing the water supply for local populations.

- ✔ Development in natural areas altering the nesting and migration patterns of bird, sea, and animal life.

These impacts put pressure on the tourism industry to develop standards that encourage greater responsibility by tour operators and tourists themselves. The terms sustainable, ethical and ecotourism evolved out of the need to do something to reduce those negative impacts without turning tourists away from areas that badly need the income.

Cutting Down on Flights

The biggest culprit in causing damage to the planet by holiday travel is flying. Air travel is the fastest growing source of greenhouse gas emissions and those gases are released into the part of the earth's atmosphere where they can do most damage. A flight from Australia to London produces as many polluting gases as three cars do in a year. Add to those greenhouse gases pumping into the atmosphere the noise experienced by people living below the flight paths of planes and near busy airports, and you can see why many experts think that air travel should be reduced.

While you're reading this nearly half a million people are in the air over Europe on planes to all sorts of destinations. Flying has become second nature for many people. Half the population of the UK flies somewhere at least once a year and it's predicted that that level of air traffic will multiply by three by 2040. About a quarter of that travel is for business but that leaves a lot of holiday flights – creating a lot of carbon emissions. All of which means more planes, more runways, more airports, and more fuel. New, modern planes, built using the latest technology, are cleaner, less noisy, and more environmentally friendly, but they are still few and far between.

If you do nothing else to get greener on holiday, cut down on the number of flights you take each year. The first question to consider when you decide you need a holiday is how far you need to travel. If you have to get to the other side of the earth to see friends and relations then doing it without a flight may not be an option – but if you have the choice, and can go somewhere nearer home, think about other forms of travel before you book flights.

So before you fly think about whether or not you really need to make that flight. Everyone who flies can help the environment by reducing the number of flights they take each year.

Counting the costs of budget airlines

Budget airlines have made air travel cheap so people who couldn't previously afford to fly now can and those who can afford it are flying more often. Because air travel is highly subsidised and there's no tax on aviation fuel the people buying those cheap flights aren't paying the full cost of their journeys. If the airlines had to charge the true cost, air travel would fall.

If you have to fly, try to take direct flights. Cheaper flights may go via a third location. Taking off and landing use up more fuel than cruising at high altitude so if your trip includes a few hops you'll be responsible for more carbon emissions.

Boarding a train instead

There may be a greener way to get where you want to go. Taking the train is slower if you're travelling long distances but there's not a lot of difference in terms of time taking a train from Glasgow to London and vice versa, after you add in the check-in time at the airport and the time it takes to collect your bags. If you fly from London to Glasgow you're responsible for six times as many emissions as if you let the train take the strain.

You can take wonderful holidays in the UK and Europe where travelling by train adds to the enjoyment. You don't have to worry about your bags getting lost for a start and you get to see a lot of your home countryside. The train is a greener mode of transport – but not as green as cycling or walking holidays.

Boats and buses are worth thinking about too – greener and often cheaper, if slower.

Flying carbon neutral

No matter how green you want to be, sometimes you really do need to take a flight. As with any other aspect of being greener, every little helps and you shouldn't set yourself unrealistic targets. If you cut down on the number of flights you make each year and take the train, go on holidays locally, and fly only when necessary, you're doing your bit.

But you can make up for some of the environmental damage done by each flight you take. You can offset the greenhouse gases your flight pumps into the atmosphere by planting trees, or paying for trees to be planted, that will absorb the carbon in those gases. For example, if you fly from London to Australia and pay for five trees to be planted you can claim to be carbon neutral.

Of course the more carbon emissions you own up to, the more trees you have to plant or pay for and that can get quite expensive. Sites such as www.climatecare.org calculate the equivalent cost of your emissions and invest in a carbon reduction project to offset them. The CarbonNeutral Company is one of the biggest tree-planting organisations in the UK. There are also schemes where instead of paying for trees you pay for energy-efficient appliances or energy conservation schemes in developing countries helping local people. You can get more information from the Web site at www.carbonneutral.com Chapter 1 explains how you can make up for some of the carbon your lifestyle is responsible for pumping into the atmosphere – from heating your home to travelling by car.

Find out before you book your flights how much your tree planting will cost and factor that into your air ticket price. It currently costs about £9 a tree on average (examples of specific costs are £8 if you fly to Morocco and back and about £1 every time you fly from London to Glasgow).

Being carbon neutral is the next best solution to stopping flying. But it can't soak up all the emissions of airline travel. And there's not enough room to go on planting trees to make up for the carbon emitted by the ever-increasing rate of air travel – the earth isn't big enough. With people in China and India expected to travel more in future too, the air routes and the areas available for woodland will run out of space. Cutting down air travel is the only realistic option. Use less polluting options like the train if you must travel.

Being a Responsible Green Holidaymaker

The greenest holidays are those spent at home – enjoying the countryside around you without travelling long distances and adding to environmental damage. But sometimes you need to go farther afield. So make your break as green as possible.

Sorting out types of green travel

The travel industry is responding to increasing demand for green or responsible holidays and has come up with a variety of options:

- ✔ A **sustainable holiday** doesn't have a negative impact on the environment.

- ✔ An **ethical holiday** goes a bit further – it's sustainable but also about treating the local people fairly and equitably and making sure that the money you spend goes to the local economy.

  Much of the income generated by tourism in the developing world never reaches the local people.

- ✔ **Ecotourism** is sustainable and ethical but in a natural environment away from hotels and resorts. There's more on this increasingly popular type of holiday later in this chapter in the section 'Discovering Ecotourism'.

Local economies can benefit hugely from some types of tourism, and tourism provides some communities with their main source of income. But tourism that isn't managed sustainably and ethically can be very damaging, bringing pollution, cultural exploitation, environmental damage, and overdependence on tourism as a source of income.

Ask your tour operator if they have an ethical policy. Are they committed to reducing waste and water use, and to minimising damage to wildlife and marine environments? Do they use local staff and, wherever possible, locally sourced produce? Do they pay fair wages to their local staff? Tourism Concern at www.tourismconcern.org.uk can give you more information on some of the campaigns it runs to encourage ethical tourism, or have a look at *The Ethical Travel Guide* by Polly Pattullo, available from www.earthscan.co.uk.

The greenest holidays are sustainable, ethical, and ecofriendly. If you want to be truly green make sure that your holiday is as kind as possible to the environment and benefits the local community and economy at your destination.

Reducing the impact of your holiday

Holiday locally or choose the greenest travel option – take the train instead of the plane or car if possible. If you have to fly offset your carbon emissions (see the earlier section on 'Flying carbon neutral').

Stay in small hotels, bed and breakfast places, or self-catering accommodation – anywhere that's not part of a big chain. That way the money is likely to go to local people. If you take an all-inclusive holiday through a UK company little of what you spend is likely to stay in the local economy.

Check out the accommodation ahead of your trip to find the greenest possible – more places are using renewable energy, have wind turbines, and encourage you to reuse your towels instead of having them changed every day.

Eat in local restaurants which buy their food locally – fresh fish straight from the fishing boat and meat and vegetables from the local farmer so you cut out the air miles (see Chapter 7).

Get around using local public transport, walk, or hire bikes instead of polluting the atmosphere with a hire car.

Stick to the same green principles you use at home: Switch lights and appliances off at the wall when you're not using them; dry clothes in the fresh air rather than sending them to the hotel laundry; take a solar-powered phone charger with you (they use energy from sunlight in a way similar to solar panels and can be plugged into your mobile phone to charge it up. You'll find retailers if you type 'solar mobile phone charger' into a search engine or ask at walking, mountaineering, or climbing shops); stick to the marked paths and trails to save wear and tear on the countryside; find local recycling facilities and take your litter away with you.

Planning a Green Holiday

Some of the things to think about if you're travelling green:

- ✔ Making all the bookings – for travel and accommodation – yourself means that you can make the greenest choices.

✔ Getting there and back greenly involves looking at alternative ways of travelling.

✔ Choosing a green, responsible tour company to book through means going to one of their locations and trusting them to have already made the greenest choices.

✔ Going away for longer than usual and making that the only long-distance trip of the year cuts down carbon emissions.

If you book through a tour operator go for one that is a member of the Association of Independent Tour Operators – www.aito.co.uk and 020 8744 9280. Members of AITO have to protect the environment and natural resources, keep down pollution, make sure that local communities benefit from tourism, and that local cultures and customs are respected by visitors. Some tour operators give money to community projects in the countries they organise trips to. Ask before you book.

Choosing your location

The first step when planning a green holiday is to find out as much as possible about your destination. You'd be surprised how many people know nothing about a place before they arrive there – sometimes not even where it is on a map of the world.

Where you choose to go depends largely on what you want to do when you get there – diving, playing sport, lounging by the pool, and so on. Some things to take into consideration are

✔ Looking for somewhere that you can be as green as you are at home

✔ Doing something different – such as helping out on a local project while you're away

✔ Trying a working or volunteering holiday for a change, such as working on an organic farm

Do some research into what life is like for the local people. You deserve a bit of luxury on holiday but in some of the most luxurious holiday resorts local people live below the poverty line. Sometimes the only people living in luxury are holidaymakers in five-star hotels. If you book into one of those hotels on full board or for an all-inclusive trip very little of the money you spend ever reaches those local people and you leave again knowing almost as little as you did when you arrived.

Even if you're staying in the UK it's worth remembering that the big tourist towns and cities such as London and Edinburgh fare better than others in terms of attracting visitors and in some rural areas local people can be living on the breadline. Think about getting into less touristy areas and spending your money there.

Getting there and back

Local holidays are the greenest especially if you can use trains, buses, or bicycles to get you there. If there's a choice between flying, driving, and taking a train or bus, go for the train or bus. Flying and driving are the most polluting options.

Staying there

Whether you decide to spend some time in the world's great cities or towns or on top of a mountain, check out the accommodation options carefully. Camping is one of the greenest alternatives. Self-catering is next greenest, as you can buy and prepare local food and control the amount of energy you use. Apart from those that encourage you to reuse your towels you can book hotels these days that have their own renewable energy sources, bore holes for water, have water-saving devices, are decorated with environmentally friendly and recycled materials, and use only locally produced foodstuffs in their kitchens.

You may want to know how well hotels treat their staff and that hotels abroad employ local people on fair wages. When you find a place you may like to stay call and ask how green they are or ask your tour operator. Remember to research how accessible accommodation is to public transport.

Choose somewhere you can get to from the airport or train station without having to hire a car, and in the centre of everything you want to see so you can walk, cycle, or use public transport.

If you need to drive, hire a fuel hybrid car as described in Chapter 13.

You may find the following Web sites worth a visit before you book somewhere to stay: www.allstays.com lists green resort, hotel, and B&B accommodation around the world and www.specialplacestostay.com includes a guide to green places to stay.

When in Rome . . .

Whether you are on holiday in a big bustling city like Rome or in a tiny village in Patagonia make sure that your money is supporting local businesses and communities. Before you book find out whether the hotel, lodge, or hostel works with the local community and provides employment opportunities to locals. When you get there do your bit by:

- ✔ Using local guides.

- ✔ Buying locally made crafts and products. Avoid large tourist shops that make cheap copies or are imported from elsewhere. Try local market-places instead.

- ✔ Learning some of the local language so you can communicate and learn about the local community.

- ✔ Respecting the local culture by dressing appropriately. A good guide-book should give you advice.

- ✔ Finding out about the local environmental issues – you may have to con-serve water and energy, particularly in many remote developing parts of the world.

The best way to get to know a place is to try to do what the locals do:

- ✔ Buy food from local markets and shops to cook in your self-catering apartment. If you see a queue of local people, join it!

- ✔ Walk everywhere! The only people you mix with on tour buses are other tourists.

- ✔ Visit the local cafés and bars rather than stay in the hotels or tourist areas.

- ✔ Buy the local newspaper and tune in to some local radio and TV. Even if you don't understand a word the pictures and sounds give you a surpris-ingly good idea of local life.

Discovering Ecotourism

There's a lot of confusion, even in the travel industry itself, as to what eco-tourism is. Every company that offers a tour, accommodations, or service in unspoiled natural locations like national parks, wildlife areas, beaches, lakes, and even remote islands, claims to be an ecotour company.

The International Ecotourism Society (TIES) says that ecotourism is 'Responsible travel to natural areas that conserves the environment and sustains the wellbeing of the local people'.

The European Travel Commission at `www.etc-corporate.org` says that for a trip to be considered ecotourism:

- The destination is usually an unpolluted natural area.
- Its attractions are the flora and fauna and its entire biodiversity.
- Ecotourism should support the local economy and its indigenous atmosphere.
- It should contribute to the preservation of the environment, and promote the importance of conserving nature.
- Eco-trips often include a learning experience.

The International Ecotourism Society (TIES) at `www.ecotourism.org` says that ecotourism should:

- Minimise impact
- Build cultural and environmental awareness and respect
- Provide positive experiences for both visitors and hosts
- Provide direct financial benefits for conservation
- Provide financial benefits and empowerment for local people
- Raise sensitivity to a host country's political, environmental, and social climate
- Support international human rights and labour agreements.

As you can imagine, it's not easy to achieve all these objectives, and if you're trying to book a much-needed quick break at the last minute you're not likely to find the eco-holiday the cheapest and more accessible option. But demand for eco-holidays is on the increase as travellers become more aware of their impact on local environments and actively look for green holiday options. Local communities see ecotourism as a way to bring in travellers who will pay a bit extra which can go towards saving endangered species or conserve their natural ecosystems.

Ecotourism is a long way from the type of holiday where everything is paid for before leaving the UK and very little of the money spent ever reaches the local communities. The problem is that not everyone involved in providing eco-holidays, or the people who opt for them, agrees on how all these criteria should be measured. Ecotourism is being increasingly audited and there are now several accreditation systems in place to help you choose the right eco-tour service.

Getting help and information

If you're convinced that your next holiday should be greener than some you've taken in the past and want more information, try a few of the following Web sites:

✔ Ethical Escape – www.ethicalescape.com

✔ Sustainable Travel International – www.sustainabletravelinternational.org

✔ Responsible Travel – www.responsibletravel.com

✔ The European VISIT (Voluntary Initiative for Sustainability in Tourism) initiative – www.yourvisit.info

✔ Green Globe – www.greenglobe.org

✔ Eco Club – www.ecoclub.com

✔ The Centre for Environmentally Responsible Tourism – www.c-e-r-t.org

✔ Ethical Traveller – www.ethicaltraveller.com

✔ Conservation International – www.ecotour.org

It's up to you to do your own research to be sure that the holiday you're buying is a ecofriendly as possible. Don't take the word of the company you're booking through – it could claim to meet all the ecotourism principles but the issue comes down to whether a self-proclaimed ecotourism company is actually adding value rather than having a negative impact. You can't take their word for it. It may do absolutely nothing to conserve the environment and add value to the local community. Unfortunately there's no large-scale international certification scheme for eco-holidays – there's lots of different labels, many only relevant to specific countries and regions.

Two of the best-known and trusted international labels out there are:

✔ The Blue Flag label (www.blueflag.org) – a label for companies operating at beaches and marinas that meet strict criteria relating to water quality, environmental management, education and information, and safety.

✔ Green Globe 21 (www.greenglobe21.com) – a label based on the UN's Agenda 21 sustainability principles, Green Globe provides certification under four sustainability standards and is not limited to just ecotour companies but all tourism, whether it be in cities or natural areas.

Do your own research with the help of some of the organisations listed in the section 'Getting help and information'.

Hitting the ecotourism hotspots

The first question you may ask when thinking of an eco-holiday is where to go? Of course, it's best to travel locally if you can to cut down the damage caused by flying but there are also many cultural and economic advantages to travelling internationally, especially if local economies benefit.

Internationally, a growing number of countries and regions are becoming popular ecotourism regions. Some of the most popular locations with an increasing number of ecotourism attractions and services include:

- **Africa:** Kenya and Swaziland have become two of the most popular hotspots. Their national parks, deserts, and forests as well as their rich wildlife and traditional culture (such as the Kenyan Masai warriors) make them extremely popular places to visit but also put huge pressure on the tourism industry to make sure that the recent marked increase in tourism is managed sensitively.

- **South-East Asia:** Indonesia and Thailand are still the most popular destinations, with their rainforests and mountain ranges contrasting with stunning beaches. An increasing number of ecotourists are also starting to visit the relatively untouched countries of Cambodia, Laos, and Nepal.

- **Caribbean and Central America:** Some of the fastest-growing ecotourism spots in the world are popping up in beach and rainforest areas found in small countries like the Dominican Republic, Belize, and Costa Rica. Costa Rica has become one the most popular ecotourism destinations in the Americas due to its government support for tourism and its unmatched variety of rainforests, volcanoes, mountain ranges, and beaches.

- **South America:** Ecuador, Peru, and Brazil are high up the ecotourism lists, with the Amazon region in Brazil, the snow-capped volcano mountains and indigenous populations in Ecuador, and the Andes in Peru still the dream destinations for many travellers.

- **North America:** The beautiful, extensive but increasingly overcrowded national parks continue to attract visitors, with Alaska and Canada increasing in popularity.

An increasing number of guidebooks highlight the attractions of these natural parts of the world (check out the travel titles in the For Dummies series) as well as Web sites such as www.greenglobe21.com and www.blueflag.org. The international tour group co-ordinator Intrepid (www.intrepidtravel.com) is one of many that provide responsible adventure and eco-travel services. Type 'ecotourism' into a search engine and you'll find lots more.

Acting naturally

There's no point using the services of a company that sells eco-holidays if you have no intention of being an ecotourist. There are seven principles for leaving no trace when you travel to natural areas. Have a look at the Leave No Trace Center for Outdoor Ethics in the USA at www.lnt.org.

- ✔ **Plan ahead and prepare:** This principle includes scheduling your trip to avoid times of high use, only visiting in small groups, and working out how to take food and drink with you so that you will cause as little waste as possible.

- ✔ **Travel and camp on durable surfaces:** Choose ready-made campsites, don't alter a site to suit your purposes, and stick to existing trails. Walk in single file, and avoid places where you can see that impacts of use are starting to damage an area.

- ✔ **Dispose of waste properly:** If you bring it with you, take it away again. For washing and cleaning, use biodegradable products.

- ✔ **Leave what you find:** Don't take any rocks, plants, or other potentially valuable artefacts in your backpack when you leave.

- ✔ **Minimise the damage of campfires:** Light a campfire only if permitted and try to use established fire mounds when you do. Burn everything to ash just in case.

- ✔ **Respect wildlife:** Don't feed animals or other wildlife – it can alter their natural behaviour. Just view them from a distance.

- ✔ **Be considerate of others:** Respect and give way to other people on a trail.

Part VI
The Part of Tens

'They may be slow but they're eco-friendly and they also fertilise the lawn at the same time.'

In this part . . .

Every *For Dummies* book has a Part of Tens. In this one you'll find ten great things you can do today to be greener; ten great Web sites to look at; ten green ideas to try out for yourself; ten things to tell your children about being greener; and ten green projects you could get your own community involved in.

Chapter 15

Ten Great Sustainable Actions You Can Take Today

In This Chapter

▶ Getting started on being green without spending money

▶ Changing your behaviour in the long term

▶ Planning ahead for an even greener lifestyle

Many of the suggestions throughout this book require some planning and help to put into practice, but there are plenty you can get stuck into right now. This chapter lists the most easily doable that won't make any impact on your pocket and just require a bit of time and commitment.

Organising Your Recycling

Get your recycling organised and make life easy for yourself. You're more likely to recycle if it's convenient and that means in and out of your home. It helps if you have separate boxes or bags organised in your home so that you can simply drop your various items to be recycled into the right receptacle as you go along. It's so much easier than sorting them all out later.

You can recycle cardboard, newspapers, magazines, paper, glass, plastic, cans, and clothes. Check out the recycling facilities in your area. Call your local council's offices and ask to be put through to the appropriate person. Some local authorities provide big recycling bins at various points around their area and expect you to take your materials for recycling to those recycling points. Others provide special bins or boxes which you fill with the appropriate materials and these are then collected by the council on particular days.

If you have a garden, designate a bin for leftover food and peelings from fruit and vegetables and assign the task of adding the contents to your compost heap or composting bin.

You can recycle other household items by reusing them rather than just dumping them in the bin. For example, recycle your supermarket plastic bags by taking them with you the next time you go to the supermarket or using them as bin bags rather than buying new ones.

Cutting Down Your Car Use

Plan your driving schedule for the next week to cut down on the use of your car. If you have to drive your children to and from school, do your shopping on the way home or on the way to collect them in the afternoon. If you have to drive to and from work, do any other journeys that require the car on your way to or from work. Share journeys with other people you work with or take other people's children with yours to school. Take your car to the nearest bus or train station and use public transport for part of the journey. Think carefully about whether you can walk or cycle instead.

Even if you leave the car in the garage for only the shortest journeys you'll be doing your bit. Short journeys are often the most environmentally damaging as when the car engine is cold it uses more fuel and pumps out more damaging emissions.

Short journeys are often to the nearest shops and part of the reason for taking the car is because the items you need are too heavy to carry back. Check whether you have an old rucksack in the shed or on top of the wardrobe which you can carry your shopping home in. Tartan shopping trolleys with wheels may seem deeply unfashionable but they're very useful – you may start a new trend! And you'll be able to say 'no thank you' when you're offered a carrier bag in the shop.

If you have to use the car think about how you drive. Rapid acceleration and breaking use up more fuel. A smooth driving style is less damaging for the environment. Don't let the engine idle when you can turn it off.

Determining to Be Energy-Efficient

Decide here and now to become more energy-efficient. Look around your home at all the appliances you own. Many of them are plugged in and switched on even though you aren't using them. Go round switching them off. Many are on standby but unless appliances are switched off at the electrical socket they are likely to still be using some electricity. Leaving televisions, computers, and so on, on standby uses up about £150 million worth of electricity each year in the UK, which is utterly wasted and pushing up your bills.

Leaving your mobile phone charger plugged in and switched on even though there's no phone charging on the end of it uses about three quarters of the electricity the phone uses while charging.

Turn out lights in rooms no one is using, and turn down the central heating thermostat and the temperature of your hot water. The whole family can wear jumpers around the house instead of basking in shirt sleeves. Check the temperature setting of your fridge. It's wasting energy if it's set lower than 3 degrees C. Take a look at the back of the fridge too. If the elements at the back are covered in dust it will be struggling to do its job properly and using more electricity than it needs to.

The fridge and freezer are more energy-efficient if they are full. If your freezer has empty spaces fill them with newspaper.

When you put your washing on, go for a lower temperature wash. It uses less energy and there's a lot less risk of everything turning out blue or pink. And if you can dry the load outside or on a drying rack not only will you save energy by not using the tumble dryer but your clothes will smell fresher and be less likely to shrink.

Think about whether there's a more energy-efficient way of using your appliances. For example if you only boil the amount of water in the kettle that you're going to use rather than boiling a full kettle each time you want a cup of tea you save energy. If you have a fan-assisted oven using it with the fan on uses a lot more electricity then using it without. Make sure that your washing machine and dishwasher are full rather than doing small loads.

Over a longer period of time you can do a complete audit of the amount of energy each of your appliances uses. You can buy a simple gadget from electrical shops to plug your appliances into which measures how much is used. You can then see clearly where your electricity is going and get a clearer picture of what savings you can make.

Seeing the Light

When you're out at the shops buy some low-energy light bulbs. As your normal light bulbs blow you can replace them with ones that use up to a fifth less energy while giving out just as much light. They are more expensive but they last a lot longer than ordinary bulbs – up to 12 years – and so will save you money in the long run. If you can afford to replace all your existing light bulbs with low-energy ones today that will be one of the biggest energy efficiency steps you can take but if your budget won't stretch to that replace them one at a time.

Changing Your Energy Supplier

Some energy suppliers can sell you electricity generated by renewable sources such as wind power. Call your own supplier today and see if it offers a green energy package. Most of the big companies do. With some tariffs every unit you use and pay for is from a renewable source. With other packages you may pay a small premium on each unit which goes towards a renewable project. Every time you switch on a light or a kettle using non-green electricity you're responsible for carbon dioxide emissions.

With green electricity there are hardly any carbon emissions. If your own supplier can't come up with something suitable call around other suppliers until you find one that can, and switch.

Turning the Tap Off

Water is the most precious of natural resources and it has been taken for granted. From today you can reduce the amount of water you use just by cutting down on the amount you waste. The biggest waste comes from leaving the tap running while brushing your teeth. If everyone in the family gets out of that habit it's a good start to a greener household.

When you run the tap to get hot water the cold you're running off goes down the sink. Collect that water – in the kettle, in bottles if you like to have chilled water from the fridge, or a second basin so that you can use it to water your plants.

Make sure that the washing machine and dishwasher are full when you use them so you use them less often. If you're washing up by hand don't do it under a running tap. Take quick showers instead of baths but if you have a power shower or stay in the shower for longer than ten minutes you may use more water than for a bath. You can use bath water to water the garden (any bubble bath will be very dilute), wash the windows, floors, and the car.

Collect rainwater in a rainwater butt or a big plastic bin to use in the garden or for washing the car or bicycle. You may be able to collect the rainwater coming off the roof and down the spouting in a water butt. Keep a lid on it so it doesn't evaporate on sunny days.

Buying Only What You Need

If you're like anyone else you've probably bought many things over the years that you didn't really need and didn't get much use out of. Everything you buy has a tally of carbon emissions – emissions in the manufacturing process, emissions from the packaging, and emissions from transporting it to and from the store. The more you buy the more emissions you're responsible for. And many unwanted items are likely to end their days in a landfill site where they take thousands of years to degrade. If you really want to save the planet you simply have to buy less and use up less of the planet's natural resources.

The key to green living is to reduce, recycle, reuse, and repair. Think carefully about whether you need to buy something. If you don't buy it you reduce the impact you're having on the environment because you aren't responsible for any carbon emissions involved in the item's manufacture, you won't be using up the earth's resources, you won't be filling up landfill sites with unwanted packaging, and ultimately you won't have to dispose of it and release more emissions while it decays. You may already have something that would do the job as well if you repaired it. But be realistic! Life is too short for most people to darn socks these days, though you can use old socks for household cleaning.

Instead of buying, think about whether you can borrow the item from someone else or share one belonging to a friend. When you buy, consider whether the item can be recycled when you're finished with it. Maybe a friend can make use of it and pass it on, or a charity shop may be able to find it a good home.

Things like paper from presents and material from clothes can be reused, and gifts you've been given but don't want can be regifted to friends who would appreciate them.

Getting Everyone in the Household Onside

It's all very well taking the decision to lead a green lifestyle but it won't do much good unless everyone in your household agrees that it's a good idea.

Talk over your plans with everyone and your reasons for going green. Explain how you'd like everyone to play their part. Maybe each can have particular green responsibilities. It will take a while before all the mobile phone chargers are switched off at the socket when they're not being used but it's about changing behaviour until it becomes second nature and by doing it yourself and setting an example you'll find you create a new green culture around the home.

Children at school get more information about green issues than most adults so you can give your children the job of making sure that you are kept up to date with any practical tips they pick up that you can use at home. That way they feel as if they're leading the green revolution in your home.

Staying Informed

There is so much information around about leading a greener lifestyle that it's hard to know where to start. I hope this book gives you some practical tips and starts you thinking, but it just scratches the surface.

The best ways to contribute to saving the planet change from time to time as new evidence emerges of just what effect we are having on our environment. You can keep informed through the Internet and the wealth of green-related Web sites. Just type *green living* into any search engine and you'll find all sorts of useful information. Newspapers and radio and television programmes are all taking the issues much more seriously than they did a couple of years ago and they're useful for keeping up to date. It needn't cost you anything to keep yourself informed.

In Chapter 16 there are 20 Web sites that will give you enough information to be going on with, so the next step – after you finish this chapter – is to pay them a visit.

Planning to Take Bigger Steps to a Greener Lifestyle

Once you've started to think about leading a greener lifestyle and read the arguments about why everyone must become greener for the good of others and the planet, you may find that you want to do more.

The steps in this chapter don't take money to put into operation so if you can afford it, now's the time to plan what you'd ideally like to do if and when you can save up the money. Most of the green steps you can take that cost money to implement ultimately turn out to be a good investment. For example, you'll save money on your bills by getting rid of old appliances that can be replaced by much more energy-efficient models. Your food bills will come down if you can convert some of your garden to grow your own vegetables and that will pay dividends in terms of giving you healthier food and more exercise.

If you want to become dark green, instead of light or mid-green, you can produce some of your own power from solar panels or a domestic wind turbine. Research the grants you may be able to apply for and factor those into the amount you have to save. There's information on grants in Chapter 3. If your car is about to give up the ghost and you intend to replace it check out the greener options on the forecourts.

There's no need to rush into spending a lot of money on being green but with planning you may well find that it doesn't cost much more and will save you money in the long run.

Another way to play your part is to become involved in some of the local environmental schemes in your area. You can find some if you do a bit of research and if there aren't any that appeal to you think about starting up one of your own. Chapter 20 has some examples. You can help raise awareness of environmental concerns, inform other people, and bring about a culture change in the way other people think about their environment.

If you can change behaviour – of other people as well as yourself – you can consider yourself well and truly green and you'll make new friends into the bargain.

Chapter 16

Ten (Or So) Informative and Fun Web Sites

- -

In This Chapter

▶ Using the Internet as a source of green information

▶ Researching ideas to make your life greener

▶ Shopping over the Internet for green goods

▶ Finding Web sites that offer green things to get involved in

- -

*T*he Internet is a gold mine of information about green living. Anything you don't understand you can get an explanation for there. You can find all the information you need to join or set up different green schemes. There are Web sites for every aspect of green living from car-sharing as explained in Chapter 12, to getting grants to make green changes to your home as discussed in Chapter 3, to where to buy the green version of just about everything under the sun.

As a bonus, using the Internet is a fairly green way of finding out what you need to know, and buying the green items you want to use, because it uses up less energy and pumps out fewer greenhouse gases (see Chapter 1) than the alternative of getting in the car and driving around researching and shopping. The Web sites in this chapter are just a sample of what's available.

Assessing Your Impact on the Planet: www.myfootprint.org

Find out what impact you make on the planet by doing the Ecological Footprint Quiz. You answer 15 easy questions in whatever language you prefer. The Web site calculates the amount of land needed to support your consumption of the planet's resources – such as food and energy – as you go about your everyday life. You compare your results to those of people in other parts of the world. It's thought-provoking and helps you see where you can make a few changes.

Any change that makes your life a bit greener is better than no change at all.

Women's Environmental Network: www.wen.org.uk

This Web site aims to educate both women and men – despite its title – about environment issues, from the use of disposable nappies and renewable energy from wind and solar power to how to prevent waste and tips on household cleaning. The Women's Environmental Network is a charity and campaigns on health as well as environmental issues.

Freecycling: www.freecycle.org

The Freecycle Network (more in Chapter 17) promotes giving away items you no longer want to people who do want them. You keep your unwanted items out of landfill sites and recipients avoid buying the same thing new.

Freecycle groups are run by local volunteers who arrange the exchange of goods within each local group. It started off as one community based in Tucson, Arizona and has grown to 3,700 communities around the world.

Making the Modern World: www.makingthemodernworld.org.uk

The Web site for the British Science Museum shows how the modern world developed and explains the impact humans have had on the planet from the 18th century up to the present. The Web site has stories about science and inventions, learning modules, guided tours, information about all sorts of everyday objects from toothbrushes to teddy bears, and animated explanations of scientific discoveries and events such as the computer and the space race. You can spend a day out without leaving home!

Green Choices: www.greenchoices.org

Green choices is a not-for-profit company which aims to give you direct, simple information on green alternatives that help protect the environment.

The Web site gives you tips on every aspect of leading a greener life from what to feed your dog to how to reduce energy use in the office. It also has details of various college, university, professional, home study, and practical conservation courses available in the UK if you'd like to study or learn a skill relevant to greener living.

The Green Consumer Guide: www.greenconsumerguide.com

This site has information on all sorts of consumer issues from energy efficiency and insulation to green cleaning products and pension funds. The guide is run by a publishing company and the Web site has all the latest on the current environmental news stories such as genetically modified rice and seal culling.

The Green Directory: www.allthingsgreen.net

This is a Web site where, as the name suggests, you can buy all things green, from cards and organic cotton to elephant poo and ecofriendly garden furniture. If you have to shop, shop green.

The Woodland Trust: www.woodland-trust.org.uk

The Woodland Trust is a charity dedicated to the conservation of native woodlands in the UK. It campaigns on green issues. You can join and become involved in its work as a volunteer, helping to map the whereabouts of ancient trees, plant trees, or help with woodland surveys.

There are activities for children during the school holidays where they can make things or enjoy wet days splashing around outside, playing games and learning about the importance of woodland to wildlife.

The WWF: www.wwf.org.uk

The World Wildlife Fund is a charity dedicated to conserving the world's wildlife. Your whole family can join, which is great for children who are particularly attached to animals. You can help with the organisation's campaigns, adopt an animal, volunteer to help out at WWF events such as sponsored walks, or even take part and raise funds.

As soon as you see the tiger and panda on the site you'll be hooked.

And Some More for Good Measure

This list has ten more sites with varying functions and green perspectives:

- www.ethicalconsumer.org rates companies as to how green they are.

- www.soilassociation.org gives information about organic food production.

- www.farmersmarkets.net locates farmers' markets around the UK.

- www.est.org.uk offers advice on saving energy in your home.

- www.clear-skies.org provides information on renewable energy grants.

- www.envocare.co.uk posts easy tips on being greener – they believe that light green is better than not green at all.

- www.recycledproducts.org.uk contains a guide to recycled products.

- www.wasteonline.org.uk gives tips on reducing waste.

- www.ethical-junction.org offers information on all things green and ethical from organic compost to being an environmentally responsible tourist.

- www.environment-agency.gov.uk gives the Government's take on what's happening to the environment.

Chapter 17

Ten Green Ideas to Try

A s the green revolution gathers momentum, you can buy food and gadgets that make your life greener, donate unwanted goods, throw green parties, and even exercise with the environment in mind.

Being green doesn't always involve spending money. It can be about putting good ideas into practice and about helping other people by behaving ethically.

This chapter outlines just a few green ideas to try.

Freecycling

Freecycling is about getting rid of stuff you don't want and giving it away for free to someone who does want it. You can freecycle just about anything – clothes and shoes, handbags, electrical goods, furniture. Of course, you can make money selling on Internet auction Web sites but freecycling is a greener alternative. And, as well as offering your white elephants to others, you can pick up things you want that others are giving away free.

Advertise your unwanted items for free on www.freecycling.co.uk or www.gumtree.com – just two of the many freecycling Web sites around. Or join one of about 340 freecycling groups around the UK in which members freecycle their goods. The Freecycle Network at www.freecycle.org has details of the 3,700-plus freecycling groups all around the world.

Schemes like this cut down on the number of new goods that people buy and the amount of energy that goes into their production.

As a bonus, giving away what you no longer want makes you feel good and you're doing your bit to stop the landfill sites filling up.

Buying Organic Vegetable Boxes

Buying locally grown, organically produced food is the greenest way to eat. Chapter 7 explains that local food travels short distances and if it's organic very few if any chemicals are used to grow it. Most areas have Organic Vegetable Box schemes so there's likely to be one near you.

Some schemes deliver only locally grown produce so you get what's in season and you may not have as much variety as you'd like. Other schemes include some imported organic food so you have better variety, but the food has to travel long distances so it isn't as green.

Check out and compare the schemes carefully before deciding which to sign up to.

You can get more information about these schemes from the Soil Association, which is the main organisation in the UK for certifying produce as organic. Take a look at their Web site, www.soilassociation.org.

The supermarkets are also offering box schemes but the produce they deliver is likely to include a higher percentage of imported products, plus they're competing with local farmers. Buy directly from a local farmer if you can.

Eating with Your Children

If your children are involved in shopping for food and cooking it, they have much more of an idea where it's come from and what's good and bad for them. Take them to visit local farms or city farms that have open days so they understand the link between food and the countryside. If they're used to eating fresh foods, including fruit and vegetables, they're less likely to develop a taste for processed food.

Buying Fairtrade Goods

As explained in Chapter 7, Fairtrade is a trading scheme that works to make sure that producers in the developing world get equitable prices for their products, and that workers have reasonable working conditions and fair terms of trade with the firms they supply.

Shops and supermarkets carry an ever-expanding range of Fairtrade goods – around 300 at the time of writing – including tea, coffee, chocolate, bananas, herbs and spices, flowers, cotton, and footballs, and the list is growing as the scheme extends its reach. You can find more information about Fairtrade on their Web site at www.fairtrade.org.uk.

Traidcraft is the UK's main fair trade organisation and sells a whole range of goods produced under similar principles but without the Fairtrade logo. Find out more at www.traidcraft.org.uk.

Shopping for Green Gadgets

There are thousands of green gadgets on sale. More and more companies are getting in on the green revolution – coming up with new ideas every day. Just a few you may be interested in are:

- **Pouches** for your cigarette butts and used chewing gum while you're out of reach of litter bins. Find pouches to fit in your bag or pocket at www.buttsandgum.co.uk.

  Litter is not just antisocial but cost councils a fortune to clean up. Cigarettes butts don't degrade. At best they just cause unsightly litter; at worst they start forest fires. Chewing gum is notoriously difficult to get off the pavement, or your shoes and clothes if you happen to stick to it.

- **Solar powered or wind-up chargers** for your mobile phone and iPod. These used to be the preserve of hill walkers and mountaineers but they're more widely available now. You can get them from specialist shops for walkers or over the Internet. Type 'solar mobile phone charger' into a search engine and all sorts of retailers will pop up.

- **Bio-degradable mobile phones** are one of the latest inventions. They're made from bio-degradable plastic and have a sunflower seed in their innards. When you've finished with your phone, you compost it and a sunflower grows. Look out for them reaching the shops.

Going for Green Energy

Green energy is energy that comes from renewable sources – wind or solar power, for example. Most energy suppliers can sell you green energy and if yours can't, try switching to another that can. You can also make the most of the energy you have coming into your home by cutting down on the amount you use, switching off appliances at the wall instead of leaving them on standby (which still uses electricity), turning the heating down, and using more energy-efficient appliances.

Check out these green energy ideas:

- **Low-energy light bulbs** cut your electricity bills and save a lot of energy. They're more expensive than ordinary light bulbs but they last a lot longer. You can get them in DIY and hardware shops, and supermarkets.

- **Wind-up radios and clocks** are green – they use no energy and there are no batteries to dispose of.

Celebrating with Green Parties

Every big event in life – births, birthdays, anniversaries, weddings, Christmas and other religious festivals – deserves a party. Parties mean spending money and buying goods but make sure you buy green goods. Buy Fairtrade, Traidcraft, or locally produced organic food, drink, flowers, party supplies, and gifts. (Chapter 4 talks about ecofriendly entertaining and funerals.)

When it comes to gifts, make your own cards and do without wrapping paper – reusable gift bags produce less waste. Give presents that don't need lots of energy to operate, or that operate on solar power or are energy saving. Regift things you haven't used and don't want, or give ethical presents. Other low-impact gifts include artwork, tickets for the theatre or a restaurant, and donations to charity. Take a look at www.greenconsumerguide.com and www.greenchoices.org for more green ideas.

When it comes to posh parties outside your home, a good hotel should be willing to provide you with organic, locally produced food. Try www.green weddings.co.uk for ideas on how to keep your wedding green. Don't forget that the farther guests have to travel the more fuel they use and the more greenhouse gases they pump into the atmosphere.

Hen and stag parties in foreign cities mean air travel which has a big environmental impact – see Chapter 12 for more on this.

Limbering Up with Green Exercise

Exercise is important for health and keeping weight down. Many people go to a gym, but gyms aren't the greenest places to exercise. Gyms use a huge amount of energy in lighting, air conditioning, operating the equipment, and heating pools, saunas, and Jacuzzis. On top of that, pools are full of chemicals and the towels have to be constantly washed and dried. If you do use the gym, walk or cycle there instead of driving.

You can get greener exercise in the nearest park or at home. Exercise in the park and there's no energy involved apart from your own. Exercise at home and unless you use electrical equipment you'll use no more power then you normally would. Housework is a good form of exercise and it's no more boring than spending time on the treadmill. Plus, you save on those gym fees.

The British Trust for Conservation Volunteers has a list of Green Gyms where you get your exercise through helping to conserve buildings, repair footpaths, and cut down trees. Contact the Trust at www.btcv.org/greengym or call 01302 572244.

Letting Your Green Hair Down

Relax, I'm talking about washing your hair without shampoo rather than dying your hair green. The greenest option is to do without shampoo and wash your hair in water only or don't wash it at all. You may find your hair gets greasy and smells, though the greasiness usually lasts for just a month or so; or you may find your hair feels better.

If you stop washing your hair, you are saving on the cost of shampoo and conditioner and on heating water, and saving water itself – as well as reducing the chemicals you flush away.

Aside from the fact that shampoos are often tested on animals, they're usually full of chemicals, so every time you wash your hair you flush chemicals down the plughole. In addition, because of the demand for palm oil in all sorts of products, including shampoos, natural forests in areas like Borneo and Malaysia have been ripped up and replaced with palm tree plantations, leaving some wildlife under threat of extinction.

If you use shampoo try to buy palm-oil-free, green ones. Specialist shops such as health food and natural products chains have quite good ranges and some regular shops carry them as well. Try Green People at www.greenpeople.com or Yaoh shampoo at www.yaoh.co.uk.

Taking in Green Tenants

If you are lucky enough to have a house, flat, or room to rent out think about 'green renting'. It costs money to add green features to a house or flat but you can get ahead of the game. (Find out about green changes to make to your home in Chapter 3.)

So far, very few landlords have taken up the green-renting idea in the UK, but some estate agents say they're getting more and more enquiries from people who want the home they rent to be ecofriendly. Green renters are likely to pay a bit extra for a green home that's cheaper to run. They're also likely to stay longer, so you don't have so many periods when the property is empty while you look for a new tenant.

Chapter 18

Ten (Or So) Things to Tell Your Kids about Sustainable Living

- -

In This Chapter

▶ Sharing the basics of conservation

▶ Giving children an understanding of how the world around them works

▶ Bringing children up with a respect for the earth's resources

▶ Equipping children to get involved in doing something to protect the planet

- -

*O*ften interest in green living starts with children. They're taught about being green in schools and pass information on to their parents. They may already know more than you! The more you discuss with each other the need for living a greener lifestyle and the more responsibility children have for leading the way at home, the more chance they'll continue to spread the message.

It takes patience to get children to behave in the way you want. Decide from the beginning that any move towards a greener lifestyle is better than none and applaud your child for every achievement along the way. No child will turn dark green overnight so take it one small step at a time.

Starting with the 3 Rs

Reducing, reusing, and recycling are the basics of green living (see Chapter 6 for more detail). Recycling is something most children learn about in school and is second nature to many. At home, let your children do much of the sorting out of recyclable items and make them responsible for their own rubbish. Reducing and reusing are harder ideas to get to grips with.

Children usually want what their friends have, so encouraging them to go without the latest toys and gadgets, or to go on using the ones they've got, can be difficult. They're more likely to get the message if you explain to them that children just like themselves, in other parts of the world, or animals, may be negatively affected – that the carbon emissions that come from making new goods could result in floods or melting ice and children or animals could lose their homes as a result.

Paring Down Packaging

Explain when you buy anything why you think it's the best choice out of the options available to you. Agree to buy the toy without packaging rather than the one in a box with several layers of plastic. If you do have to buy goods in packaging ask your children to look on the shelves for the brand with recyclable packaging.

If you can't do without something and it comes in packaging that can't be recycled or reused and has to go in the rubbish bin, explain what happens to it next and why you feel that's a waste and bad for the environment.

Say no to the offer of bags in shops and take your own with you. Children soon get used to making sure you've got your reusable bags with you when you go shopping. Keep on doing what you believe in and lead by example and the messages will get through. Children learn from each other and yours will teach their friends good habits.

Finding Out About Food

Talk to your children about what goes into the foods they eat and why you buy the foods you do. Explain where the food starts its life. If you buy locally produced foods find out if you can visit one of the farms and let the children ask questions. If they can pick their own they'll enjoy eating it too. You – or the farmer – can explain the link between the countryside, the animals, the fruits and vegetables, and the food on their plates. Help your children understand why some farming methods are better for the environment than others.

When you shop ask your children to find various items to go in your trolley. Show your children how to read food labels to discover how the food was produced and where it comes from as well as the contents. Ask them to check the labels for the lowest salt, sugar, or fat content. You need a lot of patience with younger ones but it's not long before they pick up the idea. Ask them to let you know if new products appear on the shelves so that you can compare the ingredients together and decide if new is better or not.

When you get the food home let them help you cook it. Schools don't teach as much about food and cooking as they used to, so children miss out on the joys of creating a mess in the kitchen. You can't do this every day, or you'll never have time to do anything else, but if you can do it even occasionally children will be more interested in what they're eating.

Helping Grow Your Garden

The garden is a great place for children to discover the environment. Water recycling and composting systems are good examples of the three Rs in practice. (Chapter 5 explores these topics.)

If you have space, grow some vegetables and perhaps plant a couple of fruit trees. Growing your own food – even only a tiny percentage of it – clearly establishes the link between food and the environment. It also gives you a chance to explain why some people use chemicals in the growing of food and others prefer not to. Give over a small area of the vegetable patch to the children and let them grow what they like. They may never successfully produce anything edible, and they may lose interest, but if things do grow the sense of achievement may spur them on to bigger and better enterprises.

If you have a showpiece garden with perfect lawns and flowerbeds that require a lot of attention, children get the idea it's all very hard work. Set aside an area where wild flowers can grow naturally and attract butterflies and bees. A bird feeder will attract birds and you can help the children identify all the different species that fly in.

A worm farm is fun for children and a small pond attracting a few frogs is worth thinking about when the children get a bit older.

Being Green Is Trendy

It's hard to keep up with the latest trends and at the same time reduce the number of items you buy and keep reusing them. But you can try to strike a balance with items such as games consoles and MP3 players by negotiating. Explain that you think new electronic equipment uses up precious resources and get an agreement to greener behaviour in some other aspect of life – such as giving up the longed-for fake fur jacket that takes gallons of oil to produce. And give the old games console to someone who will appreciate it so it's reused and recycled.

Though the fashion industry certainly encourages consumption, at the moment vintage clothes are fashionable and celebrities often sport second-hand items mixed with the latest off the catwalk. Buying second-hand goods is green because it's reusing, recycling, and reducing the number of new items produced. So, this is a good time to convince your children to follow their style icons.

Show your children how to take care of their clothes. If you have the time and are handy with a needle, brainstorm ways to alter out-of-fashion items to keep them fashionable for longer – like turning long trousers into cropped ones or into shorts.

Children do need to feel they're the same as their peers so if you take too firm a stand on clothes and they feel left out they may rebel against all your green ideals. Don't put them off being green by being too rigid – you may win the battle and lose the war.

Whether being green will continue to be trendy remains to be seen, but if children become aware of the issues when they're young, they're more likely to continue to take them seriously – so take this opportunity.

Cutting the Electricity Bills

Getting children to turn off lights when they're not in their rooms, or to switch mobile phone chargers and computers off at the wall when they're not using them, is a near impossible task. (Getting yourself in the habit didn't happen in a day, did it?)

Discuss with your children the different ways of producing electricity and how the ever-increasing demand for electricity around the world is putting pressure on the world's resources of oil, gas, and coal. Explain the possible link between burning those fossil fuels to make electricity and climate change. It gets children thinking when you explain how (if scientists are right) something we do in this country may affect the lives of children the same age in other countries – possibly leading to longer periods of drought and greater food shortages.

Don't scare your children or make them feel personally responsible for all the world's problems. Discuss with them the things they can do to help make sure bad things don't happen.

Closer to home explain how shortages of gas and high world oil prices are pushing up the household fuel bills. Give them a degree of responsibility over finding ways to keep those bills down. Make it the job of one child to switch off all the mobile phone chargers that aren't being used. Ask another to check all the lights are off before you go out for the day.

Ask them all to keep thinking about ways to keep the bills down and to let you know of any tips they hear at school or in friends' homes. Children respond to having a role to play in the family.

Counting the Cost of Car and Air Travel

If there's no choice but to use your car for most journeys ask your children to think of ways to cut down using the car. If children get used to going to school by car and never walk or take the bus, it's hard to break the habit. But they may have friends who also go to school by car and whose parents can share the journeys with you. If there are several families who can share the driving, ask the children to work out the rota once they're old enough to remember what's been arranged. Children can take pride of ownership in a plan they've come up with.

Often children actually prefer to walk or cycle but parents are reluctant to allow them out alone. Ask if there are friends who would like to walk or cycle together. Arrange for them to go on a cycling proficiency course and everyone will feel safer.

Cycling is good exercise, but if it isn't fun, all the messages about reducing pollution and greenhouse gases, and using a cheap means of transport, fall on deaf ears. Your children will demand a car as soon as they're old enough to drive. Be flexible about reverting to a lift in the car occasionally when the weather's bad or cycling is just too much of a struggle.

Talk to your children about holidays they would like to have in the UK and explain why it's good for the environment to cut down on the number of flights you make. Explain to them about offsetting the amount of carbon your travel produces (Chapter 1 talks about becoming carbon neutral) and work out how much that costs for each journey. Ask your children to think about that cost and help you to decide as a family whether to pay the extra or to cut down on the travelling you do.

Reining in the Water Use

Most children love water as long as they don't have to wash too often. Remember that when you're nagging your children to have a shower and brush their teeth you're asking them to use water. When you're telling them to turn off the tap while brushing their teeth and have showers instead of baths to save water, you're sending out a fairly mixed message. If possible go for reusing and recycling water. Collect rainwater in a butt in the garden and use that for flushing the toilet. Teach your children to flush the loo when there's brown matter in it but leave it when there isn't. If you can install a system to collect bath and shower water before it reaches the sewage system and reuse it, they'll see that their used water can be used for washing the car and the windows, and watering the garden. Keep the messages simple.

Getting Involved in Projects That Protect the Planet

Trips to any projects concerned with the planet and how it works will whet your children's appetite to know more. Camping, and visits to farms, museums, landfill sites, and recycling plants are interactive demonstrations that get them interested.

If they do show an interest set them the task of checking in their local area and on the Internet for projects that they'd like to become involved in that give them practical experience. You'll find a few suggestions of the kinds of local projects you're likely to find in Chapter 19 and various Web sites to visit in Chapter 16.

Respecting Other Cultures

Appreciating how people in other cultures live and what problems they face can help children understand why adults are getting so worked up about the environment and leading a greener lifestyle. Explain the ideas behind fair trade, air miles, locally grown food, and saving local environments such as the rainforests. Discuss with them how demands for more and more oil and wood, for example, take valuable resources out of the earth that can't be put back. Show them what our demands do to the areas these resources are taken from. Talk to them about the alternatives. Relating the need to use alternatives to the effects our lifestyles have on other people will give them a picture that's easier to understand.

Making a Career Out of Green Living

Careers teachers in schools don't always mention careers in conservation and environmental protection when giving children advice, even though this growing sector has a lot of job opportunities.

Natural Talent (www2.btcv.org.uk/display/naturaltalent) is a training programme of apprenticeships for the next generation of naturalists. It's based in Scotland and Northern Ireland and gives young people with an interest in the natural world the opportunity to learn specialist conservation skills. There are apprenticeships in beetles, freshwater and grassland conservation, lichens, and more.

Apprentices get money from a bursary scheme and extra money for training and equipment. You don't need any qualifications to apply, and the training lasts for 12 to 18 months depending on which apprenticeship you choose.

Chapter 19

Ten Green Projects to Get the Whole Community Involved

Community involvement brings together like-minded people who all have ideas about how to improve the environment around them, and several minds are usually better than one. New community-based environmental projects are springing up every day all over the UK as concern grows. They range from groups that campaign for change on a big scale – for example lobbying the government to change its policy on public transport so that people can leave their cars at home and travel by bus or train – to groups of local people who roll up their sleeves and rebuild a crumbling old building so that the local ecosystem isn't damaged, because it's home to a colony of bats.

This chapter gives a few examples of the kinds of projects going on in different parts of the UK. Contact your own local authority for information on what's going on around you or check the Internet, your library, and local papers, or set up a project of your own with neighbours in your street. Real interest and concern for the environment grows out of small schemes, organised to do something like clean up the park nearby or plant trees in local woodland. And getting the community involved no longer has to mean being involved in a scheme going on in the same street or town – you can be involved in something on the other side of the world or in a network of projects that span the globe. The world is your oyster.

Taking Action for Nature

Action for Nature (www.actionfornature.org) is a worldwide community project that encourages young people to do their bit to protect the environment wherever they are. Children set up recycling schemes in their communities among friends and families, or campaign for their school to use recyclable plates and cups instead of plastic ones and to buy food in recyclable packaging. The list of projects and ideas is endless.

Action for Nature collects the stories young people tell them about what they've been doing that's green, publish those stories and gives eco-awards each year for the best projects.

The messages the group gives to children about recycling are the same as in this book – like using public transport, buying less, and protecting the wider environment – but it is a practical project that encourages *doing* instead of just talking about the issues. It also encourages children to spread the messages to friends and members of their families.

Cleaning Up the UK

Thames21 (www.thames21.org.uk) is an environmental charity working with communities in London to clean up the Thames and the other rivers and canals in the capital and turn them into places that everyone can use and enjoy. Thousands of volunteers get involved every year to clean up messy beaches along the riverside, remove graffiti, and create new habitats for wildlife. Local groups join their own area's Adopt-a-River or Adopt-a-Canal project and take responsibility for caring for their own stretch of the river or canal. Frequent river clean-ups are open to everybody to join in, with training and equipment provided. At the same time, Canalkeeper Volunteers work to change things in the long term.

Keep Wales Tidy (www.keepwalestidy.org) runs a Renewal Area Environmental Project which aims to involve communities in caring for their local environment and to work more closely with the local authorities to reduce the problem of litter on the streets, in the countryside, in rivers and other waterways, or on the coast. Their aims are to work with communities to assess the condition of the local environment and work out where improvements can be made. Local people are asked for their views on what the priorities should be, and then community groups are set up, trained, and supported to take on practical environmental projects.

Where there are rivers and canals, areas of common land, pathways, and neglected parks, there are projects like these. Waterways in particular seem to attract plastic bags and supermarket trolleys, old sofas, and even the odd burnt-out car. Anything that releases chemicals into the water endangers the fish and birds, which get tangled up and die in rubbish-infested waters. Clean rivers and canals are havens for wildlife. If your local stretch of river looks neglected and in need of tender loving care, ask your local authority and local conservation groups what plans they have for cleaning it up. If there are none start a group to campaign and get local charities and businesses involved. Go on-line to www.btcv.org and contact the British Trust for Conservation Volunteers. It's the biggest organisation in the UK promoting practical conservation work.

Getting Schools to Lead the Way

E Schools is a project for local schools in the Bradford district under the banner of the Bradford Community Environmental Project that involves developing the school grounds to enhance children's learning. The aim is to support schoolwork and act as outdoor classrooms, as well as improving the school environment. Pupils are involved at every stage, from consultation to installing and maintaining the areas.

Some of the innovative ideas being worked on at the seven primary schools and one secondary school are making habitat boxes – which provide homes for birds and other wildlife and encourages them to move into the school grounds; planting fruit orchards; creating adventurous play areas with green gyms, where you can get fit out in the open, and quiet seating areas; growing food, wildflower meadows, and butterfly and sensory herb gardens; promoting pond and bog areas; and developing a sculpture/nature trail.

Other groups in the area are also involved with E Schools. Local theatre groups plan to deliver a programme of environmentally themed drama workshops. Leeds Development Education Centre is introducing 'Global Footprints', a project where children calculate their personal impact on the environment. And an Environmental Education Officer is teaching the 3 Rs – Reduce, Reuse, and Recycle! Check out www.bcep.org.uk to find out more and see how you can get involved.

These kinds of projects aren't confined to Bradford. Ask your local authority what's going on in schools in your area and how you can get involved. The Centre for Alternative Technology offers a range of resources for schoolchildren and students (www.cat.org.uk/education).

Building Centres for Change

Craigencalt Ecology Centre (CEC) is a community-based project in Fife in Scotland. It was set up in 1998 and is run mainly by volunteers. The centre provides direct experience of the environment to school groups, community organisations, and individuals. It aims to use nature as a tool to improve people's lives in the countryside and in towns and cities, and it works with people with learning and physical disabilities. It offers training for teachers and talks and tours for pupils. The volunteers raise awareness of environmental issues and encourage the rest of the community to get involved.

Over the years the centre has developed areas of community woodland and installed footpaths, and created an organic market garden. There are various events and social gatherings and practical demonstrations of environmental developments, such as renewable energy production. Members of the local community are encouraged to visit and the centre hopes to attract more visitors from outside the area. The site is open so you can wander around, free of charge, and see if volunteering to help appeals to you.

The UK's first Earthship is also at Craigencalt. An *Earthship* is a building made from natural and recycled materials, including tyres and aluminium cans. It uses renewable energy, such as wind, water, and solar power to provide heating and electricity. It catches its own water supply from rainwater, and treats its own sewage. An Earthship allows people to build homes and live in a way that is as easy as possible on the surrounding environment. See the centre's Web site at www.cfec.org.uk to find out more or have a look at www.earth ship.co.uk where a short video explains the idea.

Community Webnet (www.communitywebnet.org.uk) is an organisation that helps and supports community environmental projects in Scotland – like the Graigencault Ecology Centre – to get started, find funds, and develop. Take a look at their Web site for details of all sorts of projects and what they've achieved. The Centre for Alternative Technology at www.cat.org.uk has information and advice on all sorts of environmental projects around the UK – it's the UK's leading eco-centre and has been trying to reduce the impact people have on the environment for the past 30 years.

Restoring the Past

Rebuilding, restoring, or upgrading sites or buildings of importance to an area's history is a good way of contributing to your local environment, and you can join in one of thousands of projects going on at any one time around the UK.

Turn is a village in East Lancashire. The groups behind the restoration project there have been given ownership of an old mill pond and three fields around it. Members of the local community and two schools nearby are restoring and upgrading the site to a wetland wildlife reserve, and producing information boards and booklets about the local industrial and natural heritage. There will be a newsletter and workshops, guided walks, a willow maze, seats, and bird and bat boxes. There are also plans for a *yurt,* an all-weather shelter, for the exhibition boards and workshops.

Projects like this may get help from the Local Heritage Initiative (LHI) – a scheme of small grants ranging from £3,000 to £25,000 which aim to bring local heritage to life. The LHI provides funds, advice, and support to help local community groups research and care for local landmarks, landscape, traditions, and culture. Take a look at www.lhi.org.uk to find out more.

Regenerating Communities

There are thousands of examples up and down the UK where local people make big contributions to their villages and towns by giving their time to projects. Just one example is the Bishops Green Project Team, which includes local residents and representatives from the nearby town, parish and county councils, housing groups, police and health services, all working together to improve the environmental, social, and economic wellbeing of the Bishops Green area of Basingstoke and its residents.

The results include improved play areas and youth facilities; a new village hall and shop unit in a more central location within Bishops Green; planning for redevelopment in the village; and provision of temporary additional car parking, pending development, to ease some of the parking problems that exist. The Basingstoke local authority Web site at www.basingstoke.gov.uk/planning/regeneration/bishopsgreenproject has more information.

Green Waste Recycling Projects

Conservation Volunteers Northern Ireland (www.cvni.org) run a large-scale recycling project, based in the town of Coleraine. They have all the necessary equipment – shredder, tractor, screener, lorry, and more – funded through various grants.

The project recycles all of Coleraine Council's green (garden) waste – around 4,500 tons per year. This waste doesn't end up in landfill sites and brings the organisation revenue for this and other environmental projects. The volunteers operate a kerbside collection scheme around some local housing estates, which will bring in another 500 tons of waste a year. They also work to involve the community in the project and bring recycling to people's attention.

One of their aims is to make good-quality compost for use as natural fertilisers, mulch for gardens, and as an alternative to peat-based composts, so reducing pressure on peat bogs which are very valuable wildlife habitats in Northern Ireland.

Elsewhere in the UK, conservation volunteers are needed for similar recycling projects and a whole range of others. The British Trust for Conservation Volunteers (www.btcv.org) can give you more information about volunteering.

Car-sharing

If you live in a big city there are probably several car-sharing schemes to join. Check www.nationalcarshare.co.uk for your nearest ones.

In rural areas, car-sharing schemes are fewer and farther between. There are only two listed on the Web site www.villagecarshare.com at the time of writing, but the Web site has all the information you need to start up one of your own. Talk to your neighbours and other people in your village to see what they think of the idea. If there's enthusiasm for setting up a scheme the Web site answers all the questions you're likely to ask and tells you about getting funding with parish council grants, finding people to share journeys with, and marketing the scheme. Even if you have just two members in your scheme you're cutting down car use, and as fuel prices rise and more people become used to the idea that car use has to be reduced, membership will rise.

Trading Locally

LETS – Local Exchange Trading Schemes – are local trading networks. People in the community exchange all kinds of goods and services with one another without money being involved. You trade your goods and services for the alternative currency and use it to pay for items and services you want. (Chapter 9 has more on LETS.)

These trading schemes are green for all sorts of reasons: members buy fewer new goods; goods traded between members are being reused and recycled; often someone involved repairs broken goods so they don't end up in a land-fill site; members living locally don't have to travel far to provide their services; and fewer service people have to travel into the community to do jobs the members can do. It all reduces the local community's impact on the environment.

If there's no scheme in your area already talk to friends and neighbours about setting one up. Go to www.letslinkuk.net for more information.

Volunteering Virtually

Not everyone can leave home to volunteer for some of the types of projects mentioned in the rest of this chapter. If you have children, someone elderly or sick to look after, or have a disability that keeps you indoors, some schemes are out of the question. Virtual Volunteering is a new approach to involving people. You do your voluntary work over the Internet. That means you can volunteer for any project that you're interested in anywhere in the world as long as it accepts virtual volunteers. You arrange to complete the tasks at a time and place that suits you.

So far the kinds of job asked of virtual volunteers are Web site design, building databases, writing newsletters, fundraising, research, and mentoring. Find out more about how virtual volunteering works from CSV – a charity which places community service volunteers with organisations that need help – at www.newnet.org.uk. You can also try Timebank (www.timebank.org.uk), a charity dedicated to encouraging people to volunteer in their communities. (See Chapter 9 for more on Timebanks.)

If you want to get involved virtually with a particular project in your own community or farther afield, contact the organisation directly and offer your services. This type of volunteering is taking off and as you're using next-to-no energy to make your contribution, you're contributing doubly to the green revolution.

Appendix

The Best Green Web Sites

*T*hroughout this book, we've made suggestions about living a greener lifestyle – from swapping to a green energy supplier to shopping ethically. However, we can only add a limited number of ideas and Web sites in the text without the links getting in the way of the text, so this appendix points you in the right direction to explore the varied, wider world of green living, listing even more useful Web sites for you to look at.

Great Green Advice

eekos (www.eekos.com). This Web site supplies information, goods, and services that assist in building and maintaining healthy, sustainable lifestyles, and repairing and conserving natural ecosystems.

Environment Agency (www.environment-agency.gov.uk). The Web site of the leading public body for protecting and improving the environment in England and Wales.

Ethics Resource Center (www.ethics.org). The Ethics Resource Center in the US advances understanding of the practices that promote ethical conduct, and develops white papers and educational resources based on overall findings.

Friends of the Earth (www.foe.co.uk). Since 1971, Friends of the Earth has been campaigning for solutions to environmental problems. Friends of the Earth is the most extensive environmental network in the world, with almost a million supporters across five continents and more than 70 national organisations worldwide.

Greenpeace (www.greenpeace.org.uk). Greenpeace stands for positive change in the world, and has been campaigning for the environment since 1971.

Green Consumer Guide (www.greenconsumerguide.com). Offering green consumer advice in the UK.

Green Matters (www.greenmatters.com). A Web site including advice and forums on green living.

Women's Environmental Network (www.wen.org.uk). The Women's Environmental Network represents women and campaigns on green issues linking women, environment, and health.

Worldwatch Institute (www.worldwatch.org). The Worldwatch Institute offers interdisciplinary research, global focus, and accessible writing that has made it a leading source of information on the interactions amongst key environmental, social, and economic trends. Its work revolves around the transition to an environmentally sustainable and socially just society, and how to achieve it.

World Wildlife Fund (www.wwf.org.uk). This WWF isn't anything to do with wrestling! The World Wildlife Fund conserves endangered species, protects threatened habitats, and addresses global threats such as climate change.

Energy

Biodiesel Filling Stations (www.biodieselfillingstations.co.uk). Sources of biodiesel in the UK.

British Wind Energy Association (www.bwea.com). The British Wind Energy Association is the trade and professional body for the UK wind and marine renewables industries, promoting wind power on and off shore.

Centre for Alternative Technology (www.cat.org.uk). The Centre for Alternative Technology demonstrates practical ways to address environmental problems. The key areas it works in and promotes are renewable energy, environmental building, energy efficiency, organic growing, and alternative sewage systems.

Ecotricity (www.ecotricity.co.uk). Ecotricity is an electricity company dedicated to changing the way electricity is made. Taking the money its customers spend on electricity, Ecotricity invests it in clean forms of power like wind energy. Ecotricity is also the only green electricity company actually building these new renewable energy sources.

Energy 21 (www.energy21.org.uk). Energy 21 Trust is an environmental charity promoting renewable energy. This Web site also contains online issues of the charity's *ReGeneration* newsletter.

Energy Saving Trust (www.est.org.uk). Set up in 1992, the Energy Saving Trust seeks to achieve the sustainable use of energy and to cut carbon dioxide emissions.

Forest Stewardship Council (www.fsc-uk.org). The FSC is an international organisation promoting responsible management of the world's forests. Founded in 1993 it provides an environmentally friendly wood-labelling scheme. This book is printed on FSC-approved paper (check out the logo on the copyright page, and look for it in other books, too).

Green Building Store (www.greenbuildingstore.co.uk). This company provides building and energy products promoting energy-efficient, sustainable, and healthy buildings. There's an online shop, too.

Green Prices (www.greenprices.co.uk). Green Prices provides clear information about green energy and keeps you updated about the green schemes operated by energy suppliers.

Low Carbon Buildings (www.lowcarbonbuildings.org.uk). This is the Web site for the DTI's low carbon buildings programme (providing grants for low carbon buildings). You can apply for a grant whether you're a householder or managing a business, school, or charity.

National Energy Foundation (www.nef.org.uk). The NEF's objective is to work for the more efficient, innovative, and safe use of energy and to increase the public awareness of energy in all its aspects. Currently it works in the areas of renewable energy and energy efficiency.

Food

British Association of Fair Trade Shops (www.bafts.org.uk). This association promotes fair trade retailing in the UK, seeks to raise the profile of fair trade on the High Street, and provides a point of contact and communication for the exchange of ideas amongst its members. The Web site has a locator to help you find fair trade shops near to you.

Ethical Shopper (www.ethicalshopper.co.uk). This online food store aims to give you an ethical alternative for your everyday consumables without compromising on quality.

Fairtrade Foundation (www.fairtrade.org.uk). The Fairtrade Foundation's Web site provides details of Fairtrade products, suppliers, and retailers (including relevant UK supermarkets); details of their campaigns, and how you can get involved, are included too.

The Irish Organic Farmers and Growers (www.vic.ie/iofga.htm). The Irish Organic Farmers and Growers Association was established in 1981 and is the largest organic association in Ireland.

National Farmers' Retail and Markets Association (www.farmersmarkets. net). This Web site helps you to locate certified farmers' markets in your local area. FARMA, the National Farmers' Retail & Markets Association, independently assesses and certifies farmers' markets to make sure they're the real deal.

Organic Farmers and Growers (www.organicfarmers.uk.com). The Organic Farmers and Growers is an organic certification body, carrying out the inspection and licensing of organic farming and food processing across the UK. They can also provide certification for catering, transport, and other enterprises requiring organic approval.

The Organic Food Federation (www.orgfoodfed.com). The Organic Food Federation supports the interests of organic manufacturers, and has adopted the definitive UK legal organic standards.

The Scottish Organic Producers Association (www.sopa.org.uk). This association provides information on organic food producers in Scotland.

Sustain (www.sustainweb.org). Sustain – the alliance for better food and farming – advocates food and agriculture policies and practices that enhance the health and welfare of people and animals, improve the working and living environment, enrich society and culture, and promote equity.

The Vegan Society (www.vegansociety.com). This society promotes vegan lifestyles, and their Web site contains plenty of helpful advice and information including environmental advice.

The Vegetarian Society (www.vegsoc.org). The Vegetarian Society of the United Kingdom is the oldest vegetarian organisation in the world, offering advice and nutritional information (and running vegetarian cookery courses, too!).

Gardening

Elemental Solutions (www.elementalsolutions.co.uk). Elemental Solutions offers independent advice on sustainable water management.

Garden Advice (www.gardenadvice.co.uk). This Web site aims to provide simple, straightforward gardening advice, including a section on organic gardening.

Greenhouses UK (www.greenhouses-uk.com). All sorts of greenhouses are offered by this online shop, along with information on using them.

Green Fingers Trading (www.greenfingers.com). Ideas, information, advice and products for your garden, including an online store and articles on organic gardening.

The Organic Gardening Catalogue (www.organiccatalog.com). Web site of Garden Organic (HDRA), Europe's leading organic gardening organisation. Sells organic seeds and environmentally friendly gardening products.

The Soil Association (www.soilassociation.org). The Soil Association is the UK's leading campaigning and certification organisation for organic food and farming. This Web site includes a library of over 400 articles about organic issues and the association's work.

Soil Association Scotland (www.sascotland.org). Soil Association Scotland is the devolved national office of the Soil Association. Based in Edinburgh, this office brings the Soil Association's expertise closer to farmers, manufacturers, consumers, and policy-makers in Scotland.

Health

The British Complementary Medicine Association (www.bcma.co.uk). The BCMA is the leading authority in the field of complementary medicine, helping therapists in all aspects of their work.

The British Homeopathic Association (www.trusthomeopathy.org). This Web site aims to provide accurate and helpful advice about homeopathy, including a series of articles on homeopathy and a locator to find a nearby practitioner.

The British Acupuncture Council (www.acupuncture.org.uk). The UK's main regulatory body for the practice of acupuncture by over 2500 professionally qualified acupuncturists. Information on the history of acupuncture, what treatment involves, and how to find a practitioner.

The British Medical Acupuncture Society (www.medical-acupuncture.co.uk). This society is an association of medical practitioners specialising in acupuncture.

Institute for Complementary Medicine (www.i-c-m.co.uk). The ICM provides the public with information on all aspects of the safe and best practice of complementary medicine through its practitioners, courses, and research.

National Institute of Medical Herbalists (www.nimh.org.uk). NIMH is one of the world's oldest professional bodies representing qualified herbalists; their Web site helps you to locate a herbalist near you.

Holidays

Ethical Traveller (www.ethicaltraveller.com). Ethical Traveller promotes ecofriendly travel worldwide.

Responsible Travel (www.responsibletravel.com). There's a large selection of responsible travel and ecotourism holidays on offer from this company.

Tourism Concern (www.tourismconcern.org.uk). Tourism Concern works with communities in destination countries to reduce social and environmental problems connected to tourism, with the outbound tourism industry in the UK to find ways of improving tourism so that local benefits are increased, and fights exploitation in tourism.

Treesponsibility (www.treesponsibility.com). Offers tree-planting holidays in the Pennines.

Magazines

The Ecologist **(www.theecologist.org).** Forums, news, and a free newsletter for this green magazine.

The Environmental Post **(www.environmentpost.co.uk).** Fortnightly magazine advertising jobs in the environmental sector.

Ethical Consumer **(www.ethicalconsumer.org).** *Ethical Consumer* magazine publishes buyer's guides and features to help you shop ethically.

The Green Parent Magazine **(www.thegreenparent.co.uk).** Green lifestyle magazine covering all aspects of family life from birth to alternative education, eco-house and garden, to nutrition.

Living Earth **(www.soilassociation.org).** The Soil Association's membership magazine.

Permaculture Magazine **(www.permaculture.co.uk).** This magazine features articles, news, and reviews focusing on sustainable living, along with a link to their Green Shopping catalogue.

Recycled Goods

Freecycle (www.freecycle.org). An online guide by the Freecycling Network, with more than three million members at the time of writing. Includes a UK-specific site at uk.freecycle.org.

Furniture Re-use Network (www.frn.org.uk). The Furniture Re-use Network supports, assists and develops charitable reuse organisations across the UK.

Recycle Now (www.recyclenow.com). Operated by the Waste & Resources Action Programme, this Web site offers practical advice on recycling, and includes a recycling locator based on your postcode.

Waste Aware Scotland (www.wascot.org.uk). Waste Aware Scotland is a national campaign that aims to change public attitudes and behaviour towards waste, with details of campaigns currently running in your local area.

WRAP (www.recycledproducts.org.uk). The Waste & Resources Action Programme provides a national, comprehensive database of consumer products made from recycled materials and items that help you to recycle more stuff, more often. At the time of writing, WRAP has around 450 companies listed.

Shopping

A Lot of Organics (www.alotoforganics.co.uk). A UK-based organic search engine for all sorts of ethical products.

Adili (www.adili.com). Ethical clothes and fashion.

Animal Free shopper (www.animalfreeshopper.com). The Vegan Society's Animal Free Shopper Web site allows you to purchase vegan products online.

Ecocentric (www.ecocentric.co.uk). Ethical, ecofriendly products available online.

Ecotopia (www.ecotopia.co.uk). Ecotopia prides itself on supplying a massive range of interesting and useful environmentally friendly and natural products.

Ecozone (www.ecozone.co.uk). Ecozone offers health and household items, along with eco-gadgets.

The Ethical Partnership (www.the-ethical-partnership.co.uk). The Ethical Partnership offers independent financial advice specialising in ethical and socially responsible investment.

Get Ethical (www.getethical.com). Get Ethical finds the best ethical, fair trade, and environmentally friendly products and services and brings them together in its online shop.

Go Green (www.gogreen.cellande.co.uk). Offering natural and ecofriendly products.

Green Choices (www.greenchoices.org). Offering a wide range of links to environmentally friendly shops, along with green discussion.

The Green Directory (www.greendirectory.net). Published annually as a book and also online, the *Green Directory* offers a unique blend of people, organisations, and businesses involved in the green sectors.

Green Guide (www.greenguide.co.uk). The Green Guide strives to change patterns of consumption and seeks out greener, natural, and ethical alternatives to every conceivable type of product and service.

Green Metropolis (www.greenmetropolis.com). Online bookseller who plants new trees.

The Green Shop (www.greenshop.co.uk). Sustainable-living shopping online.

The National Association of Nappy Services (www.changeanappy.co.uk). For all your nappy needs!

The Natural Death Centre (www.naturaldeath.org.uk). The Natural Death Centre is a charitable project launched in 1991. It aims to support those dying at home and their carers, and to help people arrange inexpensive, family-organised, and environmentally friendly funerals. On the Web site you'll find information about natural burial sites.

Planet Organic (www.planetorganic.com). London's organic supermarket, with three stores at the time of writing.

Rendona (www.rendona.co.uk). A manufacturer of environmentally friendly paints.

The World Wildlife Fund Shop (shop.wwf.org.uk). The WWF online shop includes natural and fair-trade goods, a plant-a-tree gift, and more goodies with beautiful animals on them than you can shake a stick at!

Transport and Travel

Autoholics Anonymous (www.autoholics.org). A 12 month self-help course to make you less dependant on your four-wheeled friend.

Carfree Cities (www.carfree.com). A Web site dedicated to the idea that urban life is not only possible, but also better, if transport is organised so that private automobiles are not used on the city's streets.

Conservation International (www.ecotour.org). Conservation International's online guide to ecotourism, ethical travelling, and biodiversity.

Cycle Campaign Network (www.cyclenetwork.org.uk). The Cycle Campaign Network is the UK's national federation of cycle campaign groups, supporting cycling locally, regionally, nationally, and in Europe.

Environmental Transport Association (www.ets.co.uk). The Environmental Transport Association campaigns for a sustainable transport system and offers advice on green motoring issues and its own motoring services.

Freewheelers (www.freewheelers.co.uk). The ultimate in car-sharing! Freewheelers is a free service only available via the Internet, providing an online database of people offering or requiring lifts (including a special section for travelling to festivals and other big events).

The Low Impact Living Initiative (www.lowimpact.org). This Web site helps you to reduce your impact on the environment, live in a healthier and more satisfying way, have fun, and save money . . . all at the same time.

The Man in Seat 61 (www.seat61.com). Mark Smith is the man in seat 61, and he offers all sorts of terrific advice about travelling by rail and sea, worldwide.

National Federation of Bus Users (www.nfbu.org). The NFBU is an independent group formed to give bus passengers a voice.

National Rail Enquiries (www.nationalrail.co.uk). Using the train? This Web site helps you to plan your journey and book your tickets online.

Rail Passengers Council (www.railpassengers.org.uk). This council is an independent public body set up by the government to protect the interests of Britain's rail passengers.

Sustrans (www.sustrans.org.uk). Sustrans is the UK's leading sustainable transport charity. They work on practical, innovative ways of dealing with the transport challenges that affect the UK, running their own events and cycle rides.

Transport 2000 (www.transport2000.org.uk). Transport 2000 is the independent national body concerned with sustainable transport. It looks for answers to transport problems and aims to reduce the environmental and social impact of transport by encouraging less use of cars and more use of public transport, walking and cycling.

Transport Impact Calculator (www.travelcalculator.org). This online calculator encourages you to reduce the environmental impact of your travel. It aims to show how using transport with a relatively low environmental impact can help you to reduce air pollution, improve your health, and in some cases save money. There are three calculators: to calculate your pollutant emissions from your journeys; calculate the energy you use on your journeys (in calories); and calculate the full annual cost of car ownership.

UK Public Transport Information (www.pti.org.uk). The national portal for regional public transport journey planning services across Great Britain.

Index

• C •

• *E* •

• F •

• *I* •

• X •

• Y •

• Z •

Notes

Notes

Notes

FOR DUMMIES

Do Anything. Just Add Dummies

PROPERTY

UK editions

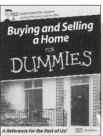
0-7645-7027-7

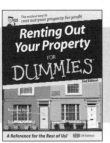
0-470-02921-8

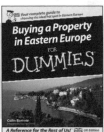
0-7645-7047-1

PERSONAL FINANCE

0-7645-7023-4

0-470-05815-3

0-7645-7039-0

BUSINESS

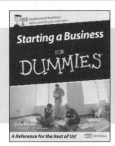
0-7645-7018-8

0-7645-7056-0

0-7645-7026-9

Answering Tough Interview
Questions For Dummies
(0-470-01903-4)

Arthritis For Dummies
(0-470-02582-4)

Being the Best Man
For Dummies
(0-470-02657-X)

British History
For Dummies
(0-470-03536-6)

Building Confidence
For Dummies
(0-470-01669-8)

Buying a Home on a Budget
For Dummies
(0-7645-7035-8)

Children's Health
For Dummies
(0-470-02735-5)

Cognitive Behavioural Therapy
For Dummies
(0-470-01838-0)

Cricket For Dummies
(0-470-03454-8)

CVs For Dummies
(0-7645-7017-X)

Detox For Dummies
(0-470-01908-5)

Diabetes For Dummies
(0-7645-7019-6)

Divorce For Dummies
(0-7645-7030-7)

DJing For Dummies
(0-470-03275-8)

eBay.co.uk For Dummies
(0-7645-7059-5)

European History
For Dummies
(0-7645-7060-9)

Gardening For Dummies
(0-470-01843-7)

Genealogy Online
For Dummies
(0-7645-7061-7)

Golf For Dummies
(0-470-01811-9)

Hypnotherapy For Dummies
(0-470-01930-1)

Irish History For Dummies
(0-7645-7040-4)

Neuro-linguistic Programming
For Dummies
(0-7645-7028-5)

Nutrition For Dummies
(0-7645-7058-7)

Parenting For Dummies
(0-470-02714-2)

Pregnancy For Dummies
(0-7645-7042-0)

Retiring Wealthy For Dummies
(0-470-02632-4)

Rugby Union For Dummies
(0-470-03537-4)

Small Business Employment
Law For Dummies
(0-7645-7052-8)

Starting a Business on
eBay.co.uk For Dummies
(0-470-02666-9)

Su Doku For Dummies
(0-470-01892-5)

The GL Diet For Dummies
(0-470-02753-3)

The Romans For Dummies
(0-470-03077-1)

Thyroid For Dummies
(0-470-03172-7)

UK Law and Your Rights
For Dummies
(0-470-02796-7)

Winning on Betfair
For Dummies
(0-470-02856-4)

FOR DUMMIES®

Do Anything. Just Add Dummies

HOBBIES

0-7645-5232-5

0-7645-6847-7

0-7645-5476-X

Also available:

Art For Dummies
(0-7645-5104-3)
Aromatherapy For Dummies
(0-7645-5171-X)
Bridge For Dummies
(0-471-92426-1)
Card Games For Dummies
(0-7645-9910-0)
Chess For Dummies
(0-7645-8404-9)

Improving Your Memory
For Dummies
(0-7645-5435-2)
Massage For Dummies
(0-7645-5172-8)
Meditation For Dummies
(0-471-77774-9)
Photography For Dummies
(0-7645-4116-1)
Quilting For Dummies
(0-7645-9799-X)

EDUCATION

0-7645-7206-7

0-7645-5581-2

0-7645-5422-0

Also available:

Algebra For Dummies
(0-7645-5325-9)
Algebra II For Dummies
(0-471-77581-9)
Astronomy For Dummies
(0-7645-8465-0)
Buddhism For Dummies
(0-7645-5359-3)
Calculus For Dummies
(0-7645-2498-4)

Forensics For Dummies
(0-7645-5580-4)
Islam For Dummies
(0-7645-5503-0)
Philosophy For Dummies
(0-7645-5153-1)
Religion For Dummies
(0-7645-5264-3)
Trigonometry For Dummies
(0-7645-6903-1)

PETS

0-470-03717-2

0-7645-8418-9

0-7645-5275-9

Also available:

Labrador Retrievers
For Dummies
(0-7645-5281-3)
Aquariums For Dummies
(0-7645-5156-6)
Birds For Dummies
(0-7645-5139-6)
Dogs For Dummies
(0-7645-5274-0)
Ferrets For Dummies
(0-7645-5259-7)

Golden Retrievers
For Dummies
(0-7645-5267-8)
Horses For Dummies
(0-7645-9797-3)
Jack Russell Terriers
For Dummies
(0-7645-5268-6)
Puppies Raising & Training
Diary For Dummies
(0-7645-0876-8)

FOR DUMMIES®

The easy way to get more done and have more fun

LANGUAGES

0-7645-5194-9

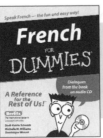

0-7645-5193-0

0-7645-5196-5

Also available:

Chinese For Dummies
(0-471-78897-X)

Chinese Phrases
For Dummies
(0-7645-8477-4)

French Phrases For Dummies
(0-7645-7202-4)

German For Dummies
(0-7645-5195-7)

Italian Phrases For Dummies
(0-7645-7203-2)

Japanese For Dummies
(0-7645-5429-8)

Latin For Dummies
(0-7645-5431-X)

Spanish Phrases
For Dummies
(0-7645-7204-0)

Spanish Verbs For Dummies
(0-471-76872-3)

Hebrew For Dummies
(0-7645-5489-1)

MUSIC AND FILM

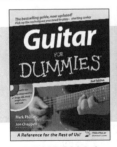

0-7645-9904-6

0-7645-2476-3

0-7645-5105-1

Also available:

Bass Guitar For Dummies
(0-7645-2487-9)

Blues For Dummies
(0-7645-5080-2)

Classical Music For Dummies
(0-7645-5009-8)

Drums For Dummies
(0-471-79411-2)

Jazz For Dummies
(0-471-76844-8)

Opera For Dummies
(0-7645-5010-1)

Rock Guitar For Dummies
(0-7645-5356-9)

Screenwriting For Dummies
(0-7645-5486-7)

Songwriting For Dummies
(0-7645-5404-2)

Singing For Dummies
(0-7645-2475-5)

HEALTH, SPORTS & FITNESS

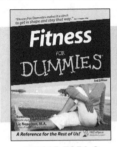

0-7645-7851-0

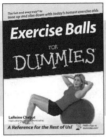

0-7645-5623-1

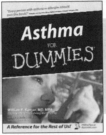

0-7645-4233-8

Also available:

Controlling Cholesterol
For Dummies
(0-7645-5440-9)

Dieting For Dummies
(0-7645-4149-8)

High Blood Pressure
For Dummies
(0-7645-5424-7)

Martial Arts For Dummies
(0-7645-5358-5)

Menopause For Dummies
(0-7645-5458-1)

Power Yoga For Dummies
(0-7645-5342-9)

Weight Training
For Dummies
(0-471-76845-6)

Yoga For Dummies
(0-7645-5117-5)

Available wherever books are sold. For more information or to order direct go to www.wiley.com or call 0800 243407 (Non UK call +44 1243 843296)

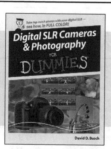